RETURN TO
DRAGON MOUNTAIN

Memories of a Late Ming Man

JONATHAN D. SPENCE

PENGUIN BOOKS

PENGUIN BOOKS

Published by the Penguin Group

Penguin Group (USA) Inc., 375 Hudson Street, New York, New York 10014, U.S.A.

Penguin Group (Canada), 90 Eglinton Avenue East, Suite 700, Toronto,
Ontario, Canada M4P 2Y3 (a division of Pearson Penguin Canada Inc.)

Penguin Books Ltd, 80 Strand, London WC2R 0RL, England

Penguin Ireland, 25 St Stephen's Green, Dublin 2, Ireland (a division of Penguin Books Ltd)

Penguin Group (Australia), 250 Camberwell Road, Camberwell,
Victoria 3124, Australia (a division of Pearson Australia Group Pty Ltd)

Penguin Books India Pvt Ltd, 11 Community Centre, Panchsheel Park, New Delhi – 110 017, India

Penguin Group (NZ), 67 Apollo Drive, Rosedale, North Shore 0632,
New Zealand (a division of Pearson New Zealand Ltd)

Penguin Books (South Africa) (Pty) Ltd, 24 Sturdee Avenue, Rosebank, Johannesburg 2196, South Africa

Penguin Books Ltd, Registered Offices:
80 Strand, London WC2R 0RL, England

First published in the United States of America by Viking Penguin,
a member of Penguin Group (USA) Inc. 2007
Published in Penguin Books 2008

1   3   5   7   9   10   8   6   4   2

Grateful acknowledgment is made for permission to reprint excerpts from the following copyrighted works:
"The Body of the Way Is Without Edges: Zhang Dai (1597–1684) and his Four Book Epiphanies"
by Duncan Campbell, *New Zealand Journal of Asian Studies*, June 1998. Used with permission of the publisher.
In Limpid Dreams: Nostalgia and Zhang Dai's Reminiscences of the Ming by Philip Kafalas.
Used by permission of East Bridge Books, Norwalk, Connecticut.
Remembrances: The Experience of Past in Classical Chinese Literature by Stephen Owen,
Cambridge, Mass.: Harvard University Press. Copyright © 1986 by the President and
Fellows of Harvard College. Reprinted by permission of the publisher.
The Poetry of T'ao Ch'ien, translated by James Robert Hightower. By permission of Oxford University Press.

THE LIBRARY OF CONGRESS HAS CATALOGED THE HARDCOVER EDITION AS FOLLOWS:
Spence, Jonathan D.
Return to dragon mountain : memories of a late Ming man / Jonathan D. Spence.
p.   cm.
ISBN 978-0-670-06357-4 (hc.)
ISBN 978-0-14-311445-1 (pbk.)
1. Zhang, Dai, 1597–1679.   2. Authors, Chinese—Biography.
I. Title.   II. Title: Memories of a late Ming man.
PL2698.C33Z8 2007
895.1'84809—dc22   200610203

Printed in the United States of America
Designed by Nancy Resnick
Map and family tree by David Lindroth

PENGUIN BOOKS

RETURN TO DRAGON MOUNTAIN

Jonathan Spence is the author of more than a dozen books on China, including *Mao* (A Penguin Life), *Treason by the Book*, *The Gate of Heavenly Peace*, *The Death of Woman Wang*, *The Memory Palace of Matteo Ricci*, and *To Change China*, all available from Penguin. A Sterling Professor of History at Yale, he is a past president of the American Historical Association and has been awarded a Guggenheim and a MacArthur fellowship. He is a member of the American Academy of Arts and Sciences and the American Philosophical Society.

Praise for *Return to Dragon Mountain*

Chosen as a Best Book of the Year by *The Washington Post*

"Westerners seeking to understand China should shelve that big pile of anxious new volumes on China's economic ascent, and read instead *Return to Dragon Mountain*. Jonathan Spence is arguably the best living English-language Chinese historian. . . . An extraordinary life and a fascinating story. It's also an intriguing topic for Spence, with his exceptional sensitivity for nuance, writing about a historian with an exceptional sensitivity for nuance. . . . Spence has again reflected China through Chinese prisms, and has added to a clearer view of the whole mountain." —*The Cleveland Plain Dealer*

"The great China historian Jonathan Spence has for years guided us on journeys into the worldviews and dreams of emperors and rebels, traitors and traders, mandarins and missionaries. Now, in *Return to Dragon Mountain*, Spence takes us inside the mind of a fellow historian. . . . [Zhang Dai] left a timelessly human record of a pivotal and fascinating era, and Spence has employed patience and empathy to bring him back to life." —*The Washington Post*

"Impressive." —*The New York Review of Books*

"I have read Jonathan Spence's many previous books and reread several of them, but *Return to Dragon Mountain* is his masterpiece, to date. As with Spence's best earlier works, *Return to Dragon Mountain* is authentic history, but also a sustained personal meditation upon the self and its struggle for spiritual survival. Spence's protagonist and surrogate, Zhang Dai, an important historian of the Late Ming Dynasty, China's Golden Age, is so rendered by *Return to Dragon Mountain* that I am reminded of the narrator in Marcel Proust and also of Joseph Conrad's heroic but darkly fated heroes. Jonathan Spence is a distinguished historian of China, but his literary gifts enhance every page of his new book. The reader encounters an authorial voice that yields the pleasures and insights given by such supreme novelists as Proust and Conrad."   —Harold Bloom

"Spence never loses sight of the life he is recounting in all its prosaic majesty."   —*The Columbus Dispatch*

"Absorbing and evocative."   —*Publishers Weekly*

For
Annping

CONTENTS

ACKNOWLEDGMENTS

When I blithely set off in pursuit of Zhang Dai some six years ago, I had no idea that he would prove to be so elusive and so subtle. And even now, after several years of trying, I still cannot feel that I have penetrated his defenses or grasped the full force of his erudition. Nevertheless, the hunt has been a compelling one, and it is a pleasure to acknowledge the aid of those who helped me to get a better understanding of Zhang's many layers.

Like other readers before me, I was first drawn to Zhang Dai because of the intriguing reputation of a short book of essays he drafted in 1646, titled *Taoan mengyi*, which can be translated as *The Dream Recollections of Taoan*. Here I had two crucial guides who helped to prepare me for a reading of the Chinese text. One was Brigitte Teboul-Wang, whose complete annotated translation into French of the *Taoan mengyi*, under the title *Souvenirs rêvés de Tao'an*, had been published in Paris in 1995. The other was Philip Kafalas, who had completed his own intricate and scholarly analysis of the structure and meanings of the *Taoan mengyi* in that same year, in the form of a PhD for the department of Asian languages at Stanford University, under the title "Nostalgia and the Reading of the Late Ming Essay: Zhang Dai's *Tao'an mengyi*." In addition to analyzing the *Taoan mengyi* in depth, Kafalas's study contained numerous extended translations from the same work. Some subsequent searching led me to other scholars who had published their own translations of selected essays from the same Zhang Dai volume, most notably Martin Huang, Victor Mair, Stephen Owen, David Pollard, Richard Strassberg and Ye Yang. The cumulative sense I got from these various translations was that though translating Zhang was clearly intensely difficult, it was also deeply rewarding, and that one might be able to use the *Taoan mengyi* to some extent as a jumping off point for a reflection on Zhang's life as a whole, and as an entry point into the broad expanse of Zhang's other writings that did not appear to have received anything like the same critical attention. As of this writing, though several biographical studies of Zhang have been published in China recently, and are listed in the bibliography, there still does not seem to have been any extended study in English, with the exception of Philip Kafalas's revised and expanded version of his dissertation, published in the spring of 2007 with the title *In Limpid Dream: Nostalgia and Zhang Dai's Reminiscences of the Ming* (EastBridge).

In addition to those scholars mentioned above, many other people have helped me in my attempts to understand Zhang. In the spring of 2005 John Delury helped orchestrate my visit to Shaoxing, Zhang's original hometown, so that I was able to walk the shaded paths on Dragon Mountain, take a night boat trip along the narrow streams that still meander through the old parts of the town, and tour the rugged hills to the southwest of the city, where Zhang Dai hid out in 1646. John also introduced me to She Deyu, professor in the College of Humanities at Shaoxing University, and the author of a recent study of Zhang Dai's family. Professor She in turn gave me helpful leads to some rare manuscripts and printed materials on Zhang that were held in the Shaoxing rare book library; and the staff there echoed his generosity by letting me have photocopies of several choice items.

At Yale's Sterling Memorial Library, Sarah Elman and Tao Yang were especially helpful, tracking down the various editions of the newly available Stone Casket History, and obtaining copies or microfilms of rare materials from the Library of Congress, Princeton, Harvard and Columbia. They also helped in locating materials on the Jesuit priest Matteo Ricci written by Zhang Dai's grandfather Zhang Rulin, a process speeded thanks to the generous sharing of information by professors Hsu Kuang-tai and Ad Dudink. Antony Marr, previous curator of Yale's Chinese collection, helped with countless leads to Chinese historical journals and newspapers that carried materials on Zhang. Andrew Wylie and my editor Carolyn Carlson were enthusiastic supporters. Mei Chin kindly read and commented on slices of my drafts, and helped me with computer searches. Pamela Carney battled with her own heavy workload and schedules to type the whole of the final recensions of the manuscript.

I also benefited greatly from the help of several students at Yale's graduate school and law school and at Yale College who worked with me at different times as research assistants. Foremost among them were Dong Xin, Huang Hongyu, Liu Shi-yee and Zhang Taisu, who generously shared their language skills and scholarship, both by translating extensive passages for me, and by helping to check my own or others' translations. At an earlier stage of exploration, I also benefited from the help of Yeewan Koon, Anastasia Liu, Xin Ma and Danni Wang. In tracking paintings by Zhang Dai's friend Chen Hongshou, I received crucial help from the accomplished art collector Weng Wan-go, who also granted me the rights to use the haunting painting by Chen that graces the book's jacket.

Another group of those who helped me must remain in part anonymous, since they were members of the audiences at various universities where I was invited to give talks on Zhang Dai and his times, as my work slowly progressed. Especially helpful were those who commented on my first attempts to share my thoughts on Zhang at the Radcliffe Institute for Advanced Study at Harvard, and subsequently at the University of California, Berkeley. But many other audiences also helped me think things through in new ways, including those at the University of San Diego, Notre Dame, East Carolina University, the University of Wisconsin in Madison, the University of Connecticut in Storrs, the University of Michigan and Peking University. I also presented some of my emerging thoughts on Zhang Dai and his family in the form of the presidential address to the American Historical Association, delivered in January 2005 in Seattle.

Throughout this entire project Annping Chin has been my companion and my instructor, trying to steer me clear of the worst pitfalls and to show me when and how Zhang was using the past in his own special and personal ways. I tried not to ruin her own research with my petty laments, but I know that at regular intervals I asked too much of her. Despite that, she seems to have kept the faith that something might come out of it all. If something has, it is due to her, and so it is to her that this book is dedicated.

March 9, 2007
West Haven, Connecticut

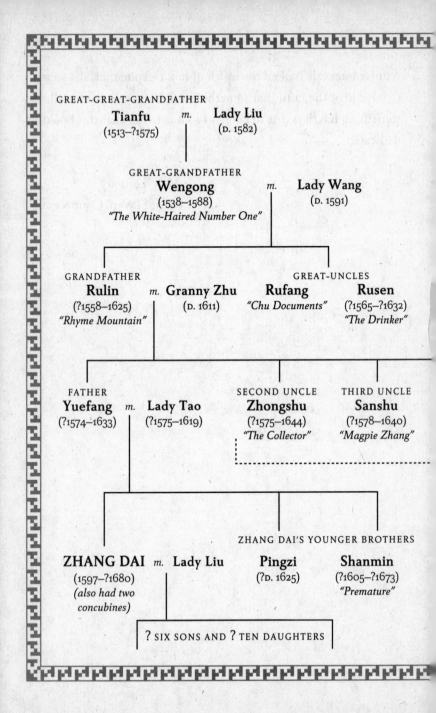

GREAT-GREAT-GRANDFATHER
Tianfu
(1513–?1575)
m.
Lady Liu
(D. 1582)

GREAT-GRANDFATHER
Wengong
(1538–1588)
m.
Lady Wang
(D. 1591)
"The White-Haired Number One"

GRANDFATHER
Rulin
(?1558–1625)
m. **Granny Zhu**
(D. 1611)
"Rhyme Mountain"

GREAT-UNCLES
Rufang
"Chu Documents"
Rusen
(?1565–?1632)
"The Drinker"

FATHER
Yuefang
(?1574–1633)
m. **Lady Tao**
(?1575–1619)

SECOND UNCLE
Zhongshu
(?1575–1644)
"The Collector"

THIRD UNCLE
Sanshu
(?1578–1640)
"Magpie Zhang"

ZHANG DAI *m.* **Lady Liu**
(1597–?1680)
(also had two concubines)

ZHANG DAI'S YOUNGER BROTHERS
Pingzi
(?D. 1625)
Shanmin
(?1605–?1673)
"Premature"

? SIX SONS AND ? TEN DAUGHTERS

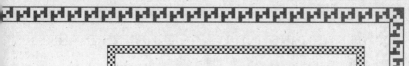

THE ZHANG FAMILY TREE

"m" = marriage

SEVENTH UNCLE
Jishu
(?1585–1615)
"The Thousand-Mile Horse"

NINTH UNCLE
Jiushan
(?D. 1642)
"The Auditor"

TENTH UNCLE
Shishu
(?D. 1644)
"Blind Rage"

ZHANG DAI'S COUSINS

Yanke
(?D. 1646)
"Emperor Who Lost It All"

Pei
(1607–1663)
"Blind Physician"

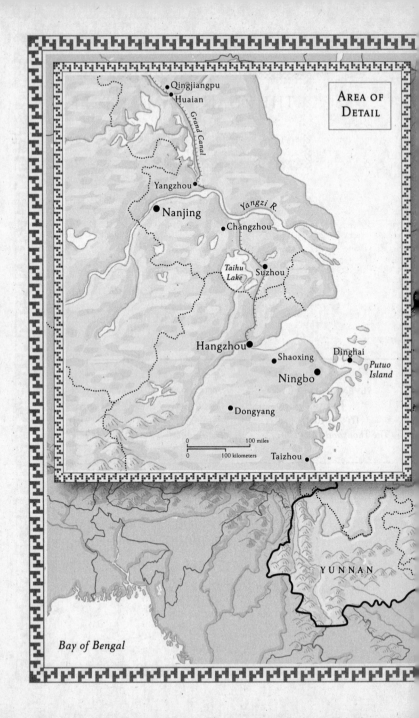

AREA OF DETAIL

Qingjiangpu
Huaian
Grand Canal
Yangzhou
Nanjing
Changzhou
Yangzi R.
Taihu Lake
Suzhou
Hangzhou
Shaoxing
Dinghai
Putuo Island
Ningbo
Dongyang

0   100 miles
0   100 kilometers

Taizhou

YUNNAN

Bay of Bengal

PROLOGUE

When Zhang Dai was born, in 1597, the Ming dynasty had been in place for 229 years. Time measured on a Ming framework was the only time Zhang knew—until, that is, it all ended in 1644 with the dynasty's fall. We might think that as Zhang Dai was growing up, such a great span of time past would have distanced him from the dynasty's roots, creating a conceptual space almost impossible to grasp; but for Zhang such a great vista of years seems to have offered, not severe dislocation, but a satisfying sense of age and constancy. Most of the underpinnings of everyday life in the late Ming would have been without surprise for him.

As it had for so long, family life revolved around intersecting hierarchies. The young lived with their elders and were expected to obey them. Marriages were arranged by senior relatives, and though wealthier men might take secondary consorts or concubines if they chose, the children from such alliances had secondary status within the family. The senior males in the family had formal authority, though in reality women often supervised the details of family finances as well as the nurturing of their family. In wealthier families, mothers or other female relatives would also supervise their children's early education, though the senior male relatives would gradually assume responsibility for the young males' preparation for the competitive examinations based on classical philosophical texts that were a staple factor in elite male life. Since women were not permitted to serve in the bureaucracy or to sit for the examinations, they tended—when literate, as elite women very often were—to be readers of more popular fictions and histories, and avid writers of poetry and letters.

Omens and prognostications about family prospects and possible problems were taken seriously and became part of family lore. Religion was practiced widely but eclectically, with devotion to the Buddha fitting comfortably with homage to one's own human ancestors and appropriate celebration of the domestic spirits of the kitchen, the home and the community. Death took many children in infancy and many women in childbirth, but men, too, died young and it was both an honor and an achievement to be alive and spry in one's fifties or later.

Technologically, too, there had been no especially dramatic shifts since the dynasty was founded. Silk production and porcelain manufacture already had an illustrious history in China and continued to be made to the highest standards, exceeding anything available elsewhere in the world. Hosts of artisans were skilled in metallurgy, jade carving, lanterns and lacquer ware, along with the production of more prosaic goods such as tea, salt, cotton, pottery and household furniture. Hydraulic engineering was a major preoccupation due to the massive burdens of silt carried by China's major rivers and canals, and the need for constant dredging, diking and drainage. Astronomy and geography also were widely studied, since the formulation of accurate calendars was essential to the imperial court's prestige and the efficacy of its astrological calculations, just as reliable maps were needed for land surveying, taxation rosters and precise charting of border regions and provincial jurisdictions. But though refinements were constantly made in all these areas of concern, there was no fundamental reordering of the country's basic activities.

Yet there was nothing static about the Ming in the cultural realm, even though many continuities with the past remained firmly in place. When Zhang Dai was growing up, Ming society, despite its many political and economic problems, was in an ebullient mode, and this sense of joy and stylishness permeated the culture of the late sixteenth and early seventeenth centuries. It was a time of religious and philosophical eclecticism that saw the flourishing of reformist schools of Buddhism and wide-scale philanthropy, along with the expansion of education for women, penetrating investigations of the concept of individualism and a broad-based examination of the grounds for moral action. Bold experiments in landscape painting, the creation of several of China's most celebrated operatic dramas and most powerful novels, unusually subtle expositions of statecraft and political theory and the codification of botanical, medical and philological terms all marked the world of his childhood. As part of this zestful sense of intellectual and personal possibility, Catholic missionaries from Europe also found a hearing, made converts, translated catechisms and works of moral philosophy along with astronomical and mathematical texts into Chinese and mingled companionably with scholars from elite families in both Beijing and the provinces. To varying extents, Zhang Dai was aware of all these intercultural adventures, and he reflected openly on many of them, writing in pretty much every mode that was prevalent at the time, with the exception of novels and short stories.

Despite such continuities with the past, there were certain undercurrents of change affecting Zhang's world. One of these currents was the inexorable expansion of the Ming population. Though there are no precise figures available, various local and imperial records suggest that when the Ming was founded in 1368, there were around 85 million people in China. By the time Zhang Dai was born, that figure had risen to somewhere in the range of 180 million, perhaps more. This inevitably brought new pressures on the land and on farming practice, pressures partly alleviated by improved strains of rice, double or even treble cropping of fields, enclosure and draining of marshlands and coastal flats and the clearing of upland forests as well as patterns of internal migration, especially to the southwest and northeast. Though few at the time could gauge their future significance, there were also various new crops being brought across the Pacific as a corollary to Spanish and Portuguese penetration into the South American continent and the Caribbean. These included sweet potatoes, maize and peanuts; medicinal plants such as qinchona bark (quinine), which was already known for its effectiveness in checking malaria; and other crops that flourished on Chinese soil, such as tobacco. Some western trading vessels also brought New World silver with which to purchase Chinese luxury goods; a handful of others brought spices and rare medicinal plants, including opium, which was used mainly for its efficacy in checking dysentery.

Zhang Dai's family had moved, perhaps a century or more before, from the southwestern province of Sichuan, bordering on Tibet, and relocated in the city of Shaoxing, near the east coast, about 150 miles southwest of Shanghai. In those days Shanghai was a prosperous market town, but not yet a major commercial center, whereas Shaoxing was an important cultural and economic hub. The Zhang family's move to Shaoxing coincided with a major sixteenth-century change in farming and landholding patterns in the region: due to the rapid population increase there were diminishing per capita returns from farming, and little new land to be reclaimed with dikes or dredging. Many wealthy families that had formerly lived in the countryside and functioned as managerial landlords in their home regions moved to the cities. Thus the class formerly most willing and able to play a leadership role in local rural society, and to act as a social and economic buffer between the small farmers and the acquisitive imperial state, became divorced from the realities and challenges of the entrepreneurial side of farming life; they slid instead into the agreeable but unchallenging role of absentee landlords, leaving the management of their estates to a new group of middlemen, the professional managers and bailiffs. The Zhang family may well have followed this trajectory, bringing Zhang Dai plenty of spending money but little or no clear sense of social obligation.

Rural revenues sparked a dramatic increase in the stylishness of urban living, in the cultural diversity of the towns and in the size and prosperity of cities such as Shaoxing, but little of this accumulated largesse returned to the countryside in the form of investment in improved farming techniques or large-scale irrigation and drainage works. Though some peasant entrepreneurs undoubtedly were able to raise their incomes by marketing their produce in these new urban centers—especially in regions like Shaoxing, where bulk water transport on the local rivers and canals had long been a fact of life—the basis was laid for a sharper separation of interests and lifestyle between countryside and metropole.

Scholars of the past, especially those Zhang Dai tells us he most admired, had all seen things wrong with their own society and had often said so, even at the risk of losing their jobs or sometimes their lives. Certainly the power of the central imperial state, and of the educated bureaucracy that staffed and sustained it, was as much a reality for Zhang Dai as it had been to his scholarly progenitors. It was partly with their help that Zhang was able to penetrate the state's façade and see the weakness it concealed, rather as the light of the lanterns he so much loved as a child could penetrate the penumbra of the city in which he dwelt.

The spectacular eccentricities of many of the Ming emperors were common knowledge in China due to the compilation of court histories and the circulation of news from the capital through weekly gazettes: The fourteenth ruler of the Ming imperial line, Wanli, was on the throne when Zhang was born and was destined to reign with increasing ineffectiveness until 1620. It may well have been the vagaries of this ruler that prompted Zhang Dai to undertake serious study of Chinese history, especially through biography, which became his lifetime passion. By the time Zhang was in his teens, it was clear that power was speedily accruing to the castrated male eunuchs in the palace bureaucracy, since they were the only males allowed access to the emperor should he choose not to leave the precincts of his inner palace compound. Eunuchs had been powerful throughout the Ming, but since the moralistic bickerings of his regular bureaucracy irritated Wanli unbearably, he often refused for months on end to hold audiences with the career officials in the outer court. In protest, scholars and former administrators began to form associations pushing for reform, and court politics grew fractured and perilous, since the arguments were heated and penalties for opposition to the throne or the eunuchs were often savage.

Zhang Dai knew the Ming dynastic history in detail. Back in the mid-fourteenth century, the founding emperor of the Ming— once an itinerant Buddhist monk from a poor rural background— had proved to be a ferocious and tenacious military leader as well as a man with an awesome determination to reunite the country after a lengthy civil war and the ouster of the alien Mongol regime. Though enfeoffing his own numerous sons with large estates, the founder also reestablished a powerful bureaucracy in his capital at Nanjing and attempted to install a new kind of meaningful social compact in the countryside through the organizational labors of prominent local landlords. The founder's tempestuous character led him to be known as much for his excesses and violence as for his shrewdness and vision, and he ensconced a new kind of leadership at the imperial center, passing the throne on to his own grandson, a man of scholarly attainments who shared his own sense of an ideal centralized government for China. But this newly installed heir was killed by one of the founder's sons— the heir's uncle—who installed himself on the throne, moved the capital from Nanjing to Beijing and ordered the construction of a fleet that took proof of Chinese power and attainment to the east coast of Africa and the Persian Gulf.

Even though these dramatic excursions were cancelled on grounds of cost, later emperors inherited these founding rulers' love for the pomp and display of warfare although they lacked either the strategic sense or the tactical skills of the founders. Even the later Ming emperors' expensive reconstruction of the fragmented northern defensive system of walls into one continuous structure, known to later generations as China's "Great Wall," proved totally inadequate to keep still-potent Mongol cavalry forces out of the northern provinces. One mid-fifteenth-century Ming ruler, infatuated by his own belief in his military prowess, was captured by the Mongols during a clumsy campaign and held for ransom until he was released. Eventually he reclaimed his throne from the man who had succeeded him, but the memory of the humiliation to the imperial family could not be erased. Another ruler early in the sixteenth century conducted vast maneuvers with eunuchs in the palace grounds, lived in yurts with his palace women and wasted millions on absurd campaigns.

Other mid-sixteenth-century rulers watched helplessly as large expanses of China's eastern coast were laid waste by seaborne marauders, disaffected local leaders and coastal dwellers, whom the court lumped under the vivid if misleading name of "Japanese pirates." On the northeastern frontier, just before Zhang Dai was born, Emperor Wanli did make the bold and ultimately successful decision to send Chinese military and naval forces to Korea to help the Korean ruler expel a Japanese invading army. Despite the success of this military intervention, by the first years of the seventeenth century a coalition of tribes from the area west of the Korean border began to organize a new and potentially rival state on China's own northern frontier. It was these forces—

working with Chinese collaborators and massed under the military banner of a new hybrid military organization—who took the name of Manchus, declared the formation of their own dynasty (the Qing) and in 1644 seized the capital of Beijing for themselves and brought an end to the Ming dynasty.

All of this Zhang Dai read about, or knew about from his family, just as he knew the ins and outs of the vast and complex world of the Ming imperial bureaucracy in Beijing. Indeed, several members of his own family, spanning the century from the 1540s to the 1640s, served in the six ministries of that bureaucracy at different times and at different levels, and were on close terms with some of the so-called Grand Secretaries, who served at the apex of the government. Other Zhang family relatives worked in the provincial bureaucracy, the tightly integrated series of offices that ran from the county level, through the major cities such as Shaoxing, upward to the provincial capitals of the empire and thence to Beijing. Zhang Dai knew all the intricacies of these chains of command, and of the perils and opportunities that came from serving the state. The many tales he heard of his family's experiences in Beijing and elsewhere percolated in his mind from childhood onward, and in his own way Zhang Dai decided to attempt a depiction of the way that deceit or outright dishonesty could be at the very heart of service to the state. In pursuit of this truth, Zhang Dai saw no need to exonerate his own family. Indeed, one of the startling things about Zhang's writing is the apparent frankness with which he depicted the travails of his own relatives, a frankness from which he did not exempt even his own father and ancestral line.

Until Zhang Dai was in his forties, his life had revolved

around the twin poles of scholarship and pleasure, though to Zhang Dai that might have been the wrong way to phrase it, since so much of scholarship was pleasure to him. Not, it is true, the daily grind of examination preparation, at which he labored unsuccessfully for so many years, but rather the idea and reality of reading, cogitating and remembering, the glorious and inescapable fact of knowing that he could walk with the acknowledged masters of the past. For Zhang, the great historians, poets and essayists of the Chinese past were never far away, and though the standards they had set were often utterly unattainable, the mere act of reaching out toward them was thrilling in its own right.

After the Ming dynasty fell in 1644, however, when Zhang was forty-seven years old, he had to face the harsh reality that the glorious Ming dynasty, in whose shelter he had lived so grandly, had sputtered out to an ignominious end, torn by competing forces of violence, ambition, desperation and greed. In retrospect, things became clear to him: the signposts became visible through the mists that had shrouded them; forgotten whispers of trouble became sharp as cries. His task now, for the second half of his life, became to recollect and to shore up the world before the ruins; he had lost his home, his comforts, his books, many relatives and friends. The foreign Manchu conquerors now ruled his land. Zhang was too old to be a resister or a fugitive for long, and became instead a tenant on a former great estate known once as the Happiness Garden. Life had to be begun again.

The year 1644 thus marked a seismic shift in Zhang Dai's life: his earlier dream of writing a history of the Ming had to be replaced by the bleaker reality of explaining the reasons behind the dynasty's fall. He claimed that in the years of his flight from the civil wars and chaos that accompanied the Manchu invasion of China, when he moved secretly from temple to temple in the southern mountains, sheltered by the monks, he always carried with him the bulky draft manuscript of his Ming history. That may well be so, and he completed the huge work sometime in the 1670s. Yet, though the surviving copy of that draft shows evidence that it was being readied for printing, the whole work only became available in China during the 1990s. Instead of achieving his major fame from his historical works, Zhang became best known for a very different kind of writing, the creation of brief aphoristic essays.

The writing of such essays had been a central part of the late Ming creative universe. Designed to be stylistically polished to a high gloss, so as to show the author's versatility, to explore a mood or a moment with deft, swift, strokes, to beguile but also to shock the reader with their contrasting or suddenly shifting tones, such essays had a boundless popularity when Zhang Dai was growing up, and he in turn became a master of the genre. In many cases, the most admired practitioners of this genre were travel writers, famous for their peripatetic ways, moving from one elite scholarly home to another, constantly restless and constantly alert to tonality and to paradox, to the shading of a view and the shattering of a mood. Despite their brevity and compact format, such essays could also be—and often were—densely erudite and allusive.

But what Zhang came to see in the postconquest years of 1645 and 1646 was that such essays offered a special opportunity to memorialize the past, to save it from extinction by recapturing each sensation of the worlds he had believed to be lost. It was in this way that the greatest catastrophe of his life, the fall of the Ming to the twin forces of northern peasant rebels and Manchu invaders, turned out to be the key to unlock the chambers of his mind and allow the accumulated memories to come bursting out. And because his friends preserved the short but passionate manuscript he wrote as a fugitive, known as *The Dream Recollections of Taoan*, we are able, from our later vantage point, to share the restless probings of his mind.

Nevertheless, it is hard to catch the essence of Zhang Dai. He certainly lived to the full and also suffered greatly, but his various surviving writings suggest that he was most contented when allowed to stay within the confines of his own mind. He wrote for his own children and their young friends as much as for his own comrades from the snuffed-out world of the Ming, and he can be either praised or blamed for putting nostalgia ahead of more practical concerns. He was born and raised on the flank of Dragon Mountain, and he returned there in middle age to make some sense of what he felt he knew.

One cannot say Zhang Dai was an ordinary man, but he was surely closer to ordinariness than he was to celebrity. He was a lover of history as much as he was a historian, an observer as much as an actor, a fugitive as much as a fighter, a son as much as a father. He had passions for many things and many people, as most of us do, but he tried to get into the deep and dark places as well, to be an excavator. He sensed that nothing need vanish if only someone can remember it, and he was determined to rescue as much of the Ming as he could from oblivion. We cannot be sure that everything he tells us is true, but we can be sure that he wanted later generations to know about the things he shares with us here.

CHAPTER ONE

CIRCLES OF PLEASURE

Zhang Dai lived a parade when the moon came out and the lanterns shone. "How could a moment be thought wasted," he asked, "when one had so many choices of lodging, so many places to make assignations, so many chances of sexual adventure?" Cost was no object in such a world. So Zhang Dai savored the sights and sounds of excess, the decorated boats that swirled around each other on the waterways crisscrossing the pleasure quarters of Nanjing, while the flutes and drums played. Behind painted lattice balconies and dangling bamboo shades, the jasmine scent of the freshly bathed revelers filled the summer air. One could look for the courtesans with their round fans, dressed in light silks, hair tousled around their temples. Above the water where the newly lighted lanterns strung around the boats glimmered like necklaces of pearls, "young men and women leaned over the balustrades roaring with laughter, the lights and sounds became blurred till one lost track of sight and hearing." Only when night was well advanced did the lanterns flicker out and "the stars disperse."

There were few limits to the realms where light or water could transport Zhang Dai, and indeed the earliest memories that he recorded were linked to one or the other. He was only three years old, Zhang tells us, when one of the older family servants had taken him on an outing to see the lantern display outside the house of one of his mother's friends, a connoisseur and art collector called Wang. Zhang was still small enough to ride atop the servant's shoulders, and from that lofty vantage point he could take in the whole panorama: lanterns of translucent crystal, lanterns festooned with beads, lanterns of paper coated with crushed sheep horn, lanterns highlighted with paintings picked out in gold, lanterns with dangling tassels, well over a hundred of them in all. Yet—at least in the memory of the adult Zhang Dai, recorded many years later—despite the splendor of the scene, something seemed wrong to the little child's eyes. It was that the lanterns were not bright enough, nor close enough to each other; there were dark spaces between the bright patches, so that people had to pick their way with care or even light a lantern of their own to see the scattered lanterns with greater clarity. One could hear some of the spectators grumbling about these inconveniences, despite the moment's glories.

Those who, like Zhang Dai and his family, lived in the city of Shaoxing were almost innately connoisseurs of the lantern arts, for Shaoxing was a comfortable, prosperous town filled with craftsmen and their potential customers. As Zhang Dai wrote later, there was nothing surprising about the local people's passion for lanterns: "It was just that bamboo was cheap, lanterns were cheap, candles were cheap. On account of the cheapness, every household could have its own lanterns; and on account of that cheapness any household that did not display lanterns felt ashamed." At the time of the spring and autumn festivals, lanterns graced every street, from the widest boulevards to the meanest alleyways. The Shaoxing residents usually hung their lanterns from a stout but simple scaffolding, composed of two bamboo poles at each end, tied together, with one sturdy cross-piece linking them. From this central beam seven lanterns could be hung at a time—one large central lantern called the "snow lantern" with three round "globe lanterns" on each side.

Such memories stayed fresh in Zhang Dai's mind: "From the end of each street, if one turned around to look back down its length, one could see the close-folded rows piled up in order, freshly beautiful, stirring and shivering in the wind; and that alone was enough to move one." At the major crossroads within Shaoxing a single giant lantern would be hung from a massive framework of painted timber, the lantern itself painted with up-lifting scenes from the well-known texts of Chinese history and poetry, and adorned with riddles that the crowds, drawn up in circles around the lantern, would endeavor to solve. Lanterns hung, too, in the monasteries and temples, dangling from the beams, illuminating the religious inscriptions written on the lintels of the gateways and adding extra luster to the decorative lotus flowers of red paper and the rows of little glass lamps inter-laced with garlands and the Buddha's effigy. Villagers dressed in their best clothes came crowding in from the surrounding countryside, thronging the residential streets and shopping dis-tricts, while the local women and girls ambled arm-in-arm among the visitors or sat in the doorways of their houses and shacks, nibbling melon seeds and sweets made from bean paste, until the night was well advanced.

Zhang Dai's first recorded memory of water also came from his early childhood. He was about five when his mother took him with her to offer prayers to the Buddha in a temple to the east of their hometown of Shaoxing. The temple was perched above a lake that had been excavated and filled with fish by Zhang Dai's maternal grandfather thirty years before. The day was hot, and as mother and son drifted on the lake in a small boat, they hung a bamboo basket containing four melons to keep cool in the water. Without warning, a fish—"huge as the boat" in Zhang Dai's memory—slammed up under the boat, almost swamping it, grabbed the whole basket of melons and vanished with a wave of its tail, as swiftly as it came, leaving the worshipers and their boatmen shaken and bewildered.

Many years later, when Zhang Dai was forty-one, the moment was repeated, but on a more awe-inspiring scale. Zhang was at the funeral of a family friend, not far from the city of Hangzhou, when someone called out from the top of the seawall that he could see the crest of the tidal bore bearing down on them from the estuary beyond. Zhang Dai had heard this promise made before, for the tidal bore was a famous sight in the region, much celebrated by local poets and essayists, but hitherto he had always been disappointed. Nevertheless he ran out again to the seawall and clambered up, with two of his friends hurrying after. And this time it was true—the solid wall of water was hurtling across the bay toward them.

Zhang Dai described the moment this way: "We saw the crest

line of the wave coming toward us from the direction of Haining, heading straight for the seawall. As it drew nearer one could see a blurred mass of white, like a huge flock of tiny geese beating their wings in frightened flight. Nearer still, flakes of foam like crushed ice sprang up, as if countless snow lions coated the surface and were goaded on by the rumbling thunder, heads thrust forward. Closer yet, a howling gale pushed the wave onwards, determined to strike the wall and overleap it. We watchers could hold out no more, and left our perch to hide behind the shelter of the seawall. Reaching the wall, the tidal bore smashed into it with all its force, the water soaring up for scores of feet, soaking all our faces. Careening off to the right, the wave struck Turtle Rock in cascading rage—a cannon's roar in the dragon's cavern, a snow dance in the demi-void. We watchers were scared and dizzy, and sat there for a long time before our color came back to normal."

Suddenly recollected, almost any moment from the past could hold Zhang Dai's attention, at least until he had probed it for its full range of possibilities. "It was in the summer of 1614," he noted in one of his informal jottings, "passing by the Speckled Bamboo Shrine, that I took some water from the spring and tasted it. It had the bitter tang of phosphorous and startled me. When I looked more carefully at the color of the water, it was as if an autumn moon in frosty space were spurting forth its whiteness, or as if the lightest of fogs wreathed a mountain, curving round the pines and rocks before fading away altogether." Curious as to what this water would taste like in making tea, Zhang Dai found after some experimentation that the stony taste vanished after one had let the springwater sit for three days, and that then the full aroma of the tea became accentuated. If one swirled the water around against one's cheeks while pressing the tongue against the palate, the special taste of this particular spring was unmistakable.

Zhang Dai's worldly-wise third uncle shared his highly developed taste with his nephew, and between them they explored a wide range of possibilities, checking which tea from which celebrated region went best with certain kinds of water. Their final conclusion was that the springwater from the Speckled Bamboo Shrine, when allowed to sit for a recommended three days, brought out the richest aromas from the choicest leaves, and that when it was prepared in the finest of white porcelain, the color of the brew—the purest and palest of greens—was incomparable. The two men debated whether to add a petal or two of jasmine to the leaves, and agreed that adding the freshly boiled water to a little of the same water that had been allowed to cool in the same pot was the perfect method: watching the leaves stretch and unfold was like "seeing one hundred white orchid flowers open their petals in a wave of snow," and so it was that they named their discovery Snow Orchid tea.

Ever curious to expand the range of tastes, Zhang Dai experimented with other uses for his Snow Orchid tea. For some time he had been exploring ways to make cheese after obtaining a supply of cow's milk and letting the cream separate overnight. Into one pound of this separated cream he blended four cups of the Snow Orchid tea and boiled the two together for a long period in a bronze pot until the mixture became sticky and thick, "like liquid jade or pearls." When chilled, the flavor and aroma were to Zhang "sumptuous as snow," delicate as the scent of orchids, "silky as the hoar frost." Further experiments showed a variety of other uses for this enticing mixture: it could be steamed with the rich local wine in an earthenware crock, mixed with soybean flour and fermented, shaped into fritters or rolls, steeped in spirits or preserved in vinegar. It could even be simmered with cane sugar, strained and molded into delicate conch-shell shapes. However you treated it, Zhang wrote, this was something so good that the recipes "had to be held under lock and key, written on sheets of paper that one kept hidden away, and were not lightly to be passed on even from father to son."

Within five years, by 1620 or so, this tea that Zhang and his uncle had named Snow Orchid had ousted its rivals from the connoisseurs' circles. But it was not long before unscrupulous businessmen began to market inferior teas under the Snow Orchid brand name, and those who drank it seemed not to know they were being gulled. A short time later, even the water source itself was lost. First, entrepreneurs from Shaoxing tried to use the water for wine making or else opened tea shops right by the spring itself. Next, a greedy local official tried to monopolize the spring's water for his own use and sealed it off for a while. But that increased the spring's reputation to such an extent that rowdy crowds began to gather at the shrine, demanding food, firewood and other handouts from the monks there and then brawling when they were refused. At last, to regain their earlier tranquility, the monks polluted their spring by filling it with manure, rotting bamboo and the overflow from their own drains. Three times Zhang Dai came with his household attendants to try to clear the spring, and three times the monks polluted it as soon as he had departed. Finally he gave up, though noting with sardonic amusement that many ordinary people, still remembering the magic of the old name, continued to brew their tea from the utterly contaminated Speck-led Bamboo Shrine water and declared it fine.

But Zhang was a realist about such matters, and he knew how water circulated. As he wrote of another source esteemed for its purity, "The water from the spring bubbles on its way; from the well it flows to the brook, from the brook to the creek, from the creek to the pond, and thence to the kitchens, to the public bath house, to cleaning the yards, to washing off grime, to watering the garden, to bathing oneself, to sluicing out the night-soil buckets." So it had to be, Zhang concluded: "Those who live in a garden give equal weight to the delicious and the crude."

Other aspects of his taste changed to match the opportunities for deepening a particular sensation. Thus it was logical for his quest for a perfect light to be followed by his search for the perfect lantern maker. The hunt led the adult Zhang Dai to a carver of Buddhist statues in Fujian province far to the south. The carver was a man of exquisite skill who had been persuaded by an official patron to make ten lanterns, a task that took him two years to complete. Since the patron died before the commission was finished, one of the junior officials in the area—a man named Li, also a native of Shaoxing city—brought the lanterns back to Shaoxing in wooden crates. Knowing of Zhang Dai's fascination with lanterns, he offered them to Zhang as a gift. Zhang however insisted on paying, giving Li fifty taels of silver on the spot. This was a lordly sum for those days, when each tael of silver weighed a full ounce, but it was a price Zhang contentedly assessed as being less than one-tenth of the pieces' true worth. The Buddhist carver's lanterns became, to Zhang, the corner-stone of his rapidly growing collection.

There were other artists to help Zhang's lantern collection reach its apogee. One Shaoxing craftsman called Xia excelled at cutting flower designs out of colored silks and sewing them onto the back of thin pieces of ice-colored silk; Zhang found the effect astounding, "like seeing a peony through mist." Xia also created designs from molded metal, in a huge range of curious shapes, which he covered with multicolored silks from Sichuan, far to the west. For each year's main religious festivals Xia would create at least one perfect lantern, and once the ceremonies were over he would sell it to Zhang Dai for what Zhang considered an "agreeable" price. Zhang purchased other pieces for his Dragon Mountain displays from famous makers like Zhao in Nanjing, whose pressed silk screens and sets of lantern holders were without rival in the region. As his lantern collection increased, Zhang found the perfect person to conserve it, a young servant in his household "with a gift for looking after things: even if the lanterns were made of paper, they could be used for ten years without ever being damaged, and thus my lantern collection grew ever richer."

Zhang Dai's enthusiasms were often fleeting, yet he wrote about them as if they were intense enough to have provided the markers that gave structure to his life. Just two years after his first experiments with the Snow Orchid tea, he conceived a passion for the form of long zither known as the *qin*. During 1616, when he was nineteen, he convinced a group of six like-minded young relatives and friends to study the instrument with him. Zhang Dai's premise was that good musicians were scarce in Shaoxing, and that if one did not pledge oneself to play regularly throughout the year, one would never raise the general standard. The goal of the members of the *qin* club, he wrote in an elegant prose manifesto, should be to meet three times in every month, which would be far better for all of them than "to sit around idle in fine weather." If they practiced regularly, their music would form a triad with those other standard Shaoxing sounds, the wind in the pines and the rushing waters; if successful, they might even "catch an echo from the surrounding mountain peaks." Filled with a sense of purpose, they would "expand their very being" and make it their "highest ambition to have their hearts live through their hands on the strings."

Not everyone was up to these lofty standards. Zhang Dai's cousin Yanke, who joined them for a while, was simply no good at music. Nor was their friend the orchid grower Fan Yulan, though Fan was at least interesting in his badness. For a while Fan would devote himself passionately to a particular teacher, striving to catch his every nuance, until another teacher caught his fancy. Then he would unlearn everything he had just learned and start all over again, repeating the pattern at intervals. "As for those pieces Fan had studied previously," wrote Zhang, "he worked so hard at forgetting them that he truly could recall nothing of them; and finally he could not play anything at all. At night he just cradled his *qin* and tuned the strings, that was it." Zhang Dai claimed that he himself did better, learning the techniques from his teachers until he had mastered them, at which point he was able to "move back to a more natural tone," deliberately cultivating a slightly roughened sound. With a favorite teacher and the two friends who played the best, Zhang Dai formed a quartet that gave performances from time to time: "Our four instruments sounded as if played by a single hand. Our audience was spellbound."

By the year 1622, when he was twenty-five, Zhang Dai had added cockfighting to his interests, founding a club for fellow enthusiasts. Cockfighting already had been popular in China for at least two millennia and had built up an entire mystique of training and courage. Cockfights were usually in three rounds and were carried through to the death. Stories told of celebrated bird handlers in the past who had taught their high-strung charges to contain their reflexes behind a calm exterior, to be unresponsive to sound or shadow, to reveal no emotions to their antagonists. Ideally the true fighting cock would be a machine, "a wooden gamecock," from whom all lesser birds would turn and flee. As one early text put it, the best trained birds "made their feathers stand up and flapped their wings, sharpened their beaks and whetted their spurs, restrained their anger and awaited victory." The ideal fighting cock could be easily identified by its key characteristics: feathers "sparse and short," head "strong and small," feet "straight and large," eyes "deep-set" and the skin "thick."

As he had with the music club, Zhang Dai wrote a manifesto for the members of the cockfight club, though this time he used a model from the past, one written initially in the eighth century by the poet Wang Bo. Among the club regulars was Zhang's second uncle Zhongshu, who, though younger than Zhang Dai's father, was already famous in the region as an art collector and connoisseur. Uncle and nephew bet heavily on the fights—their wagers included "ancient art objects, calligraphy, paintings, brocades, fans"—and, according to Zhang Dai, his uncle lost steadily, growing angrier every time. Finally uncle Zhongshu went so far as to fasten metal spurs onto the claws of his fighting birds and to place mustard powder under their wings—practices known and condoned in fights since ancient times. Uncle Zhongshu even scoured the region for those who might have descendants of the great fighting cocks of times past, but it was to no avail. Only when Zhang Dai abandoned the club he had founded, claiming that the omens were inauspicious—the Tang emperor who had most loved cockfights was born under the same astrological signs as Zhang Dai and subsequently lost his kingdom—did the two become close friends once again.

For a time, starting in 1623, Zhang made up for the demise of the cockfights by taking his younger brothers and a chosen group of friends to watch performances of football. This was not football as a contact sport but an art form featuring extraordinary dexterity and grace, in which individual players sought to keep the ball in contact with their bodies for as long as possible. Again, there was a long tradition of such skills being practiced by both men and women, by courtiers and by commoners, sometimes in conjunction with other forms of sport and gambling. As Zhang wrote of one contemporary expert, "Kicking the ball with his feet he began to roll it over his whole body, as if it were fastened to him with glue, or held in place with a string." Some of the best ballplayers were also professional actors, a few of them from Zhang Dai's own troupes, for he was becoming a lover of the theater, too, along with its interlocking skills of voice, gesture, costume and motion.

One of the longest-lived groups was a poetry circle of Zhang Dai's relatives and friends. They would meet at intervals to write verses on common themes and to dream up erudite and apposite names for rare art objects and curiosities that they had purchased. When that palled, there was a group that met to play cards, using flexible paper cards of Zhang's own design rather than the thicker variants made of bone that had been common previously. These playing cards were focused around the themes, so standard a part of Ming dynasty life, of the cultured scholar and the extrovert military man. Zhang Dai's cousin Yanke, who had been such a failure as a musician, was an imaginative, even brilliant deviser of new card games, drawing countless elements from the familiar repertory into fresh competitive patterns of dazzling complexity.

Zhang Dai mentions other clubs or groups that his own relatives convened: his grandfather had a history club, one of his uncles had a humor club and Zhang's own father loved to meet with a select group to discuss alternate etymologies of old place names and to set geographical conundrums. And, though Zhang does not tell us when he first convened it, one of his favorites was the Crab-eating Club. This select group met only on certain afternoons in the tenth lunar month, at the perfect point in the freshwater crab gathering season, when the crab claws were purple and at their plumpest. What was so special to Zhang Dai about the crabs at this autumnal time of year was that they contained within themselves every one of the five basic flavors without needing even the tiniest bit of salt or vinegar. The rules were that each member of the club would receive six crabs, so cooked as to emphasize the flavor of every part: the succulent "jade-cream" juices, the long violet claws, the shining little legs, the flesh "sweet and velvety." But for fear that reheating them would ruin the subtlety of the taste and aroma, each crab was cooked separately and in sequence for each member of the club.

Zhang Dai granted somewhat similar virtues of exquisite transformation to the snow itself. Snow fell rarely in Shaoxing, but when it did Zhang was enraptured. He loved both what fresh snow did to landscapes and what it did to people. And he tracked the effect of snow on his moods by depicting both the shift in perspective that accompanied the movement from the small group to the solitary observer, and its opposite, in which the solitary observer found his comfort in the small group.

The first of these moments to which he gave a date was in late January of 1627. Close to three feet of snow had covered the city of Shaoxing, and when the sky cleared at evening, Zhang Dai called together five of the actresses from his little drama troupe to come and sit with him on the flat platform above the lofty main gate of the City God Temple, whence they could look out over the snow-covered landscape. "Every mountain was coated in snow," he wrote, "and the brightness of the moon draped everything so that the moon's own light could not be seen since the snow shone so brightly. After we had been sitting for some time we were frozen, and one of my old servants brought us some heated wine. I forced myself to drink a full measure, so as to ward off the chill. The hot vapors of the wine were swallowed up by all that accumulation of snow, with the result that I did not get drunk. Ma Xiaoqing sang us an aria while Li Jiesheng accompanied her on the flute. The music, subdued by the extreme cold, was muted and roughened, so that we could hardly hear it. At the third watch we came home to sleep. Ma Xiaoqing and Pan Xiaofei, holding each other tightly, rolled all the way down the hill from Hundred Paces Road to the very bottom. When they picked themselves up they were completely bathed in snow. As for me, I hired a small wheel-barrow cart, and came home dragging a great lump of ice."

Six years later, also in the twelfth lunar month, there was another major snowfall, large flakes that fell for three days. This time

Zhang Dai was across the estuary from Shaoxing, in the city of Hangzhou, where his family and several of their friends and relatives had villas, on the edge of West Lake. It was already dusk when, wrapped in a fur coat and carrying a charcoal-filled hand warmer, he clambered into a boat and told the boatman to pole out to Lake's Heart Pavilion. One could hear no human voices, not even a birdcall. With the cold mist wreathing the lake, the sky, the hills, the water itself, everything above and below was white, and the world was transfigured in the way Zhang Dai most loved: "The only shadowy forms one could make out on the lake surface were the ridged scar of the long embankment, the lone dot of Lake's Heart Pavilion, the mustard seed that was our boat, and the two grains of rice that were on the boat." When they reached the pavilion, to Zhang's surprise two men were already there, sitting on rugs while their servant heated the wine. They turned out to be travelers from Nanjing, 150 miles away, and they persuaded Zhang to take three full cups with them before he parted. As the boatman pushed off at last from the island, Zhang Dai could hear him mutter, "One can't accuse young master of being a total fool, for here are two others even more foolish than him."

Servants and boatmen were more often the silent partners in Zhang Dai's quests, the main spoken lines being reserved for Zhang himself along with his relatives and friends. But sometimes, even when not speaking, these quiet, hardworking figures became an integral part of the mood itself, inseparable from the ways a moment blossomed and flourished. When he was a student, Zhang had a study near a place in Shaoxing known as Lord Pang's Lake and there, he tells us, he always kept a boat moored so he could go out whenever the mood took him. The small lake fed into the tangled network of creeks and streams that cut through the town behind the houses and alleyways. No matter whether the moon was shining or the skies were dark, and without regard to the hour, Zhang Dai would have his boatman convey him along a circuitous route of a mile or two, while he stretched out, lazily watching as the darkened houses and the landscape glided by.

He caught one such outing with these words: "On the slopes of the hills, the house gates were all closed and people were sleeping deeply, one could not see the light from a single lamp. In the silent darkness, the mood was somber. I laid out a clean mat in the boat so I could lie there and look at the moon; in the prow of the boat, one of my young serving companions began to chant a song. The drinking I had done blurred with the dream I was having, the sound of the song seemed to recede, the moon itself also seemed to grow paler. Suddenly I was asleep. The song ended, I was as swiftly awake, and mumbled a few words of thanks, but almost at once was snoring yet again. My little singer too was yawning with tiredness and stretched out, and we each pillowed ourselves on the other. The boatman poled us back to the shore, beating out a rhythm with the pole to tell us it was time to go to bed. At that moment my mind was huge as the ocean, I could feel no trace of any resentment." Even after "sleeping the following day around," Zhang wrote, "I still could not grasp what this thing was that people call sorrow."

Despite the apparent intimacy of this tranquil moment, Zhang always harbored the conviction that people remained self-conscious even when they seemed the most self-absorbed. He knew that in our minds we are never far away from scrutinizing the image we are conveying to others, and moon viewing provided no exception to this rule of life. As he drifted one evening at leisure on Hangzhou's West Lake, at the time of the September moon festival, despite the varied delights of the occasion there was nothing more absorbing to Zhang than watching the other people who were also out on the lake watching the moon.

Zhang categorized the moon watchers into five classes, each of which he sketched in words. There were the very rich, in their formal clothes, entertained by actors as they ate their banquets. Distracted by their many pleasures, though they were indeed floating under the moon, "they never really saw it, though they themselves were worth watching." There were those distracted by their efforts at seduction, as they sought the attention of the courtesans and pretty boys bunched on the decks of their vessels: "Though their bodies were under the moon, they never really looked at it, though they too were worth watching." There were those who reclined on their boats and sipped their wine in the company of women and Buddhist priests, talking quietly as the music softly played. "They did watch the moon, but they wanted others to watch them watching the moon." Then there were the onshore rowdies, who owned no boats but racketed along the lakeshore, stuffed with food and pretending to be drunker than they really were, shouting and singing out of key. These were the eclectic ones, watching the moon to some extent, and also watching others who were watching the moon, "but also watching those who were not watching the moon, and themselves seeing nothing." And lastly there were the studiedly elegant aesthetes, who traveled in small boats, their figures sheltered behind fine curtains, sipping tea from delicate white porcelain with their female companions, quietly watching the moon but in such a way that others could not view them watching it. Since "they did not watch the moon self-consciously, they too were worth watching."

Zhang wrote also of those who took their pleasure in esoteric ways. It was grandfather's friend Bao, for example, who created three multistoried boats just for his and his guests' pleasure: one boat was for his troupe of singers, one for his art collection and one for other diversions with his chosen companions. At intervals Bao might sail off with a group of guests for ten days or more at a time, with no one knowing when or where they would come back to land. This same Bao, Zhang was told, had erected an eight-sided pavilion, which he called his Chamber of the Eight Trigrams. Bao's room was in the center with eight rooms encircling it. Each of those eight rooms was enclosed by curtains that Bao could raise or lower when he chose, to watch the beauties as they lay. There in his chamber old Bao could recline on his pillow, light some incense and play with the curtains. Thus his last twenty years sped by.

Playing at hunting was another way Zhang gained pleasure. Zhang described in the lushest terms one such outing that he took in 1638: how he and his friends went riding out of the city in hunting costume, with five courtesans they had chosen to accompany them, the women all "dressed as archers, in red brocade trimmed with fox fur, their hair held in place with fur headbands, mounted on horseback." With their outriders carrying the weapons of the chase, dogs straining at their leashes, falcons clutching at leather gloves, they could pretend to be chasing down musk deer and hare, pheasants and foxes, before resting their tired limbs to watch a play, staying overnight in a countryside temple and returning the next day for a new round of parties at the Zhang clan's residence.

Zhang Dai also knew of the darker shadows in the nighttime

alleyways, for with his younger cousin Zhuoru he had scoured the narrow streets of the brothel areas in Yangzhou, a hub for travelers heading to or from Beijing along the Grand Canal and the center of China's vibrant (and government-monopolized) salt trade. There were, wrote Zhang, almost one hundred of these little meandering streets twisting and turning around and across each other. Despite the narrowness of the alleys, some of the houses, especially those of the most celebrated courtesans, were quite grand, and access could only be obtained by the services of a hired go-between or guide. Such sought-after women never paraded themselves in public, as did the common prostitutes of Yangzhou, who numbered between five and six hundred by Zhang's calculation. In mock military language these women of the streets described themselves as being "on guard duty" when they worked. Brushed and bathed and perfumed, they came out into the dusk of early evening and settled in their favorite teahouses and wineshops. If overly bright lanterns were lit, or if the moon shone too strongly, those with blemishes hovered in the shadows, where darkness helped their makeup to disguise their flaws. Some withdrew further, shielding their ravaged good looks behind curtains, or concealing their country women's unbound feet behind the high lintels of the doorways. Men moved back and forth across the streets, seeking their evening partner. When they found one, the two set off for the woman's lodgings. As soon as they were sighted, her spotter at the gate would shout out, "Big sister so-and-so has a guest." From inside the house would come an answering shout, and people rushed out with lanterns to welcome the couple for their brief tryst together.

So it would go on into the night, until at last only twenty or thirty of the streetwalkers were still left at their posts. It was to these women that Zhang Dai paid the greatest attention in his words. He watched them as the darkness thickened. The lanterns burned down to a flicker, the teahouses and wineshops doused their lights, the sounds of voices stilled. He noted how the women—so the waiters would not chase them out—pooled some of their scarce money to buy a few more minutes of light, in hopes of a late client dropping by. He watched the waiters' yawns grow deeper, and he registered how the women's attempts to sing songs or tell tales interspersed with bursts of falsely cheerful laughter gradually faded into silence. "As it neared midnight," wrote Zhang Dai, "they had no choice but to leave, silently and feeling their way, like ghosts. And when they got home to their old procuress they might be deprived of food, or beaten—there is no way for us to know."

Between the luxury boats and the back lanes lay another zone, that of a human market devoted to the longer term, where young women might be sold as junior consorts or concubines to wealthy local families. Zhang Dai wrote of this world with his usual detail, in a tone that blended disquiet with sympathy. Once again, the setting he selected was the city of Yangzhou. He titled his piece "The Lean Nags of Yangzhou," using the current local slang term for the flesh market. Those who made their livelihood by battening on to such women numbered a hundred or more, Zhang calculated. These predators seemed to be everywhere—they were "like flies on rotting meat, and there was no way to brush them off." Once you had let it be known that you were interested in obtaining a woman, the go-between knocked on your front door at dawn and hurried you off to the first "nag's" house. After you were seated and had sipped a bowl of tea, the first of the women or girls was brought out for your scrutiny. Following the instructions of her owner-manager or madame, she would bow before the potential patron, pirouette, turn her face to the light, pull up her sleeves to reveal her hands and the texture of the skin on her arms. Then she would state her age, so the patron could judge the delicacy of her voice, and walk some steps so he could gauge the size of her feet. After she left the room, a new prospective partner would be brought forward—most of the houses had five or six on display, Zhang wrote—and the whole sequence of inspections would begin again.

And so it might go on, day after day, inspecting woman after woman, tipping matchmaker after matchmaker, until the girls with their powdered faces and their red dresses faded into an indistinguishable blur in which discrimination became impossible. It was just like writing the same exercises in your practice book a hundred, a thousand times, Zhang wrote, until you cannot even recognize the written characters anymore. If, either at random or for good reason, one made a choice, then there were pledges to be offered: first, a gold pin or an ornamental clasp for her hair. Next, an inventory on red paper for the man to fill in with brush and ink—so much colored silk, so much jewelry, so much cash, so many bolts of cloth. Then, if a patron had signed for enough items on the inventory, a procession of joyful hangers-on headed from the woman's lodgings to the proud purchaser's house. There were musicians and drummers, servants carrying wine, dressed meats and pastries as well as the "bride" herself, in a sedan chair, with her escort of lantern bearers, "bridesmaids," singers and cooks loaded down with more meats, vegetables and sweetmeats and all the paraphernalia of a feast—awnings, table coverings, cushions, table settings and bed curtains. The celebrations are noisy and cheerful, but also swift and efficient, for this of course is not a real wedding, nor is it taking place in real time, as Zhang Dai cannot help reminding us: before the sun is even at its zenith the hired help have pocketed their tips and are en route to another house and another client, where they will repeat the same performance.

Zhang Dai was content to leave unexplained the varying routes by which the junior consorts or concubines came into the service of the Zhang family, and it is only rarely that he even mentions their names. But there is no doubt that he was intrigued by mystery women, by those who knew how to play their parts and at the same time brought a promise of sexual surprise along with them, even if they seemed to come from nowhere and have no fixed point of return. Among such were the women who, at the lantern parties thrown by his grandfather on Dragon Mountain, left their tiny shoes dangling in the tree branches, as if gesturing nostalgically to the pleasures they had just enjoyed or bestowed. And such too were the six or seven women who suddenly appeared at the same festival, ordering an untapped flagon of wine when they were told no wine was left in the opened jars, and drinking it all as they munched the melons and other fruit they had hidden in their sleeves, before vanishing into the night.

On occasion, Zhang Dai presented these vignettes with an apparently documentary precision, as in the case of a woman who drifted into his life for a moment in 1639. Zhang Dai tells us he had been out on the West Lake of Hangzhou with one of his great-uncles, drinking on a pleasure boat, when the old man declared his wish to return home early. But Zhang Dai's close friend, the painter Chen Hongshou, was with them. He had been drinking steadily and protested at the early close to the party. So after seeing great-uncle home, Zhang Dai rented another boat—a smaller one this time—and returned to the lake to watch the moon and let Chen drink some more. A friend hailed them from the shore and offered them orange confits, which they ate with gusto. Chen Hongshou was sound asleep and snoring loudly when a young lady's servant called to them from the shore, asking Zhang Dai if he could give his mistress a ride to First Bridge. "Of course," replied Zhang Dai, and the woman climbed onto their vessel. She seemed joyful, friendly, slender in a light silk dress, and Chen Hongshou, awakening, was enchanted. He challenged her to a drinking match, which she accepted. At the second watch of the night, they reached First Bridge, and she drained her wine cup and stepped ashore. Zhang Dai and Chen Hongshou asked her where she lived. "She merely smiled in reply," wrote Zhang Dai. "Chen Hongshou clambered ashore and tried to follow her, and saw her pass by the tomb of the ancient kings of Yue. But he never caught up with her."

The swath of China with which Zhang Dai was most familiar—stretching at the northwest point from Yangzhou on the Grand Canal down in the southeast to his hometown of Shaoxing itself, with Nanjing and Hangzhou poised between the two—was then the economic and cultural heartland of China. It was also the region where a virtual cult of the studious courtesan was flourishing, one that recognized especially talented and beautiful women as much for their scholarly attainments as for their physical allure. For Zhang Dai, as for many other men of his time, the scholarly courtesan was inevitably tinged with melancholy, for she spanned two worlds that were not necessarily in harmony and indeed clashed in certain inevitable ways. The scholarly courtesan became, by her very nature, a public figure and object of scrutiny as well as of desire. She was both irresistible and remote because she was already in the public gaze. And, as a consequence, she could be written about with a freedom that would not be used in writing of one's own wife, concubine or other family members.

The woman in this category whom Zhang Dai knew the best, and who often accompanied him on his excursions outside Nanjing to beauty spots like Swallow Rock, was called Wang Yuesheng. Wang, wrote Zhang, had started out in the poorest of the brothel areas of Nanjing—the area known as the Red Market, where respectable people were ashamed to be seen. But her beauty was extraordinary and Zhang rhapsodized about her complexion, fresh as a newly opened orchid, and her tiny, pointed feet, "like the first shoots of the water chestnut."

To Zhang, Wang Yuesheng stood out from all the denizens of her quarter. She gradually made her way into more rarified regions where she would not even appear at banquets to sing unless booked in writing well in advance and paid five or even ten gold coins. More private assignations had to be booked in January or February if one was hoping for her favors within a given year. Wang Yuesheng learned to read and write, and to paint well, excelling in her renderings of orchids, bamboo and narcissi; she became a connoisseur of fine teas by sitting at the feet of the region's greatest expert, Master Min. She was especially accomplished at singing the tunes known as the songs of Wu, from the coastal region. Wang Yuesheng cultivated an image of refined distancing, keeping silent when others were raucous, remaining somber while others laughed. Zhang likened this side of her nature to "a solitary plum blossom under a cold moon, cool and distant." If forced into the company of someone she despised, Wang remained silent.

Zhang Dai sized up her character with a simple anecdote: "A man of quality once paid for her to sleep and eat with him for a spell of two weeks or so, but he failed to get a word out of her. One day her mouth moved as if she were about to speak, and those in attendance on her rushed off to tell their master, calling out, 'Yuesheng is about to speak!' There was a surge of excitement and her patron hurried to be with her. Her face grew animated for a moment, but then resumed its previous calm. The man begged her again and again to speak, and at last she graced him with just two words: 'I'm leaving.' "

Sometime, probably in the mid-1630s, Zhang Dai wrote a poem for Wang Yuesheng, trying to catch what it was about her that had kept her in such demand for close to thirty years. The poem's title was plain and frank—"For the singer-courtesan Wang Yuesheng"—and Zhang warned the reader that the exercise was a perilous one: trying to assemble apt comparisons to describe the dwellers in the brothel quarters of Nanjing would naturally be seen as an inappropriate task, and the common folk who heard about it would bare their teeth in laughter. Yet true connoisseurs would perhaps understand—most of all Wang's longtime instructor in the rigors of tea tasting, the seventy-year-old Master Min from Peach Leaf Crossing. After a lifetime of experience, Min could "conjure up the taste of a particular tea from the empty air," just as Zhang was trying to catch the essence of Wang Yuesheng from the traces in his memory:

From the white porcelain cup the aroma ascends like
    jasmine;

Its color like pear blossom glimpsed through a paper
    window.
How to describe that delicate taste on the tip of the
    tongue?
Sweetness and tartness are even better than the inner tang
    of olive.
So when I first came face to face with Wang Yuesheng,
It was almost as if the tea spoke overtly to me.
Her walking was delicate, three steps to my one;
But so restrained was her reserve, she seemed like ice.

That feeling vanished as Zhang Dai let himself succumb to the
beauty of her face, to her freshness and fragility, to the lure of her
body through her dress. These were the stock manifestations of the
definition of beauty in his day, but Zhang did not pause to mock
himself; his goal was to recapture his sense of bewilderment at the
depth of emotion he felt. This passion, this *qing* in the language of
the time, was a pure force that justified a multitude of human actions and beliefs, and Zhang claimed that he accepted it at once,
even though he had not found the exact word to describe what he
felt. He was still gazing, in silence, when his friend Junmo gave
him the tea metaphor with which to capture her inner quality.

In his closing quatrain, Zhang rounded out the metaphor and
at last brought himself back to earth:

Using the exquisiteness of tea to describe an exquisite
    woman,
Who has ever thought of such a thing down through the
    ages?

Even just saying that someone's calligraphy "is filled with
   the sound of a river"
Will lead those who hear you to spit out their food with
   laughter.

There was no concealing the theatricality of Wang Yuesheng's demeanor and gestures, and her combination of remote-
ness and accessibility clearly made her all the more alluring to
Zhang Dai and to many others. Indeed the theater was never far
from his thoughts, and he dedicated much money and effort to
the pursuit of excellence onstage. Zhang Dai was aware that this
art form was in a process of growth and change—he may have
claimed to know what the rules were, but not everyone agreed.
The melodious and enchanting form of regional drama from
Suzhou known as *kunqu* was already separating itself from local
specializations like Shaoxing theater, just as later "Beijing opera"
was to grow out of and—to many connoisseurs—to vulgarize
kunqu drama in search of a broader audience. There is little
doubt that Zhang Dai, despite his interest in music, still knew
that in important ways the drama he loved and the actresses he
admired were true to the basic demands of telling a story perfectly. The storyteller Pock-marked Liu, for instance, with his
brilliant improvisations and booming voice, marked a kind of
transition between the more ancient arts of narration and the
newer and richer theatrical techniques. Liu's base of operations
was in Nanjing, though his fame had spread far. Like Wang
Yuesheng, he had to be booked days or weeks in advance and
paid a retainer fee. He would offer one recitation each day, never
more, and would simply stop completely if he was interrupted by

his listeners' whispering—or even if they yawned. Liu's looks, though odd—he was "swarthy," and his face "covered in craters and ridges"—did not lessen his powers. "He might be remarkably ugly," wrote Zhang. "But his lips are puckish, his eyes animated, his dress quietly elegant: all of which effectively puts him on a par with Wang Yuesheng for comeliness, hence their equal drawing power as entertainers."

The Zhang family's passion for operatic drama, Zhang Dai was careful to point out, was not deeply rooted in family traditions, but originated with his grandfather around the time Zhang Dai was born. Grandfather and a small group of four friends—all of whom were from the Hangzhou area or from just across the northern border of Zhejiang province in the wealthy southern part of Jiangsu—were the ones who took the first step of forming their own troupes of singers. All of these friends were recipients of the highest literary degrees, and the fact of such prestigious men sponsoring acting troupes and "paying fastidious attention to them" was, according to Zhang Dai, "completely unprecedented." In one essay he mentioned six of these companies—two of these may well have been composed of boys and men, but three of the others certainly had actresses in them and perhaps were exclusively composed of girls and women performers. Membership of the troupes shifted over time, and on occasion a troupe changed its name but kept some original members. Actors of the caliber of those found in the troupes of his grandfather's generation had, by the time of Zhang Dai's maturity, "become as impossible to find as the jewels and ceremonial objects of the Three Dynasties."

Zhang Dai's father had several acting troupes of his own once he abandoned his ceaseless quest for examination success and embarked on the ostentatious life of a man-about-town, as did several other uncles or cousins of Zhang Dai. His younger brother Pingzi also had his own troupe, whose members appear to have come into Zhang Dai's own troupe when his brother died prematurely. As Zhang Dai tried to explain this passion, "The master of the troupe gains in insight as day follows upon day, whereas the skills and artistry of his young charges become more remarkable the more they perform." Zhang Dai loved to watch the transitions within his own troupes, as actors and actresses grew in age and in power until it came time for them to retire and be replaced by a new batch of youngsters. In some of his troupes, this process repeated itself five times. "As for myself," said Zhang Dai, "though I have now become a trembling old man, with eyes grown as green as a Persian's, I can still tell the good actors from the bad. When a man from the mountains travels across the sea and returns home again, his eyes retain all the flavor of what they have seen. Come all of you and taste them!" The joys of success were obvious to Zhang: "It was thanks to me that these actors rose in the world and became famous. Later, by way of these actors whom I had made famous I myself became famous too."

There were of course countless ways of training an apprentice actor. Zhang Dai wrote of one teacher called Zhu who never began his theater training for girls by introducing them to acting. Instead he taught them first to play a broad range of musical instruments—strings, wind and percussion—and then taught them to sing and finally to dance. The result was that some of Zhu's actresses attained a "level of perfection that could be felt through the pores." There were, however, two major problems with Zhu as a teacher. In mounting a performance, he never knew when to stop and would appeal to the crowd by piling on redundant dances and special effects. Zhu was also lascivious and possessive, and his treatment of women went beyond the bounds of decency. Zhang Dai wrote that people could hear the cries of rage from women Zhu had locked up in certain special rooms so that he could have his way with them.

Though teacher Zhu blurred the lines between artistic training and amorous demands, Zhang Dai wrote of celebrated female singers who had started off as courtesans and made the transition to the status of singers and actresses able to tackle the most demanding roles and take part in as many as seven different plays that might continue through the night. The presence in the audience of their learned and demanding teachers could paralyze some singers, depriving them of voice and motion. They likened the experience to "passing through a gateway of swords." Others had an almost impossible setting for their art, like the actresses whom Zhang Dai's father summoned to give a performance in one of his newly built "floating stages" that was tossed in a storm while moored on the lake in front of the large audience. But out of willingness to shine, and urged on by applause, most of them could overcome the difficulties of the setting and their confusion. Lengthy opera sessions held in wealthy homes, like those of the Zhangs, allowed connoisseurs to assess one another's skills as teachers and also fostered some mobility between opera troupes as aesthetes sought to recruit fresh talent for their own group.

Occasionally, however, even young actresses would perform in front of immense crowds. Zhang Dai estimated that at the autumn festival of 1634 there were at least seven hundred invited guests assembled at Ji Mountain. All of them brought their own wine and food, and carpets were spread for them to sit on under the stars. With other guests and mutual friends the number— spread across seventy mats—was close to a thousand. All had been drinking steadily for several hours and singing songs together when Zhang told his young actresses Liu Jiezhu and Ying Chuyan to perform a choice of scenes—they ended up singing around ten. The two young women had originally been in Zhang Dai's brother Pingzi's troupe, but due to the brother's death they had been taken over by Zhang Dai himself. They sang their last songs under the moonlight, which made the faces of the audience "shine as if they had just been bathing"; and as the distant mountains disappeared among clouds, the girl's voices rang out so purely "that the mosquitoes ceased to hum."

One of Zhang Dai's favorites among the actresses in his own troupe was Liu Huiji, who had developed her own approach to acting. As Zhang Dai wrote of her: "To get a following among the public, an actress needs to have charms, self-assurance, and personality. But for Liu Huiji that is not the case. Liu Huiji is full of imagination, and her desire is to remedy the failings of actors from the past." Though Zhang Dai did not spell out exactly what he meant by that depiction, it is clear that Liu was especially brilliant at acting male parts in the dramas she performed, and Zhang noted that his friend Peng Tianxi had said to him: "With an actress like Liu Huiji, what need is there any more for male actors? And what need for old Peng?" Peng Tianxi was known to be a stern judge and to give out praise sparingly, wrote Zhang, so the compliment was especially to be treasured.

A native of Jiangsu province to the north of Shaoxing, Peng Tianxi was a friend of Zhang Dai's for many years—and, like other highly refined gentry opera lovers, he was at once critic, sponsor, actor, teacher and enthusiastic viewer. In an admiring essay, Zhang succinctly summarized the expensive perfectionism of this actor-director he thought of as "the best in the world." Peng's rules were simple: he never strayed from the script to embellish it with inventions of his own; to prepare for a performance, he would invite the whole cast to his home for rehearsals, regardless of the cost, which might be dozens of taels each time; he was constantly expanding his repertoire, so that over the years he played fifty or sixty different scenes at Zhang Dai's home without ever repeating himself; and as an actor he specialized, concentrating on just two of the standard parts that were common in most dramas: those of the villain and the clown. Nobody could portray evil and cruelty like Peng: "When he puckered his brows and peered out at you, you would have sworn there was a sword in his belly and a dagger in his smile; he was so demonic, so murderous, that people shuddered with dread." Perhaps, Zhang Dai reflected, Peng had in his nature so much learning, such great vistas, so much subtlety and energy, that it was only through theater that he could give shape to it all. Peng's performances, concluded Zhang, were of such a quality and originality "that one regretted not being able to wrap each of them up in the finest brocade, so that they could be passed on and preserved forever."

The only actress who came close to matching Peng's power, in Zhang Dai's view, was Zhu Chusheng. She had been trained by an opera teacher from Ningbo named Yao, and had become a specialist in what was becoming known as the Shaoxing school of performance. Yao was a tough teacher, constantly seeking musical perfection, and he used Zhu Chusheng as the standard by which to judge all the other members of his troupe. She, in turn, had devoted her whole life to the theater and invested all her energies there. If her teacher pointed out anything that could be improved in her singing or in her recitations of the libretto, she would not rest till the flaw had been corrected. "She was not especially beautiful," Zhang wrote, "but the most beautiful woman in the world never had her special qualities. She was poignant and impetuous; one could read her independence in her brows, and read her depth of feeling in her eyes, the charm could be seen in her dreamy look, in the poise of her movement." But in Zhang's eyes, Zhu was doomed by the excess of her emotions, "by the depth of her feelings, which she was unable to control." One twilight, said Zhang, he sat beside her near the river in Shaoxing. The sun sank, mist rose over the water, the trees turned dark and she began, silently, to cry. Unlike Peng, she could not release all the turbulent forces that consumed her. She died, thought Zhang, "because she just had too much sadness in her heart."

Much of life, for Zhang Dai, was spectacle, and the great truths for him remained aesthetic ones. In the world of the spirits, as on the stage of life, there could be no clear demarcations between the ruthless play of the gods and the frail defenses of men. What we call the real world was just a meeting place in which the two struggled for attention and competed to see how well all of us could play our parts. Zhang Dai lived to explore such moments. It was late at night, he writes, one day after the midautumn festival of 1629, that he anchored his boat on the river shore below Gold Mountain. He was traveling north to visit his father, taking the Grand Canal route, and had just crossed the Yangzi River at Zhenjiang. A bright moon played on the water, which was swirled in mist. Among its surrounding trees, Gold Mountain Temple was dark and silent. Entering the temple's great hall, Zhang Dai was seized by a sense of the past, for this was the very place where the Southern Song general Han Shizhong, with only eight thousand troops, had fought for eighteen days against the Jin invaders from the north, finally beating them back from the river. Zhang called to his servants to bring lanterns and musical instruments from the boat, to light the hall and to play an accompaniment as he chanted the story of General Han and the battle for the Yangzi River long ago.

At the sound of the music, wrote Zhang, "All the monks got up from their beds to take a look, the old ones amongst them rubbing the sleep out of their eyes with the backs of their hands, their mouths agape, yawning, laughing, sneezing as they watched intently. . . . But none of them," Zhang added, "dared ask what kind of beings we were, what we were doing there, and when we had come." The performance finished, and dawn lightening the sky, Zhang Dai had the props and lanterns stowed away, the boat pushed off from the shore, and resumed his journey. All the monks, he wrote, came down to the riverbank and followed him with their eyes until they could be seen no more. And Zhang Dai was satisfied: "Whether we were humans, or emanations, or demons, they did not know."

CHAPTER TWO

CHARTING THE WAY

On ordinary days Zhang Dai studied. He never was done, and he never would be done, as he well knew, for he was locked into a system from which there was no outlet save absolute success. And even absolute success was a frail concept, since within apparent success there could always lurk an undertow of failure.

The scholarly heritage for which Zhang Dai was being groomed consisted of far more than rote learning of a few texts. At its heart lay the potential for a life immersed in the intricacies of Chinese scholarship that private libraries conferred, and the opportunity for family members to devote a goodly section of their lives and their resources to the act of reading for the examinations. Based on a curriculum of classical works drawn from the Confucian canon, higher levels of the state exams were spread over several days of intense mental testing. Success in these exams promised entry to a bureaucratic career and the prestige and profit that came with it. In the Zhangs' world there

was nothing at all surprising about members of different generations studying together side by side: fathers had rarely passed
their senior examinations before their eldest sons were born, and
in some cases the youngsters might pass before their own father
or uncles. For the wealthy, the examinations were simply a fact of
life that had to be confronted—normally at three-year intervals—
again and again across the decades: initially at the local county
level where the qualifying exams were held, then at the provincial capital level and, finally, for an elite handful, the triennial national exams held in Beijing.

In his own case, Zhang Dai attributed this sense of heritage to
his great-great-grandfather Tianfu, born in or near 1513, the
third son of a prosperous branch of the Zhang family in Shaoxing. According to family legend, as a boy Tianfu had been ordered by his father to pursue a career in business, since both his
elder brothers had already embarked on scholarly careers. But
tearfully pleading with his father that being forbidden to study
would be a catastrophe—"Am I not human, that you wish me to
be a merchant?"—Tianfu prevailed and began the protracted
period of study that brought him at last to success in the national
examinations in the year 1547.

Yet even this pioneering great-great-grandfather Tianfu had
a shadow lying over the exam success that meant so much to him.
In Zhang Dai's account, after Tianfu won the right to study because of his tearful pleas, he passed the local exams and thus
earned licentiate's rank and the right to take the qualifying exams in Hangzhou. But the examiner there was a man called Xu
who not only already had taught Tianfu in the local Shaoxing
school, but had graded him the highest among the previous

year's crop. Now this same Xu summoned Tianfu to help him scrutinize the competing students' papers from other counties, assuring Tianfu that he had already decided that he would be ranked at the top. When Tianfu demurred, fearing gossip, scandal or worse, and said that he had better leave, Xu overrode him, with the startling remark, "Your paper will be graded as the best; as for those to be ranked number two and below, I will leave those decisions to you." Though Tianfu went on to pass the higher-level exams in the regular way, the episode (even if known only to the Zhang family) certainly called great-great-grandfather's integrity into question.

The Zhang family believed that the beauty of the building where Tianfu studied had been a crucial factor in his success, and to the young Zhang Dai it was altogether appropriate that great-great-grandfather had worked in such a setting. "None of the study pavilions built later in our family were as good as this one," Zhang wrote of a visit he made to the site in 1613. "The place was called the 'Bamboo Long Life Pavilion,' and though later on our family built towers and halls and studios, they were never like this. To have made it any higher would have diminished it, just as adding another wall anywhere would have disfigured it. Great-great-grandfather created this pavilion as a perfect whole, and did not wish anyone to add a single painted rafter or ceramic tile to the outside, nor a single door or leaf to the inside. That was how he wanted it. In front of the pavilion, and behind it, with his own hands he planted trees that grew to a fine size, providing clear shade and light breezes, swaying gently like feather fans, as if one were floating in autumn waters."

To contrast with the perfection of the study pavilion, Zhang

Dai chose to highlight the realities of the examination process it-self. His source here was one of his contemporaries, Ai, who sat for the provincial-level examinations seven times between the early 1600s and the 1620s without passing. In a brief memoir transcribed by Zhang, Ai recalled how he struggled to pass the exams every three years, trying to guess at the types of scholar-ship favored by different examiners, drawing from a variety of stylistic models from different periods and eclectically shifting from classics to philosophy, from astronomy to geography, and even to military tactics and Taoism.

Ai wrote of the endless discomforts and indignities that he endured in the examination halls: joining the shivering crowds of young men at dawn, signing in at the entrance gate, shuffling forward with brush and inkstone in one hand and a coverlet in the other, enduring the cold hands of proctors giving the candi-dates body searches to check that they were not smuggling in written material with which to cheat on their answers. Then came the chore of finding the right booth and a miserable plank bench, sweating through the dust and mounting heat as the sum-mer day advanced, desperately shielding their answer papers with their clothing if a sudden rain broke through the frail roof. Even finding a time and place to urinate was hard, and the enclo-sure stank from the hundreds of sweating bodies crammed to-gether in the exam compound. One saving grace was that the proctors paraded past the candidates' seats calling out the topic aloud for those whose eyes—like those of Ai himself—were too weak or weary to read the question papers; for those hard of hearing, other proctors wrote the questions in large characters on display boards. Once the exams were finished, wrote Ai, the students had to endure the uncertainties of erratic grading before being informed of their rankings and their scores. If they failed, they knew they faced the same dreary prospect all over again. "People looked like wives or slaves," Ai noted, "deprived of all their dignity."

Zhang Dai added his own glosses to Ai's account. The formalized answer system known as "the eight-legged essays," he wrote, had been imposed by the Ming rulers to "torment scholars and discourage ambitious men." Any small slip in style or content led to demerits or failure. Even the finest of scholars would "find no use for their arsenal of talents and knowledge" unless they joined the pack, "submissive in manner, limited in scope, stale in words, poor in attire, with internal feeling rotted away." The result was damaging to the country as a whole: those who passed were "either old men waiting for death, or naïve youth who understood nothing." And yet, curiously, both Ai and Zhang felt that there was something useful in the system despite all its pressures and shortcomings: the studying and the stress did create strong bonds between teachers and students; a life of leisure was not the only significant way to spend the time; hardship could lead to greater things.

There was, of course, no guarantee that great-great-grandfather Tianfu's success would be replicated by others in the Zhang family. Indeed the health of Tianfu's eldest son, Wengong, was so poor when he was a child that his mother forbade him to carry out the intensive routine of study demanded for successful candidates. Scared of arousing her anger, Wengong would conceal a night-light in his room. Only when he knew his mother had retired to her quarters to sleep would he light his own lamp and begin to read, continuing through the night. Zhang Dai adds that the stresses to which his great-grandfather was subjected in the political realm had turned his hair completely white by the time he was thirty. So when great-grandfather Wengong astounded his family and his fellow townsmen by winning the top place in the Beijing examinations in 1571, "the white-haired number one" was the nickname that his fellow students gave to him.

Despite the fame that accrued to the Zhang family because of Wengong's startling triumph, Zhang Dai knew that Wengong's subsequent career was not especially fruitful and that his examination success weighed upon the family. "Throughout his life," Zhang Dai wrote, "my great-grandfather Wengong served the concepts of loyalty and filial behavior. He looked upon receiving the top-ranked grade in the palace examinations as being a consequence of our family's loyalty and filiality; thus his attainment of the top-ranked position was a foundation for us all, not to be seen merely as 'good fortune.' Those who looked upon his success merely as an example of good fortune were people with a consumer's view of good fortune; but those who saw it not as mere good fortune but as a foundation are the sort of people who can encourage good fortune to emerge. If that were not the case, why was it that Wengong made no attempt to eat or drink in luxury and to live palatially? And those among his later descendants who are not like him, what does that say about us?"

Even more enigmatic was the portrait that Zhang Dai painted of his own grandfather Rulin. Zhang Dai termed his grandfather's calligraphy "ugly and clumsy" and felt that a certain "unruliness" set the man apart from his fellows. It wasn't that grandfather was slow in any obvious sense. Like most of the family he was quick with words and capable of astonishingly erudite quips in the most unlikely circumstances; one case in point was when as a boy with his "hair still tied up in tufts" he was taken to see his father's friend Xu Wei in prison, after Xu had been condemned to death for murder. In a few minutes of conversation, grandfather was able to fit in two erudite allusions, which led the condemned man to murmur, "I was almost embarrassed by a child." The main problem was that grandfather always wanted to do and express things his own way. In Zhang Dai's words, his grandfather "really exerted himself to be good at classical learning, but he was always unwilling to follow superficial readings of the texts just in order to gain some easy success." Even buying his way into the imperial academy and giving up all attempts to see to the family landholdings and other pressing matters while he studied without interruption failed to smooth the rough edges or bring him prompt examination success.

Grandfather Rulin finally felt ready to take the provincial exams in the late 1580s, but was not able to do so because the deaths of his father and mother occurred almost concurrently at just this time (Wengong in 1588 and Lady Wang in 1591), and by tradition a son mourned each of his parents for a twenty-seven-month period after their deaths. During that mourning period, one could neither hold bureaucratic office nor take the state examinations. But one could still study, and so grandfather did, first in the family pavilions in Shaoxing and later, in 1594, in a final burst at Crane Call Mountain in Nanjing. But in his mountain studio grandfather "fell ill with a film that spread over his eyes, so that he had to pull coverings over the windows, and sit in contemplation for three months." Nevertheless, Zhang Dai noted, the enforced change of circumstances did not deflect grandfather from his larger goals. His friends came to discuss topics from the classics with him in his darkened room, "and after their words entered his ears, whole essays would spring forth from him." The mental drill this period of artificial darkness provided, Zhang Dai implies, helped his grandfather not only to pass the provincial exams in the summer of 1594 but to move on at once to the national exams in Beijing, which he passed in 1595 at the age of thirty-nine, not long before Zhang Dai was born.

Yet even here, Zhang Dai found strange ambiguities in the way his grandfather managed to obtain his provincial degree in 1594, and he spent some time trying to record the exact details. According to this account, which Zhang included in a brief biographical sketch, his grandfather showed up punctually for the exam, wrote his answers swiftly and finished all his answer booklets before noon. The papers were handed in to the assistant examiner, whose job it was to make a preliminary cut, and he summarily placed all grandfather's booklets in the "reject" category. As the day wore on, the assistant examiner handed in to the chief examiner, a man called Li, the first batch of answers he had felt to be the best. "But Li scolded the assistant because the batch was so poor, and told him to send in another batch. This batch also Li considered no good, so the assistant examiner was told to submit some more, and this went on four or five times until there were no more exam booklets to hand in. The assistant examiner wept with anger."

Double-checking the numbers of papers that had been handed in, Li realized that there were still seven booklets of essays that he had not seen at all, and he asked the assistant examiner what had happened to them. "Those seven booklets made no sense at all," came the reply, "so I just kept them separately here as a source of amusement." Li demanded that all seven booklets be produced and, again in Zhang Dai's words, "as soon as Li had read them clapped his hands and declared them to be profound. He used cinnabar and lead to blank out the negative comments that had been written on the seven answer booklets by the assistant examiner. Among all the answers to the question on *The Book of Changes* he adjudged grandfather's to be the best, and a candidate called Gong Sanyi's to be the second best. All the rest of the essays [in the same batch] were also high on the list."

But though it was Li's inclination to place grandfather's name at the top of the list of passing candidates, wrote Zhang, he was inhibited by the "precedent followed in the south, that the eldest son of a senior official could not be placed at the top of the listings." Accordingly, chief examiner Li put Gong's name at the top and grandfather's a few spots below, though Li later told people that in acting thus "I did something that went against my own heart." The entire examination process was full of protocols, one of which was that the successful students were expected to offer their formal thanks to the examiners who had passed them. True to this custom, "After the provincial degree list had been publicly posted, grandfather paid a visit to the assistant examiner. But the assistant examiner closed the door and would not receive him, saying: 'You are no disciple of mine, so don't confuse things.'"

Like the national examinations, the triennial provincial exams were complex and formal events, taking several days and involving many hundreds, even thousands, of students, and there is no doubt that Zhang Dai was somewhat streamlining the story for effect. But the key point for him was that chief examiner Li was the kind of man who had flexibility as well as standards of excellence, whereas the assistant examiner tried to play by the rules and penalized those of eccentric or independent views. Grandfather was lucky to have had his brilliance perceived and to have made the cut. If all seven of the previously rejected papers were indeed of excellent quality, that may also imply that the assistant examiner was biased against those from Shaoxing— who usually dominated the listings in the region—or else had some private roster of his own favorite candidates that he was trying to impose on the chief examiner. When, later on in his official career, grandfather became an examiner in his turn, he made a point of looking for signs of talent among those names of candidates assigned to the reject lists, and was eventually dismissed for doing so too often and too flagrantly.

The world of scholarship described by Zhang Dai was full of contradictions: on the one hand there might indeed be dizzying heights of fame and opportunity but on the other lay anguish, frustration and even physical collapse. Continuing with his depictions of family examinees, Zhang Dai showed how his own father had experienced a somewhat similar mixture of problems and illness. As Zhang Dai summarized in rather harsh tones, his father's early years were happy, but decline was swift. Zhang Dai wrote that his father had been born in 1574 in Shaoxing and as a boy was "quick and clever"; he learned to read early and "by nine was able to grasp the moral and logical points being made in his classical texts."At the age of fourteen, father was able to pass the preliminary level of the examinations, which qualified him for the title of "licentiate" and the right to sit for the provincial-level exams. But thereafter he spent almost forty years in various forms of study, his childhood love of books being transposed into a grim grind that bought intense depression and ulcers and almost cost him his sight, perhaps from some congenital eye disease inherited from grandfather. Zhang Dai was himself a schoolboy when the constant reading nearly blinded his father: "The pupils on both his eyes clouded over," Zhang wrote later. "Father altogether lost the ability to read texts written or printed in small characters." Apparently it was newly imported technology that saved the day, since when someone brought father "a pair of Western lenses to balance on the tip of his nose," he regained the ability to continue reading and studying. Not until father was fifty-three did he scrape out a passing grade on the supplementary list of provincial candidates.

According to Zhang Dai, his own uncles covered a whole spectrum of responses to the examination system. Seventh uncle, for instance, led a tough, wasteful and independent life, and used to look over the various primers on the exam curriculum being studied by his relatives with contempt, commenting, "This seems no big deal. Why get in such a state about it?" Just to prove he could do it if he chose, seventh uncle, around the year 1605, "lowered the screens and read the books; after three years he had mastered them completely." But he still made no attempt to sit for the exams, and never did so. More complex was the relationship between the two brothers who were Zhang Dai's ninth and tenth uncles. Tenth uncle clearly started out with plenty of advantages: "His father died when he was small, and his mother, Lady Chen, loved him deeply. By nature he was extremely obstinate and it was difficult to talk to him. As he grew older, his contrariness increased even more. And yet he enjoyed his studies, and became an able essay writer, earning the local licentiate's degree in his late teens." The senior examiner there plucked tenth uncle out from among the other students and provided him with a living allowance that permitted him to continue with his provincial-level exam studies for thirty years. Yet this comfortably subsidized life did not calm tenth uncle's notorious temper, for in the year 1628 his older brother, ninth uncle, obtained the national-level *jinshi* degree and sent a banner and an honorific tablet to be hung above the family gate of his home. Tenth uncle cursed him contemptuously, saying, "Why do you have to shove this piddling turtle of a *jinshi* degree right in front of my eyes?" Tenth uncle proceeded, in Zhang Dai's words, "to rip up the banner so that his servants could patch their pants with it, sawed up the flagstaff to be used as firewood for the cooking-stoves, and broke up the tablet, using the pieces to reinforce the gate-posts."

Despite this outburst of apparently uncontrollable rage and jealousy, tenth uncle clearly had no absolute hostility to the exam system itself, only to his own brother's success within that system. For twelve years later, in 1640, when the emperor opened up some of the places in the national exams for ambitious men of talent who wished to enter government service to solve the country's pressing problems, tenth uncle put forward his own name, and in a special exam was ranked number nineteen in the second class, being granted the title of secretary in the ministry of justice.

How then should tenth uncle be evaluated in scholarly terms? Zhang Dai was elliptical: "Tenth uncle was stubbornly angry, to such an extent that it was impossible to talk to him, and thus one could say that tenth uncle was crazy. But he also loved his studies, and was never without a book in his hand; the essays that he wrote were refined, rich and subtle, and from that point of view tenth uncle was obviously not a madman." Such were the types of paradoxes that could be present when learning and violence flowed in the same channels and within the same person.

As can be seen from the cases of both Zhang Dai's grandfather and father, the threat of blindness often hung over young men in the Zhang family as they studied. Grandfather had recovered his sight by a rigorous avoidance of all light, and father by acquiring a pair of eyeglasses, which were at the time becoming available in Ming China at around four ounces of silver a pair. But in the case of Zhang Dai's younger cousin Pei there was nothing to be done, and he lost his sight completely at the age of five. According to Zhang Dai, the cause was not too much reading but rather Pei's passion for everything sweet, itself exacerbated by indulgent relatives who gave the boy whatever sweetmeats he craved. When the rapid deterioration of Pei's sight was noticed, eminent doctors were called in, but they could do nothing to reverse the illness, even though Pei's adoring grandmother "spent several thousand taels on fees."

According to Zhang Dai's admiring account, Pei adjusted to the situation swiftly and successfully: "Though Pei was now blind, it was in his nature to love reading books, so people were hired to read to him. Everything that he heard he remembered perfectly. There was not one among the hundred or more titles listed in Zhu Xi's historical digest that he did not memorize from beginning to end, whether it was the lists of family names and the genealogies, the place names and the cyclical dates, or each individual person and the key events. From just before daylight until the hours around midnight, Pei listened intently without ever growing bored. When the tongues of his readers grew tired, even bringing in several new readers was not enough for him. The books that he arranged for people to read aloud to him were spread across all the basic categories of classics, histories, essays and belles lettres and extended to the nine basic schools of literature and philosophy, to the hundred names, and on to historical novels and romances. He absorbed them all."

In Pei's case, this remarkable eclecticism led him to carefully choose his career, one that Zhang Dai (Pei's senior by ten or eleven years) recorded in some detail: "Pei developed a particular love for discussing medical texts, and again he went through every collection completely: the Yellow Emperor's basic outline of medicine, the complete botanical compendia, the book of basic medical principles, the basic method of cinnabar streams, and the finest prescriptions for cinnabar use." Zhang described how the shelves all around Pei's study "were piled high with many hundreds of kinds of medical texts," and just as he had in the past, Pei had these read aloud to him by teams of readers and once again was able to remember all their contents. Gradually Pei found an area of concentration, what past and contemporary doctors called "the basic principles of pulse theory," and he absorbed with especial care the works by the leading analysts of the pulses, which were believed to vary significantly in different parts of the patient's body, and to be able to guide a physician into making a correct and comprehensive diagnosis of many illnesses. Study of the pulse was of course an admirable focus for one who had lost his sight: "When Pei diagnosed illnesses by the feel of the pulses, he was always composed and alert; with a touch of his hands, his knowledge was sure."

Pei amplified this basic skill by learning the efficacy of a wide range of medicinal plants, which he had people gather for him, and instructed his assistants to prepare the medicines by following the most celebrated of the famous doctors of the past: "In all his decocting, boiling, steaming and evaporating he followed the ancient methods." Some of Pei's precautions struck Zhang as being especially meticulous and admirable, such as his practice of never opening a single package of medicine "unless he first washed his hands." Pei was equally careful with the forming of the medicines into tablets and powders, and with prescribing exactly measured doses. And his generosity was unfailing, even though his own father had died young, leaving Pei with the obligation to care for numerous relatives. The result, as summarized by Zhang Dai, was that "many who were ill came to Pei's lodgings for treatment, and even if they could not offer him any money they still left with the medicine; even if dozens of them were lined up to see him, costing him hundreds of doses of medicine and dozens of taels in expenses, he never begrudged it."

It may be that the vulnerability of these family members made Rulin love his eldest grandson Zhang Dai all the more, for this particular grandson was both brilliant with words and often sickly. Zhang Dai later wrote about several of the trips he had made with grandfather, especially visits to some of the beautiful studios and gardens on the edge of Dragon Mountain. Foremost among them was the luxuriant "Happiness Garden" built at the northern foot of Dragon Mountain. It had once been the home of a senior government official, and when a member of the Zhu family married into that man's family it became his favorite place to study, a place from which happiness radiated to all around, hence its name.

Zhang Dai's memories were precise: "When I was a child, I often accompanied my grandfather to this place. The front slope of the mountain had hundreds of ancient pine trees, all grotesque and intertwining with one another like snakes. Those trees epitomized the pines' bizarre and varied appearances. At the bottom were hundreds of stags and doe, sitting or walking the steep paths. Whether it was dawn or dusk, rays of sunlight would penetrate the trees, changing color to yellow or dark red. Outside the Garden, tens of thousands of bamboo plants spurted skyward; one's face would turn green when among them. Within, small paths lined with pines and thickets of cinnamon woods were thick enough to block the rain. In the small pond before the pavilion were lush green lotus and climbing hibiscus. It was a blend of white and red." In Zhang's memory, the constantly changing scene was never dull: "Bodies of moving water swirled around like intestines, but they were never congested. The houses themselves were like scrolls of marvelous written pieces, selecting only the finest in their scope of view. Opening the door, one could see the mountain; opening the windows, one could admire the water. In the front, there were garden plots with rich soil and elevated patches, on which were planted many varieties of fruit trees. The garden was thriving with bamboo plants, mandarin orange, plum blossom, and apricot trees, as well as pear trees, haw trees, Chinese cabbage patches, and melons. It was indeed like a market even with its doors closed to the outside world." As grandfather told Zhang Dai, the Happiness Garden at Dragon Mountain "was an entirely different world, and not of the human realm."

This Dragon Mountain, which dominated the northwest section of Shaoxing within the city walls, was the focus for many of Zhang Dai's earliest memories. It was a friendly mountain, really a medium-sized hill with sharp edges, about 220 feet high along its main ridge. No one need get lost on Dragon Mountain: you could be at the top in fifteen minutes or less and stroll its whole length in twenty-five. You could wander at leisure along the paved trails and stone steps that cut through the woods, or rest in the various viewing sites, or pay a visit to one of the many artfully placed small shrines or temples. From the main ridge, if one climbed onto the viewing terraces that reached above the trees, one could look out across the city in all directions: northwest over the walls to the hills that formed a partial barrier between Hangzhou and Shaoxing, or northeast across the Qiantang River and the estuary toward the ocean, or south to the tight rows of houses that backed onto the many canals that gave the city its main transport routes for heavy goods and travelers, past the two soaring pagodas that could be seen from all over town, and beyond the crenellated walls to the looming masses of much higher and wilder hills, where the bureaucratic presence of the city barely penetrated. Like many wealthy families in Shaoxing, the Zhangs lived on estates that backed into the slopes of Dragon Mountain, with their spacious gardens, formal courtyards and carefully orchestrated living quarters separated by generation, gender and status. Zhang Dai was the eldest son of the eldest son of the eldest son; with grandfather as his guide and his guardian, his position must have seemed unassailable.

Grandfather clearly had high hopes for Zhang Dai. And perhaps with these visits to the Happiness Garden grandfather was helping his grandson get over the loss of his own cherished childhood studio, which seems to have been literally destroyed by Zhang Dai's high-living second uncle Zhongshu. As Zhang Dai later recorded, he first saw this perfect study space when he was only five: it was a pavilion so designed that it seemed to be dangling among the tree tops and for this reason had been given the name Suspended in the Branches Pavilion, borrowing a phrase from the eighth-century poet Du Shenyan, the grandfather of the great Tang lyricist Du Fu. So did education begin for many of the Zhang children, with travel and wordplay, and in homage to the past. "I remember the pavilion was situated at the foot of a sharp precipice," Zhang Dai wrote later, "perched on pilings of wood and stone. No soil had been used at all, it was a flying space in a building without mass, with the eaves aligned like combs' teeth. The edge of the cliff rose over the roof, a mass of dense trees and foliage, all tangled in confusion with the eaves and the roof tiles."

But, as Zhang Dai was always quick to point out, such moments of delight are rarely fated to endure. In this case it was second uncle Zhongshu—his father's younger brother and closest childhood friend—who brought the joy to an end. Zhang recalled, "Some time later, uncle Zhongshu decided to build a house at the foot of the same cliff and was persuaded by geomancers that the pavilion stood in the way of the benevolent natural forces. He made special arrangements to buy the pavilion, and in a single night had it demolished, leaving nothing but a tangle of wild vegetation. My boyhood delights were lodged in that spot; often in my dreams I try to make my way there once again."

Grandfather seems to have had ambitious plans for Zhang Dai's further education, and Zhang Dai left a detailed record of the journey they made together to meet the celebrated scholar-teacher Huang Zhenfu. Huang, who had obtained the top literary degree in 1598, ran a kind of informal school in his mountain retreat to the west of Hangzhou city. Grandfather may have hoped that Huang would consent to be Zhang Dai's tutor in classical Chinese, but when the two reached Huang's residence, they found that intimate study was out of the question. As Zhang Dai later recalled his childhood visit, "A thousand or more disciples from all over the country had come to study there, and the threshold of the house was as bustling as a marketplace." Huang himself was a wild-looking man, bearded, bright-eyed, full of laughter and with an uncanny ability to do a dozen things at once: "At the same moment he could listen to what his visitors were saying, run his eyes over a batch of letters, write out an immediate reply, and issue instructions to his servants. Despite the general confusion, nothing seemed to escape him." Huang's hospitality was boundless, and his generosity unquestioning; any visitor, however strange or uncouth, could be sure of a good meal and a place to sleep for the night.

It never did work out for Zhang Dai to study formally with

Huang, but off and on for twenty years Huang's career tracks crisscrossed with Zhang Dai's grandfather's, sometimes in harmony and sometimes in not-so-friendly rivalry; for a time, when both were posted to Nanjing, they ran a history reading group together and exchanged essays. In 1626, the year after grandfather died, Zhang Dai made a nostalgic trip back to Huang's once frenetic Hangzhou mountain home. As he described it, all was now desolation: Huang had died shortly after his friend Rulin, and his body lay in its coffin in the great hall of the once vibrant building that itself was now falling into decay. Even the rocks outside Huang's study, which to the visiting boy long before had seemed as beautiful as camellias—"beaten down by wind and rain but emerging out of the mud" and able to be penetrated by any visitor "as a butterfly penetrates to the heart of a flower, leaving no stamen untouched"—now seemed, to the observing adult Zhang Dai, merely blackened and sodden. Nevertheless, Zhang Dai was seized by the sudden notion that it would be grand to rent the whole of Huang's desolate property and to live there in the ruined hall all by himself, "to pile up stones across the threshold, to sleep under this roof, to stay here ten years without ever leaving," and to lead the simplest of lives "wearing coarse garments, with a jar of millet and some bits and pieces of books." But the practical demands of living pushed this whim aside.

Despite the fact that Huang clearly would not be able to tutor Zhang Dai, grandfather did all he could to help with his career. Grandfather had long been a great collector of books and manuscripts, and Zhang wrote disarmingly of how he personally came to be part owner of the family collection. "For three generations in our family the books had been piling up, until they totaled more than thirty thousand *juan*. [A *juan* was a stitched unit of anywhere from a dozen or so to sixty or more pages, a number of which were then boxed together into volumes of varying size.] Grandfather encouraged me by saying, 'Among all my grand-children, you are the only one with a passion for reading. If you want to read some of these volumes, then make your own choice.' So I made a selection from the collections of great-great-grandfather Tianfu, great-grandfather Wengong, and my grandfather, choosing those books that showed the smudges from their fingers and contained either their handwritten nota-tions or else their corrections. Once I had composed my list of books, I went to ask grandfather for them. Delighted, he let me borrow them. There were in all about two thousand *juan*."

According to Zhang Dai's later record, he had been given an education of great flexibility by his grandfather. By the strict cur-riculum rules of the time, those preparing for the exams had to prepare one formal examination field in the "Four Books," as the basic classical canon had been classified by the scholarly editor Zhu Xi at the end of the twelfth century; a second examination field was devoted to the full texts of the "Five Classics," which had allegedly been shaped by the editing of Confucius himself in the fifth century BC. Each student had to choose one of the Five Classics for deeper exegesis and, as Zhang Dai's earlier com-ments showed, grandfather's special field—at which he clearly excelled, even if eccentrically—was on *The Book of Changes*. The third examination field was on political and economic analysis, also drawn from ancient texts but also to some measure aimed at analysis of China's own needs at the time.

An enormous amount of most advanced students' time went into the mastery of the voluminous commentaries on all these texts but, according to Zhang Dai, grandfather forbade him to take that customary route: "When I was young, I followed implicitly the instructions of my grandfather not to read Zhu Xi's annotations and so whenever I read the classics I dared not do so with the opinions of the commentators foremost in my mind." From his grandfather, Zhang Dai absorbed the idea—prevalent among some scholarly circles in late-sixteenth-century China— that relying on commentaries destroyed 90 percent of the meaning, and that understanding of such ancient texts came in the form of sudden enlightenment. As Zhang recalled this phase of his education, "With all due reverence and seriousness, I would recite the text itself several dozen times before becoming suddenly aware of the meaning and significance of what I was chanting. When, occasionally, I came across a section that I could not force myself fully to understand, I would store the sentences away in my mind, as devoid of meaning and significance as they were. A year or maybe two later, when reading another book perhaps, or listening to the arguments of others, when observing the mountains and rivers or the patterns of the clouds and the stars, when watching the behavior of the birds, beasts, insects and fish, what struck my eye would arouse my mind and I would become suddenly enlightened to the meaning of the text I had been reading."

These moments of understanding could not be anticipated in advance, nor were they explicated in learned commentaries; they would appear "directly and unexpectedly along the way," and they would form hitherto unguessed-at connections, just as two snakes entwined by the side of a road or a woman's dazzling sword dance might lead a calligrapher to a truer understanding of his art. "The secret knack of such epiphanies," wrote Zhang Dai, "is not susceptible to rational understanding. To press this point somewhat further, when color, sound, fragrance and taste are aroused and issue forth, not one of such sense impressions will fail to encounter its appropriate receptacle, there to await an unexpected epiphany with a person of deep understanding and clear perception who will encounter it most unexpectedly, whereupon a lifelong affinity will be formed."

Despite all grandfather's encouragement, Zhang Dai never did pass the provincial examinations that would have permitted him to sit for the national examinations in Beijing. (The repeated failures seem, for at least one period of Zhang Dai's life, to have led to some kind of deep depression, from which it took the concerted and combined efforts of his younger brother and of his close friend Qi Biaojia to rescue him.) But even if examination success eluded him, Zhang Dai continued to be the passionate reader he had been since early childhood. And despite his jaundiced view of the whole exam system, he seems to have drawn solace from his eccentric grandfather's ability to succeed by not giving up his deeply personal views of the meaning of the classical texts. Zhang Dai even held up the hope that some examiner of the future would read Zhang's own scholarship in the kind of free way that he had expressed it. As Zhang Dai put it: "The ancients, with their fine minds and contemplative understanding, undertook research both long and painstaking before, suddenly, like a spark struck from a flint or a flash of lightning, they achieved illumination, their intellectual and spiritual powers fused and they could no longer say from whence their thoughts flowed. Likewise, the examination candidate struggles away on his books for a decade before, locked in his examination cell, exposed to the elements and within the shortest possible compass of time, he displays his perfect mastery of the seven topics and his composition happens to accord with the opinions of the presiding examiner who, despite his drunken slumber, will nonetheless be drawn to it like iron to a magnet, grass-clippings to a piece of amber, whereupon it will please him and be fully understood by him and he will proceed to devote to it his undivided attentions."

Grandfather also had a lighthearted side, which he shared at intervals with his grandson. Zhang Dai was especially struck by a splendidly phrased formal essay that grandfather wrote for his younger brother Rusen, Zhang Dai's great-uncle. At this time Zhang Dai was just fifteen, and grandfather and Rusen together must have given him a lusty portrait of the joys of Dragon Mountain and the tangential rewards of scholarship. In Zhang Dai's words: "Great-uncle Rusen was a powerfully built man with a luxuriant beard, so people called him 'Zhang the Beard.' He loved to drink, and there was no time that he was ever sober, be it day or night. After the noon hour, his kerchief would be untied, his robe hanging open, his beard braided like a whip, and sticking out from under his chin like the tail feathers of a bird. He would brusquely hail everyone he met, and drag them back home with him; and then, closing the gates, he would get madly drunk with them. He would never let the party end till late at night. Throughout the year, be it at the moon feast or the festival of flowers, he was always completely and totally drunk. People all grew scared, and fled at the sight of him." But, Zhang Dai added, Rusen also had a love for the mountains and streams and, "Whenever he heard that my grandfather was going on some trip or other he would grab a staff, put on his shoes, and be off to join him. And once they were on their way, he would forget to return home."

The friendship between the two older men was a powerful one, and Zhang Dai's grandfather was tolerant of Rusen's avocation, devoting to it one of the elegant formal essays that he loved to write, in which the dignity of the diction made a playful contrast with the raucous topic under discussion. As grandfather explained, he wrote this piece in 1612, after Rusen had built a special pavilion to shelter the guests who came to his new Shaoxing home to drink with him. Rusen asked his older brother to give the pavilion a name, and grandfather chose the characters *Yinsheng* (Luring to famous sites), and wrote out an essay explaining the choice: "My younger brother Rusen is a man who loves to drink. When he has stored a flagon in his belly he collapses onto his bed, not knowing if the sky is his mat or the earth is his curtain. I realize that Rusen has the same inclinations as Ruan Ji [a third-century poet famous for his drinking bouts]. Rusen used divination to find a site for a house on the southern side of Dragon Mountain, but before he had even finished the house, he built a pavilion to shelter his guests, declaring that 'I cannot go for a single day without drinking.' Since he asked me to give the place a name, I chose 'Luring to famous sites.' Rusen gazed fixedly at me and asked: 'What kind of name is that? I don't understand what it means, and need some further word of explanation.' So gravely I quoted the words of Wang Weijun, that 'the point of drinking is to lure people to go and visit famous sites.' Before I had even finished these words, Rusen jumped up and replied: 'I still don't understand your explanation, but once you mention drinking I get the idea.' "

Grandfather loved words and their meanings, and was at this time, as Zhang Dai described elsewhere, composing a huge and arcanely organized dictionary. Now grandfather played with the interconnection of lexicography and alcohol: "People in the world get so tied up over the exact meaning of words; with the babble of their voices they make things harder for themselves. Eventually they can't even find a use for half a word, and end up all tangled in the search for meaning. The precise meaning of words is in fact something refined; but when coarsely put they get reduced to [phrases like] 'riches and honor' or to the so-called 'big' questions of 'death and life.' Everything gets all tangled up with everything else, they are glued together and cannot be separated. To go even further: some people care so much for riches and honor that they will risk their lives to attain them; others are so concerned with matters of death and life that they cut themselves off from riches and honor. They do not understand that the two [pairs] are all intertwined. But those who are steeped in drink, do they have any of these entanglements?

"Rusen once said to me, his older brother, 'The ruler can make his people vicious in their pursuit of riches and honor, but I have no government positions and am truly light. Why should I fear the ruler? And the old god of the underworld Yama can terrify people with his talk of life and death, but if I have to go, then I'll just go. Why should I fear Yama?' . . .

"Such are the views of someone who has been made complete

by their drinking," grandfather continued, paraphrasing an earlier Taoist thinker. "Those who find they are made complete by drinking can not be startled by the gods, are not nervous of tigers, do not get hurt if they fall out of a cart, regard death and life as of no more consequence than a mustard seed. The same is true of riches and honors. Is it not even more true for the meanings of words?" Grandfather had intuitively realized that though Rusen had no understanding of the name given to the pavilion, in truth he had already understood it.

"Drink is Rusen's paradise," grandfather concluded. "How can we compete with him in that? Besides which, he really knows his way with drink, whereas you and I are groping with these mysteries, deep in our own thoughts; sinking into the world of meanings we have become ensnared there. . . . My capacity for drink is small, and compared to [the poet] Su Dongpo who could drain fifteen wine cups in a row, I am a mere mouse at this drinking business!"

Zhang Dai summarized the rest of his great-uncle Rusen's life in two short sentences: "My bearded great-uncle enjoyed himself in his 'Luring to Famous Sites' pavilion for the next twenty years. After that time the drinking made him sick, and he died at sixty-seven."

Grandfather died in 1625, when Zhang Dai—now twenty-eight years old—happened to be away in Hangzhou. There was nothing Zhang Dai could do to hold his grandfather's library together: "My father and my uncles, along with my brothers and their households, and even the lowest servants, all grabbed the books higgledy-piggledy, so effectively indeed that the heritage of three generations was entirely dissipated in the space of a single day."

If the books themselves, so painstakingly acquired, could be so quickly scattered to the winds, what of the deeper recesses of learning to which those books were meant to be the guide? Here, too, Zhang Dai grew cautious as he grew older, and he kept wondering, in his own writing, about all the time that went into these various ventures. It was not just that the examinations themselves were perhaps not worth the fuss, expense and bother. It was also that at the heart of the scholarly life itself there often lurked a real element of futility. Strangely, Zhang Dai followed up this particular theme most carefully with the example of his own grandfather, whom at many levels he had clearly loved and respected, even revered. Yet, despite all his brilliance, grandfather—according to Zhang Dai—spent his last years of life in pursuit of a truly impossible vision, the compilation of an immense dictionary that would marshal all knowledge in composite categories based on a rhyme-scheme series of classifications. As Zhang Dai wrote in an essay aptly named "Rhyme Mountain," right up to the end he rarely saw grandfather without a book in his hands, and piles of books lay in disorder all around his study, under layers of dust. When the sun was bright, grandfather took his books out of doors so he could read more easily. At dusk he lit candles and held his book right close to the flame, "leaning across the desk into the brightness." Thus he would stay far into the night, showing no signs of tiredness.

Claiming that all the previous dictionaries were inaccurate, grandfather determined to create his own, using the idea of mountains as his controlling metaphor of organization: key words were termed "high mountains," catch phrases were "little mountains," characters that had variant rhymes were termed "other mountains," proverbs were classified as "worn-out mountains" and so on. In this "Rhyme Mountain," wrote Zhang, grandfather's columns of little characters followed in tight columns "like the pleats in a skirt, on sheets of paper yellowed from the heat of the lamp"; he had filled, in this way, over three hundred notebooks, "each thick as bricks." Some rhyme schemes might fill ten books or more.

One sad day, an old friend brought grandfather a section of a huge manuscript encyclopedia from the palace library in Beijing, proving to him that all of this had been done before, better organized and on a far larger scale. Sighing, grandfather said: "The number of books is without end, and I have been like a bird seeking to fill the sea with pebbles. What can be the point of it all?" So he pushed aside his thirty years of work and never returned to his "Rhyme Mountain." And even had grandfather finished the project, Zhang Dai wrote, "Who on earth would have published it?" There was nothing left of all that work across thirty years but "a pile of writing brushes with the whiskers worn down to the wood" and "piles of paper useful only for sealing storage pots."

Zhang Dai might have agreed that one man's scholarly tenacity could never match the vast scholarly resources of the state, but even though at one level he mourned for all his grandfather's wasted efforts, at another level he respected and admired what his grandfather had tried to do. After grandfather's death,

Zhang Dai reported years later, he did not once think of destroying the huge manuscript. Instead he kept the piles of pages in his own home on Dragon Mountain. And when the violence of civil war and foreign invasion swept across Shaoxing in the 1640s, Zhang Dai packaged together the entire manuscript of "Rhyme Mountain" and concealed it as well as he could among the bundles of sutras stored in a temple out in the countryside. That way, he wrote, later generations could at least have a chance to see what his grandfather had sought, across so many years, to accomplish.

CHAPTER THREE

ON HOME GROUND

Zhang Dai's father liked to claim that the birth of his eldest son proved the efficacy of divination: Zhang Dai recorded this information in a matter-of-fact yet enigmatic way, as if his own life did indeed depend on it: "The Zhang family's divination spirit resided in a special shrine inside the Hall of Longevity; a writing brush was kept hanging right there, on the wall, and if there was some impending event the brush began to move itself. As soon as one held the brush it began to write, and its predictions were remarkable. One could ask it for a son if a woman was pregnant, or for a cure if someone was ill, or for the location of an elixir if that was needed, and it would respond at once. When father invoked it on the question of his having an heir, the spirit told him he could find the elixir inside a certain box of *linquan* writing brushes. The key to the box had long ago been lost, but when father examined it the bolt disengaged from the socket, and there was a single golden tablet. Mother swallowed it, and so became pregnant with me."

Zhang Dai's mother, however, had her own rendering of the generative moment. When Zhang Dai was just forming in her womb, she later told him, she established the habit of chanting aloud from a sacred Buddhist text titled the "White-Robed Guan Yin" sutra, so as to earn the protection of the Goddess of Mercy. The birth was difficult, and still she chanted, so that in Zhang Dai's mind his entry into the world came to the sound of his mother's prayers. And Zhang felt that the prayers were not truly lost even after his mother's too early death in 1619: "Even the blazing fire of misfortune could not erase that warmth." For, as Zhang Dai recalled in his old age, "Oftentimes, when the sounds assailing my ears are for a moment at rest, in my mind I can still hear the sound of my mother chanting those sutras." His mother's tale had become a part of him, "like being stirred by the sound of the sea tides, like having thunder poured into one's ears." And by hearing her voice in his head, he conjured up her image once again, across the great vista of the years.

A different kind of moment with his mother was also dear to Zhang Dai. When he was still a young child, she took him with her on a journey to burn incense in one of the most famous Buddhist temples in Hangzhou, the provincial capital some thirty miles to the northwest of their home. The young Zhang Dai was often sick with some kind of fluid in his lungs, and had to take a rare medicine provided by his mother's relatives, so perhaps that was the reason for their journey. Built in the tenth century, the temple was known locally as the Korean Temple in honor of a donor from the Korean royal family who had donated a precious collection of Buddhist sutras. For many years, the sutras had been stored in a great octagonal bookcase that pivoted around a central shaft: when set in motion by worshipers at the shrine, the sutras were believed to bring them merit just as if they had recited the sutras aloud. Zhang Dai could, for the rest of his life, recall the sequence of his mother's actions: "She took out a string of three hundred coins and instructed our sedan chair bearers to set the revolving storage case in motion. At first, the revolving mechanism gave out a groaning sound, like band instruments being played by a beginner. Then, as it began to spin with greater ease the stored sutras revolved as if in flight, so that those doing the pushing could no longer keep up with it."

Zhang Dai's mother came from the Tao family, whose home was in the eastern ward of Shaoxing city in an area named Kuaiji; for her wedding she only had to travel to the northwest part of town, known as Shanyin, where the Zhang residences were clustered round Dragon Mountain. This seems to have been the common procedure among the Zhang family males. Shaoxing was a large and wealthy city, so there were several families in Kuaiji with whom marriages would be arranged with mutual benefit. By marrying off their men to Kuaiji women with different surnames, the Zhangs avoided the dangers of intermarriage, while constructing a series of valuable social and financial connections in the locality. Such contacts were important to all family members, since by Chinese law no man born inside a particular province could hold office in that same province, so as to prevent graft, nepotism and undue economic influence: Thus no member of Zhang Dai's family could hold office in Zhejiang province, any more than they could in Shaoxing city.

By extrapolation of the same law, no scholar could have his examinations graded by an examiner from his own native province, even if that examiner had left home decades before. But Shaoxing residents could of course be tutored before the examinations by local scholars; in the same way, when they traveled to other provinces they could socialize or do business with officials and merchants from Shaoxing or stay in hostels run for Shaoxing natives by Shaoxing natives, where they could eat Shaoxing food, drink Shaoxing wine and be confident that their distinctive Shaoxing accent would be readily understood. Often, too, they might be accompanied by women from Shaoxing whom they had chosen as their companions. But during those absences, which often spanned years, their primary consort, elderly parents and young children would stay in their family residences in their own hometowns.

Zhang Dai was well aware of the major roles that the local women who married into the Shanyin branch of the Zhang family had played at various stages of his and his progenitors' lives, and he tried to record them with the same care that he gave to charting the examination struggles of his male ancestors. Great-great-grandfather Tianfu, for instance, had married a woman from the Liu family. Though she rejoiced at her husband's examination success—he won the provincial degree in 1543 and the national degree in 1547—Lady Liu was watchful over the vicissitudes of his official career and was cautious about the fates. She believed that a modest level of achievement was enough for any family, and that it was crucial to "know when enough was enough."

For her, that moment came in 1558, when her husband was

working at his first senior provincial posting, as the chief education supervisor for the province of Hunan, and their oldest son, Wengong (then twenty years old), performed brilliantly in the Zhejiang provincial examinations. For Lady Liu, that was the signal that her husband had risen far enough, and she urged him, politely but forcefully, to retire. He refused and received another promotion, this time to the distant border province of Yunnan. But in the new position, on account of his unbending moral stance, his career began to unravel, and he was faced with a death sentence for his alleged corruption, being saved only by his son Wengong's skillful manipulation of the legal system. Shortly afterward, in 1571, Wengong astounded his family by placing first in the national examinations in Beijing. Far from expressing joy, Lady Liu repeated, "Our good fortune is now excessive, our good fortune is now excessive." As if to prove her correct, her husband returned home in disgrace and took to excessive drinking, while her son encountered jealous enemies in Beijing and was forced to return home as well. In a suitable reminder of life's ironies, according to Zhang Dai, it was at the massive celebrations for her son's examination triumph, held on a lavish scale in Shaoxing, but also in the pouring rain, that her husband contracted an illness—perhaps some kind of glandular infection that spread to his neck—that was said to have led to his death at sixty-two.

It was in 1558, just at the time of his provincial examination success, that Lady Liu's eldest son—Zhang Dai's great-grandfather Wengong—married a woman from the Wang family. Lady Wang was "by nature frugal and restrained," in Zhang Dai's cautious words, but she would have needed to be just that to survive in the austere household of her new husband. While her father-in-law Tianfu was usually away, absorbed by his career, her own husband, Wengong, seems to have been an unusually strict disciplinarian. According to family anecdotes, the birth of several children did not soften Wengong's stance. "Great-grandfather ran his household severely," wrote Zhang Dai. He imposed rigorous rules on his own two sons, on their wives and even on his two younger half-brothers and their wives. "Every moment of their day had to be in accordance with ritual conduct. At dawn an iron gong was struck three times, and the whole family assembled in the main hall to give him their greetings. His daughters-in-law usually had no time for their ablutions at that hour, so each night they put on cloth wraps to protect their dressed hair, and to prevent its being in disarray in the morning. Everyone in the family felt worn by this." Pointing at the metal gong Wengong used to strike, they would say, "That is like his iron heart!"

On ordinary evenings, when the family was all together, his two sons had to be in his presence to ensure the incense remained lighted and to sit quietly in contemplation. Only late in the night were they allowed to go to bed. Sometimes, great-grandfather's actions were vindictive. At one of his birthday celebrations, his eldest daughter-in-law and the other young women of her generation put on their special brocaded clothes and some jewelry, both pearls and jade. Seeing them thus attired, great-grandfather flew into a rage, ordering them to change their dresses and remove all the jewelry. He then ordered the whole lot burned at the foot of the steps to the main hall. Only when the young women had dressed in plain cotton clothes did he agree to accept their birthday greetings.

Great-grandfather's wife, Lady Wang, responded to her husband's extreme sense of thrift with thrift of her own. So that there would be no arguments that she was wasting family money, she spent some time every day weaving and stitching kerchiefs. Whenever she had accumulated a small stock of them, she would send one of her servants off to the market, where each kerchief could be sold for a few dozen coppers. According to family tales, whenever the townspeople saw one of her servants heading for the market they would cry out, "These goods were woven by the wife of the top degree candidate," and they fought to buy them.

Great-grandfather's intense moralism affected not only the members of his family but also his career in the Beijing bureaucracy. The late Ming political world was frequently riven by tensions between the ruling empress and various junior consorts over the formal installation of the heir apparent. Officials who blundered into this dangerous world, where court eunuchs also played a powerful role, did so at the risk of their own lives. As a teenager, back in the 1550s, great-grandfather had made a name for himself by bravely protesting—by means of a written placard which he displayed in public—the illicit execution of a loyal minister. Once he had been awarded the top-ranking degree, great-grandfather held a series of official posts in Beijing and was named to the prestigious Confucian Study Academy in the capital. In 1573, he sent a special petition to the emperor, obviously aimed at addressing the factionalism between the court women and their various supporters, in which he asked for permission to give lectures in the inner palace on the "Biographies of Worthy Women of the Past," an uplifting text, written over a millennium before, on women's correct roles and deportment in times of hardship or danger. He also petitioned to have the first two sections, called "The Southern Collections," of the *Classic on Poetry* edited and circulated among the inner palace women. The poems in these two sections—many dating back well before the time of Confucius, perhaps to the eighth century BC—dealt with the meaning and rituals of marriage as well as the expressions (and curbing) of sexual passion between men and women. More than two millennia of analysis and exegesis by Chinese scholars had layered over the obvious sensuality of these poems with interpretations that linked their content to moral action in the government and household spheres. Great-grandfather's offer was declined by the court, but he was later asked to serve as a tutor to the recently installed heir apparent. Wengong's death, according to the official history, was a direct result of his anguish at failing to have his deceased father Tianfu completely cleared of all the charges levied against him years before, during the military campaigns in Yunnan province.

The most economically and politically important marriage made by the Zhang family was the one that linked them to the wealthy and powerful Zhu clan of Kuaiji. This came about through curious circumstances, which Zhang Dai took the trouble to record in detail. The key date was August 11, 1556. At that time Zhang Dai's great-grandfather Zhang Wengong was still an eighteen-year-old student in Shaoxing preparing intensively for his provincial examinations in the family studio on Dragon

Mountain; his study mate Zhu Geng was a close friend and fellow townsman from the Zhu clan. And it was on August 11 that the two young men made a pledge together: if at some time in the future their wives bore them children of different sexes, those two children would be pledged to marry each other in order to permanently celebrate the closeness between the two families. The pledge was sealed not only with words but with pieces of cloth cut from their summer study robes and carefully preserved. Zhang Dai later noted, "I myself actually saw one of the pieces of cloth they cut off the lapels of their robes: it was gray in color, and a bit worm-eaten, but I was able to bleach it back to its original whiteness." It was Zhang Dai's great-grandfather who got his provincial degree first, at the triennial examinations held in 1558, and right after the exams he married Lady Wang, who promptly bore him a son. Zhu Geng married around the same time and had a daughter (later to be known to Zhang Dai as his Granny Zhu). Thus did the pledge by the two young men become a lived reality. The two scholars kept in close touch as they advanced successfully through the state examinations and each launched his bureaucratic career. Their two children were duly married in the early 1570s, and Zhang Dai's father, fruit of that union, was born in 1574.

According to Zhang Dai, this same study companion, Zhu Geng, was decidedly eccentric and had come to believe that he was the reincarnation of the Southern Song dynasty scholar and statesman Zhang Jucheng, a claim that he backed with a number of stories. By means of divination, the twelfth-century scholar shared the stories of his own and various intermediate incarnations with Zhu Geng and even gave him instructions to locate a copy of a Buddhist sutra that had been left incomplete in a certain monastery. Going to the monastery, Zhu Geng did indeed find a sutra lying on one of the beams. It was written out in the Song man's calligraphy but still lacked the last two sections. Carefully and devotedly, Zhu Geng wrote out the rest of the work in calligraphy "so like those of his previous incarnation that one could in no way tell the two apart." Did Zhang record this odd story just to belittle the Zhus' most influential ancestor? That seems unlikely. Perhaps, rather, it was just Zhang's way of showing the unpredictable nature of life.

As soon as his sons had sons in their turn, Wengong played a role in shaping their lives. Zhang Dai described one such intervention in the case of the little boy who was later to become his second uncle, Zhongshu: "At birth, Zhongshu's head was slanted over to the left, and his grandfather Wengong was upset about this. So he took a steelyard weight and attached it to one of his [grandson's] childhood tufts of hair, so that it hung down on the right-hand side. And when Zhongshu went off to study in the local school, his grandfather told the young attendants there to light incense close to Zhongshu, and to his left, so that if he tilted his head to the left he would burn his forehead. After this had gone on for six months, [Zhongshu's] head no longer tilted over."

Another of great-grandfather Wengong's interventions was designed to stop the misbehavior of a different grandchild (Zhang Dai's third uncle Sanshu): "Sanshu was a mischievous youngster and liked to play around with a group of children. Whenever he saw Wengong coming, he would jump up and run away to hide in his mother's quarters, where he could not be caught. Wengong got so angry at him that he took pieces of roof tile, cut them into the shape of a shoe, and stitched them into the soles of [Sanshu's] shoes. Next time [Sanshu] saw Wengong coming he jumped down and the tiles broke into shards, so that he was [caught and] tied up and given a beating."

Such examples show that the women in the Zhang family often gave safe haven to the children when their irascible grandfather Wengong was on the prowl. On some occasions they could change the flow of events. One such case involved Zhang Dai's own father and his adored younger brother Zhongshu. The incident must have taken place around 1578, after the birth of the two children concerned, but before the death of Lady Liu (which came in 1582). At the time, Zhang Dai's father was four or five, and great-grandfather Wengong had just been recalled to active duty in Beijing. As Zhang Dai retold the family story: "Zhongshu was just one year younger than father, and the two brothers were inseparable. When Wengong's leave of absence was over, and he had to return to the capital, Zhongshu was four years old. Wengong adored my father, and decided to take him along on his return to the north. Zhongshu had therefore lost his dearest companion, and he wept fiercely and refused to eat for several days. At this time Lady Liu was living at home [with Zhongshu], and she sent a messenger to overtake them and to bring [my father] back. Only when my father got back home did Zhongshu start eating again. Thereafter [the two boys] got up and went to bed at the same time, and ate and played together; they were the wind and the rain, night and morning, and so forty years sped by like a day."

Wengong's daughter-in-law (Granny Zhu, as Zhang Dai called her) brought new resources and vistas into the Zhangs' world.

Her father, Zhu Geng, became a powerful and successful official, rising from a position among the elite scholars in the Confucian Study Academy to become the president of the ministry of rituals and a grand secretary, and thus she had to make her way in the overlapping worlds of the Zhangs and the Zhus with tact and tenacity. Her task was not made easier by the injunction passed on to her and her husband in 1604 by her own father. Worried by the many stories that he was hearing in Beijing of the wasteful excesses of his own Zhu family, Zhu Geng instructed the pledged couple to identify and keep him informed of those members of the family who behaved the most outrageously. As Zhang Dai wrote later, the scars were to be enduring: "Many of Zhu Geng's sons and grandsons were arrogant and disobedient. When he received his staff of office, he wrote a letter to grandfather, listing a whole series of rules item by item. He authorized grandfather to punish the Zhu offspring as though they were his own. Grandfather ordered his family servants to beat [the errant Zhu clan members] with the staff of office, and asked his wife, Granny Zhu, to help him identify those who were arrogant and bullying. At the cost of great pain, he drove some of them out, and showed no indulgence towards them. Those [Zhu family] sons and grandsons still resent that to this day."

Despite these difficult family tensions, Granny Zhu's brother, Zhu Shimen, was one of the Zhejiang region's leading connoisseurs and art collectors. His expensive tastes and habits had a great impact on the Zhang family as a whole. In a later comment appended to some family biographies he had written, Zhang Dai gave a negative summary of that impact: "We Zhangs were built into an enduring family by the simple habits and thrift of my great-grandfather Wengong. Our later yearnings for palatial lodgings and glorious accouterments truly began with my maternal great-uncle Zhu Shimen, and my father and my paternal uncles first imitated and then came to exceed him, to the degree that they were unable to stop."

Foremost among those Zhangs who imitated the extravagant ways of Zhu Shimen was Zhang Dai's second uncle Zhongshu, the boy whose tilted head had been artfully straightened by great-grandfather's stern commands many years before. Zhongshu, in his turn, was to become a passionate and extravagant collector of antiques, but one whose sure eye for quality also brought him a major income from the treasures he bought and sold. In an affectionate sketch, Zhang Dai gave the salient details of uncle Zhongshu's career as an art collector and dealer.

Once the inseparable boyhood friend of Zhang Dai's father—they were only one year apart in age—uncle Zhongshu personified that attraction and tension between art and money that surfaced often in the family's daily life. As Zhang Dai wrote: "Uncle Zhongshu loved ancient literature and philology, and on the side studied the art of painting. As a youngster, Zhongshu became a great favorite of his maternal uncle [Zhu] Shimen, and so was able to examine many old paintings. By the time he was sixteen or seventeen, he had become especially good at painting from nature, and at estimating the worth of things; later, he made haste to look at all the great masters, and became at home with the works of painters such as Shen Zhou, Wen Zhengming, Lu Baoshan, Dong Qichang, Li Liufang and Guan Si. Uncle

Zhongshu had a particular acuteness in appraising artworks, and along with [Zhu] Shimen labored to build up his collection—together, the two of them traveled all over the country."

Like the political world of Beijing, the art world had its share of bargains and of dangers. Shrewd buyers could make fortunes, as could contemporary artists of unusual flair; at the same time, the number of skillful fakers and forgers was growing, and the connoisseurship of those who could make honest and accurate appraisals was in high demand, bringing them large fees. Zhu Shimen must have been a great teacher for Zhang Dai's second uncle, since he had impeccable contacts in the art world and had built up an astonishing collection of his own, some of which Zhang Dai lovingly itemized. In the year 1603, after failing the provincial examinations, uncle Zhongshu made a trip to Huaian. A traveling merchant there was offering a naturally formed ironwood table for sale, and the local governor had made an offer of one hundred taels for it. But Zhongshu got it by offering two hundred, put it aboard a boat and hurried off home. The governor sent someone in pursuit, to track uncle Zhongshu down, but when the man discovered that Zhu Shimen was Zhongshu's sponsor he did not dare question the young man further and returned without the treasured art object.

Zhang Dai sketches in the details of his second uncle's rise to eminence in the richly endowed world of the late Ming Yangzi delta region. "From this time on, [Zhongshu's] art collection grew more splendid every day, and he came to be considered one of the top five collectors south of the Yangzi." In the year 1606, adds Zhang Dai, second uncle Zhongshu "built himself an elegant villa at the foot of Dragon Mountain, and kept his finest antiques and favorite pieces there. It was stuffed full of them." Perhaps here Zhang Dai was referring to his childhood dream studio that this same uncle so callously destroyed, but if so he did not push the point. Instead he flattered his uncle by equating him with the greatest of all Yuan dynasty artist-collectors: "Even Ni Zan's 'Cloudy Grove Pavilion' was no match for this." Zhongshu also maintained his own comfortable houseboat, perhaps mainly for visiting collections in the Yangzi delta and Hangzhou regions and acquiring new works as much as for getting away quickly from angry competitors. He appropriately named this craft his "Calligraphy and Painting Ship," and Zhang Dai used to sleep on this boat on some of his own journeys. Perhaps prior to building his villa on Dragon Mountain uncle Zhongshu also kept some of his treasures here.

Some of uncle Zhongshu's youthful purchases already showed his shrewdness as a dealer: Zhang Dai mentioned especially three eleventh-century Song dynasty pieces of exceptional rarity and beauty—a white porcelain incense burner from Dingzhou, a porcelain wine pitcher made in the Hangzhou region and a porcelain vase of Ru-ware—for which a local connoisseur offered five hundred taels, only to have the offer turned down by Zhongshu, who said he would keep the three treasures until he died. In 1610 Zhongshu obtained a thirty-pound piece of peerless green jade: checking out its color qualities by plunging it first into clear water and then checking it in bright sunlight, and satisfied as to its remarkable purity, he entrusted it to specialist jade carvers, instructing them to make a carved dragon cup and ceremonial marriage cup. For the marriage cup alone Zhongshu was paid three thousand taels and—as Zhang Dai noted—this sum did not include the dragon cup or the smaller pieces of jade left over, which were worth a small fortune in themselves.

Even after 1628, when Zhongshu at last embarked on the official career he had never given up seeking, he continued to keep his eyes open. He knew, for example, when posted to the Mengjin region of Henan province, that it had once been the seat of the late Zhou kings of the first millennium and hence must be a great site for ancient bronzes. By the time he had finished his service there, according to Zhang Dai, uncle Zhongshu had acquired "several wagon-loads of early bronzes including a whole set of sixteen or seventeen ritual wine goblets of different sizes, all with the purest and most striking green patina." By these various "deals," as Zhang Dai observed, his uncle Zhongshu "made colossal profits and his collection grew more valuable every day." Zhang Dai does not comment on whether any of these bronzes reached uncle Zhongshu through irregular channels. But elsewhere Zhang Dai notes that some of the most beautiful and unusual objects he had ever seen—a set of three elegant bronze wine goblets, and two ritual bronze vessels, each standing three feet tall and decorated with elaborately carved animals—had come into his wife's family because an alert official had intercepted a robber excavating items from an ancient grave site of the Three Dynasties period. Having interrupted the robbery, the official making the arrests had apparently quietly kept the objects for himself until he later sold them to Zhang Dai's father-in-law.

Zhang Dai's mother was from the Tao family in Kuaiji, in the east side of Shaoxing. The Taos, like the Zhus and the Zhangs, were well known in scholarly circles and had good records in the

examinations. Her own father received the provincial degree and
served for several years in Fujian as an official in charge of the
government salt monopoly. But he was also an austere man and
tight with money, following in the steps of his own senior relatives in the Tao family, who liked to style themselves "incorrupt-
ible and poor." As Zhang explained, their parsimony meant that
around 1596 "Mother was sent off to be married without any
dowry, and thus forfeited the affections of her mother-in-law
[Granny Zhu]. As time went by, mother devoted her energies to
running the household well; as an outsider, she took only the
poorest food for herself; she never tried to take things for her
own private gain, and never forgot her own responsibilities to
her husband. Thus my grandmother Zhu, who was by nature a
testy woman and treated mother with severity, realized that
mother followed the correct code of wifely behavior, and came
increasingly to respect her."

Whether she was respected or not, life was clearly not easy for
Zhang Dai's mother, even though giving birth to a son in 1597, so
soon after her marriage, should have brought her praise from the
Zhang family. And yet Zhang Dai talks about his parents' early
life as being full of difficulties and problems with money. Some
of the dilemma may have been that even after a decade of marriage, and well into his thirties, with twenty years of tuition behind him, Zhang Dai's father had still not passed the provincial
examinations that came as the next step on the scholarly ladder,
and thus he was especially beholden to his own family for financial support. Faced by his needs, the older generation of Zhangs
seem to have been grudging with their assistance. Zhang Dai's
paternal grandfather was a formidable figure, and his branch of

the Zhang family clearly had considerable wealth, as of course did the Zhu family, to whom he was bound by marriage. But their expenses were large, and grandfather was not a man to accept bribes as a way to expand the official stipends he received as a midlevel official. Zhang Dai observed that even after his grandfather passed the highest level of the state examinations and received a position as a county magistrate in 1595, he gave his own children and other relatives only the bare minimum for their expenses, leaving them to sell property if they had to. Thus, despite the family's prestige and influence, wrote Zhang Dai, "Father's living conditions were poor and mean, and he did not have the initiative to come up with alternate plans. He left the task of acquiring the basic necessities of life to mother. She lived a difficult life, always pressed for funds, but by saving thriftily for twenty years she was able gradually to improve the family's circumstances."

Zhang Dai seems to have had a defiantly flexible sense of the meanings of thrift, poverty and extravagance, since elsewhere he recorded a party thrown by the Zhangs in 1601 that would have been completely impossible for a poor family and must have stretched even a wealthy family's resources to the limit. Since he was only four at that time, he probably was told the details by his parents or an uncle. As Zhang described it, the extravagance began when several of Zhang Dai's uncles, together with his father, decided to light up the whole of Dragon Mountain in Shaoxing with a display that would put all other families to shame. They cut and sharpened many hundreds of wooden stakes, painted them with bright red lacquer and tied them together in threes. Each of these triangular scaffolds was garlanded with satin, and from each a lantern was suspended. Under the branches of the trees that grew in profusion on the mountain—and were also festooned with lanterns—the lines of lacquered frames with their gleaming offerings "hemmed the skirts of the mountain paths, climbed along the steep mountain steps and clothed the valleys with their radiance." As Zhang Dai remembered the scene some sixty years later, "From the gates of the City God's temple to the gullies at the Penglai ridge, there was nothing to see but lanterns. As one let one's eyes roam across the landscape from the base of the mountain it was as if the starry river of the Milky Way was flowing backwards, shimmering and luminous."

The scale of the festivities was so lavish that the local Shaoxing authorities had to issue special ordinances to curb abuses that might spring from the public's enthusiasm. At the gateway of the City God's temple on the southern edge of Dragon Mountain—that being the entry point the crowds had to take to reach the brightly lighted mountain beyond—various placards were posted: from that point onward no one was to travel by cart or on horseback, but only on foot; there was to be no use of firecrackers or other rowdy behavior; nor were the powerful families of the city to follow their customary habit of sending their personal family retainers in front of them to clear a passage through the throng. Zhang Dai's father and uncles erected a wooden platform of their own under one of the great pine trees, spread out their mats and relaxed there at their ease, eating, drinking and making music. As for the other city folk, "Those with an eye for business sold wine, and the mats laid out for people to relax on stretched all around the mountain. There was no bit of mountain that did not have its lanterns, and there were no lanterns that did not have their mats. There was no mat on which someone was not sitting. And there was no one who was not singing or beating out the music." As soon as the men and women coming to view the lanterns had passed through the gates of the City God's temple, "They had no room even to turn their heads to look behind them, no room to reverse the course of their steps. All they could do was move along with the flow, as with a tide rising and ebbing, not knowing on what shore they would be beached, but just moving on, without caring." Each day workers came up into the mountain to clean away the debris from the night before: "mounds of fruit pits, chewed over stalks of sugar cane, meat and fish bones, piles of discarded sea shells." And each night, for four nights in a row, the lanterns blazed forth once again.

When Zhang Dai was about eight years old he received a new lesson in the ways that duty and love could so easily either blend or collide. Around 1605, while his mother was in her sixth month of pregnancy, the whole family came together to celebrate the birthday of Granny Zhu. Determined not to be blamed for idleness and thus shamed in the eyes of the Zhang family members, his mother, despite her pregnancy, insisted on seeing to every detail of the old lady's celebration, planning the meals, the guest list and the presents. Exhausted by the work, she gave birth three months prematurely to a baby boy named Shanmin. He was tiny, less than a foot in length, and weighed just a few pounds; he panted constantly as he fought for every breath. Amazingly, the baby survived, and became to Zhang Dai the most beloved of his three younger brothers. But because his mother had no expectation that the baby would live, she wasted no time on it—there were more than enough other children to love and care for, ones with better chances of growing to maturity. In the Shaoxing region, the slender chances for such children surviving were acknowledged by the name given to them, "Lily pad babies." The term suggested the degree to which both their birth and their survival thereafter depended on miracles, for the lily pad was the symbol of the Buddha's footprint.

Father was equally disinterested: "As for my father," Zhang Dai wrote, "he was exhausted by his attempts to pass the examinations, and had no will left to teach this son, so my youngest brother lost the chance to receive an education. But my brother exerted all his efforts, saying, 'Can one be fully human if one has received no education?' So he proceeded to teach himself to read and made his way steadily through every kind of book." By querying whether one could be fully human if one did not have a thorough education Shanmin was—perhaps knowingly—echoing his own great-great-grandfather's comment of one hundred years before. But Zhang Dai agreed that his young brother's chances for success were frail: "Judging from appearances, one would have thought that my brother would never be any good at his studies."

Yet Shanmin, even without his parents' support, was able to succeed in many spheres: as a scholar, as a poet, as an art connoisseur and as a collector who was the last member of the Zhang family to reach the stellar realms charted out by Zhu Shimen and second uncle Zhongshu. As Zhang Dai summarized the components of his younger brother's success: "In character, my younger brother was receptive and quick; he acquired perspicacity early on, and considered things carefully and with gravity. In his reading he showed great intelligence, he was refined without undue speculation, had breadth without galloping around all over the place, and had thoroughness without conducting endless research."

Nor was Shanmin ever snobbish about where he looked for his treasures: "If some itinerant vendor or someone in the local market happened to have a special object, he focused on it with complete concentration: it had to be old and it had to be refined, the skill with which it was made was crucial. If he saw it was good, he always had to buy it; if he bought it, it had to be the best. Once an object was in his hands, he had to caress it day and night, until an unusual sheen emanated from it; he would wrap it up in rare brocade, and store it in a chest of camphor wood; he would seek out those who were known for their skill with their hands, and write eulogies about their work. At nighttime he would burn incense and boil water for tea, browsing by lamplight through his treasures; when he came across some really beautiful poem, he would smack his lips over the taste, unwilling to let it go." Clearly with his younger brother Shanmin, as in the case of his blind cousin Pei, Zhang Dai was exploring how personal strength of character could carry the individual over hurdles that would have tumbled most people to the ground.

Zhang Dai's mother faced a different kind of test when, in 1611, Granny Zhu suddenly died while on a visit to one of her children—Zhang Dai's third uncle, who lived some distance from Shaoxing. The problem here was one of ritual and propriety mixed with fear: it was not considered ritually correct to enter someone else's home in order to remove a relative's corpse back to one's own, nor was it correct to carry out the funeral rites away from the ancestral home that had been adopted by the deceased. Popular superstitions in the region warned that either course of action might lead to dire consequences for the offending person. According to Zhang Dai, the whole problem was too much for his own recently bereaved grandfather: "Grandfather was thrown into a flurry of indecision. Mother forcefully requested that they return [the body] to their ancestral home for proper burial, stating that she would take all the evil omens upon her own self. Grandfather was delighted, and said, 'My daughter-in-law is a Zengzi or Min Ziqian among women.' Later [mother] indeed had to endure various calamities, but to the end she never regretted her action." Grandfather's comment was deliberately flattering, for Zengzi and Min Ziqian were known in the classical canon as two of the most punctilious disciples of Confucius, men who could always be relied upon by their teacher to act correctly in matters of ritual deportment.

For the fifteen-year-old Zhang Dai these were difficult times, and in 1612 he responded by invoking the help of Nanzhen, the fairy spirit of dreams. Local belief held that Nanzhen resided in Kuaiji, the original home of Zhang's mother, and Zhang Dai wrote a formal petition to the spirit, asking her to send him richer dreams, ones that would accord more with the kind of varied dreams one would find recorded in history and literature. As things now stood, Zhang told the fairy, he was unable to understand the full subtleties of premonitions and intuitions. Returning from the dream experiences to one's own mundane existence "was to feel that one was pitiable, but whom could you tell that to? If people made a mock of my lot, how could I be able to bear it?" And Zhang recalled the even deeper questions that had obsessed him as a fifteen-year-old. In the same petition to Nanzhen he asked, "In order that you, the spirit, can be my teacher, should I be asleep or awake? I have had premonitions about both my departure and my destination. . . . I am eager to obtain merit and glory. It is my hope, as I scratch my head in bewilderment, to question the Heavens. I pray to you with deep conviction, and prostrate myself, forehead to the earth."

Granny Zhu's death caused no miraculous transformation of the family's predicament, and Zhang Dai later wrote frankly about the problems and of the open and unusual approach taken by his mother: "As time went on, father's constant anxiety about taking the examinations led him to become depressed and discontented, and he fell ill with stomach ulcers. Mother grieved over that, and said to me: 'Your father is turning into an aging Feng Tang. It is hard to wait for the [silt-filled] rivers to run clear. It would be better to let him do as he pleases in his gardens and pavilions, to enjoy himself with music of many kinds, and to get some respite from his reclusive life.' " His mother's reference to Feng Tang was a witty and apposite one, as Zhang Dai would have seen at once. Feng Tang was a historical figure from the Han dynasty, fifteen hundred years earlier, who was descended from a distinguished family of scholar-administrators and became celebrated for the length of time it took him to make anything of his life. When he finally got his first job, as a palace attendant, the ruler stepped down from his palanquin to inquire how anyone so old came to be working for him in the palace grounds. And when Feng Tang was ninety his name was still being circulated as a possible candidate for office, only to be rejected by the ruler's successor on the grounds that his age was excessive.

So it was in accordance with his own mother's decision, Zhang Dai tells us, that in the years following 1610 Zhang Dai's father began to indulge his passions: "creating landscape designs, building pleasure boats with multiple decks, teaching and training his young maidservants, playing the music at theatrical performances—no matter what the level of extravagance, father was allowed to pursue it as he pleased. Mother would not let herself be beaten down by her distress, but did her best to provide him with what he wanted." But to Zhang Dai, even though he also was bent on his own pleasures during the same time, the results were less than happy as his father's extravagance increased: "Thus it was that in the closing years of mother's life, father drew on the family resources so he could live like a rich man. In 1619 mother died, and father contracted a rare illness; everything grew worse and worse, and within less than three years the family fell into decline."

In a concluding comment on the structure of his father's life, Zhang increased his implied criticism by praising his mother for whatever his father had managed to achieve: "When father was young, he never really applied himself to making a livelihood; and later in life he was absorbed in the quest for longevity. The means by which mother transformed father were both strange and also like a dream. I, Zhang Dai, their unworthy son, have had this presumptuous thought: The fact that father was able to seek a place for himself among the immortals is perhaps due to the help he got from mother."

By the mid-1620s, as Zhang Dai emphasized at intervals, his father was still jobless and had grown immensely fat—a trait shared by various members of both the Zhang and Zhu clans and presumably exacerbated by their passion for staging eating competitions, where they consumed great mounds of food. Zhang Dai made no attempt to present his father's eating binges as endearing. Indeed, he went out of his way to emphasize their grosser side. "Father's body was strongly built, and he looked like his maternal uncle Zhu Shimen, though slightly shorter. In his prime, he would hold eating competitions with his mother's brother Zhu Chiaofeng. Once each of them ate a plump goose weighing more than ten pounds, and father strained the goose juices and poured them over noodles, slurping up more than ten bowls full in a row. Uncle Zhu, clutching his belly, withdrew."

As if these details were not quite enough, Zhang Dai separately wrote a detailed account of the serious illness that afflicted his father after another such goose-eating binge in 1620, complete with a step-by-step depiction of the hideous stomach and digestive disorder that followed and of the successive treatments tried by various expensive doctors. The treatment that succeeded used *dihuang* (*Rehmannia glutinosa*), which a local doctor known for his eccentricities prescribed after all the other physicians had given up on the case, "taken their fees, and departed."

Around 1616 Zhang Dai married a young woman named Liu from a moderately successful scholarly family, but he tells us nothing about his wife, a reticence supported by the conventions of the time, and almost nothing about the children she bore him. He did, however, write in passing of some of the women who had at intervals entered his family, living alongside the senior consorts and bringing up their children in the same households, yet never fully at home and always fearing for their own and their children's future. Zhang Dai had at least two such concubines of his own, and both remained living with him after his wife died. His father had several, both before and after Zhang Dai's mother died, as did Zhang's uncles. In family accounts, such women were often scheming to acquire some of the family's property, and according to Zhang Dai, the concubines sometimes got their way: "Mother devoted all her strength to keeping our family strong, and yet [after her death in 1619] the concubines, the surviving sons and daughters, along with the servants and slaves, carved everything up into three parts." The result was that in his sunset years Zhang Dai's father "had no more valuable things in his possession." But it was equally likely that concubines might be evicted from home if a sudden upsurge of morality overwhelmed an aging clansman—such, allegedly, was the procedure followed by Zhang Dai's grandfather in his last years: "In 1611, after the death of his wife, Granny Zhu, grandfather sent away all of his concubines and lived in seclusion in the Sky-bright Garden, where he had amassed a collection of thousands of volumes."

It could happen, too, that the senior consort was placated by an ingenious husband and that a kind of balance was obtained that left all parties satisfied. This at least, according to Zhang Dai, was the case with his great-grandfather's scholarly companion Zhu Geng, the father of Granny Zhu. Zhu Geng, it was said, found himself in trouble at home when he brought in several young concubines: instead of accepting the situation calmly, his wife was enraged and "roared like a lion" on hearing the news. Alarmed, Zhu Geng came to ask the Zhang family divination spirit if it could provide an elixir to counteract such jealousy. The spirit replied in writing that the task was "hard indeed," but that Zhu Geng would find the requisite tablet inside his pillow. Zhu Geng found it there and gave it to his own wife. She took it and told everyone who would listen, "My old man had a magic elixir, but instead of giving it to those women he gave it to me. Clearly he still favors me." The spirit's plan succeeded for, as Zhang Dai added, "she now got on as well with her husband as when they first married."

Sometimes after a father's death his surviving son, acting swiftly and perhaps sardonically, ousted the father's once-cherished concubine. In one of his short biographical sketches, Zhang Dai told of the initial survival campaign and eventual fate of one such woman. She was a concubine of second uncle Zhongshu, the same Zhongshu who was once Zhang Dai's father's favorite playmate. Second uncle died, vastly rich, in 1644, leaving his huge art collection and virtually everything else to his son Yanke. Apparently, in former days, this woman had convinced Zhongshu of her devotion, but the younger relatives were unimpressed. Indeed many years earlier, since second uncle "had no need for her" as Zhang Dai phrased it, he kept urging his second uncle to dismiss the woman from his service. But the woman pressed her claims to stay at second uncle's side, pleading with him by asking, "Why should your slave ever want to go? All I want is to die as a member of the Zhang family." When second uncle relayed her words to Zhang Dai, Zhang could do nothing but congratulate him on his good fortune at having such a loyal and loving woman.

After they heard of second uncle's death, Yanke and Zhang Dai hurried to the dead man's home to perform the funeral rituals. There they found the same concubine among the crowd of mourners. Seeing Zhang Dai and Yanke there, the concubine addressed them as follows: "If you will now let me go off and get married my good fortune would be complete!" Zhang Dai smiled and reminded her of her stated wish to die as a member of the Zhang clan. "Oh that was just something I said for the old master's ears," the woman replied. "I'm still young, and not yet ready to become a ghost. And even if I did become a ghost, you can be sure I would not be offering my services to the Zhang family." Her honesty got her nowhere: the two men laughed and refused to grant her request.

Zhang Dai's own father had one particular companion, Zhou, whom the son called his father's "bed chamber concubine," who sought especially to strengthen her position in the family after Zhang Dai's mother died and to make sure that the children she had borne would have a decent share of the family property. Zhang Dai described a bantering conversation he had with his father about this woman and her wiles: "Father enjoyed jokes and quips, and never stopped jesting with his children and young relatives. One day the woman Zhou fell ill, and father was fearful that she might die. I told him, 'She won't die.' Father asked me, 'How, pray, do you know she won't die?' to which I replied: 'The heavens gave birth to Bo Pi so as to destroy the kingdom of Wu. As long as the kingdom of Wu has not been destroyed, Bo Pi will not die!' Father gave me a scolding, but after thinking it over a bit he could not help smiling." The reason father smiled was because the allusion was a clever one, which referred to the determination of the counselor Bo Pi, almost two thousand years before, to stay alive until his mission was accomplished. Such historical erudition, casually shared by father and son because of their protracted education, gave the moment its touch of levity; but the economic and emotional fragility of women like Zhou was real enough.

Zhang Dai also wrote at length about his mother-in-law, whom he called his "second mother." Descended from another local family, she was to outlive his own birth mother by exactly nineteen years, and clearly filled the emotional void left in his life by his mother's death. As Zhang Dai wrote of this second mother, Lady Liu, in a funeral essay after her death, "She supported, educated, and disciplined me like a real mother. Yet in supporting and educating me she feared spoiling me; in disciplining and reprimanding me, she feared hurting my feelings. In those ways, her caution and consideration were like those of a real mother. Now my mother-in-law has passed away, and I have lost all the maternal love in my life." The strange coincidence that the two mothers in his life had died on the same day of the same month—the fourth lunar month, twentieth day—even though nineteen years apart, strengthened in Zhang Dai's mind the feeling that their maternal fates were linked: "Thus the funerals of mother and mother-in-law intersected, and when I grieve for my mother-in-law it is as if I grieve for my real mother. I thought about exhausting my whole being so that I could express my gratitude to my mother-in-law until the time of her death; it is as if I sought to requite my own mother. Yet on this day, when I cannot follow her, and feel my insides torn by the thought and regret eating me away every day, it is as if I also miss my real mother, and weep for her as well."

For the last five days of his mother-in-law's life, as she steadily weakened, Zhang hunted for the best doctors and medicines, and also tried a mixture of spiritual interventions: in front of his family shrines, and by invoking the godly powers that pervaded Mount Tai—a region to which he had gone on a kind of tourist pilgrimage a few years before. It was to no avail. Thirteen days after her death, he invited a group of priests to her coffin chamber, where they performed the rituals from the twelve books of the Water Penance (*shuichan*) to give her blessings in the afterlife. The following day Zhang Dai assembled her surviving family members—one daughter and several grandchildren, some of whom were married—to lament her passing with his own eulogy.

Zhang Dai's pen portrait of his mother-in-law was to be the longest he ever wrote on one of the women in his family. His words were affectionate but bleak: "Though born into a wealthy family," he began, "my mother-in-law did not experience a single day of good fortune or peaceful rest during her life, whether as a girl, wife, daughter-in-law, mother or aunt." Instead, she faced the miseries of losing loved ones and of loneliness. In all the years he had known her, wrote Zhang, he only saw her smile three or four times, and much of the rest of the time was filled with tears and disappointments. Indeed the story of her life could be told as a record of loss. Zhang Dai's mother-in-law had been married at the age of sixteen, but her husband died only eleven years later, in 1605, when she was twenty-seven, leaving her with two little daughters and pregnant with a third child. Throughout their brief marriage her husband had suffered from numerous ailments; after his death the son she bore turned out from

boyhood to be entirely dependent on her. Shortly after that, her
father-in-law, whom she loved deeply, drowned in a tragic accident. Of her two surviving daughters, one died young not long
after getting married, leaving no heir. Thus it was only her second daughter, married to Zhang Dai, who could extend the
family line and thus appease widow Liu's dead husband in
the underworld: yet even there, Zhang Dai wrote regretfully, the
longed-for grandchild "took long in the making," leaving her all
the more anguished and her "brows troubled." In her darkest
moments, Zhang Dai wrote, this second mother of his did not
even enjoy the happiness of an "old woman gatekeeper," who,
despite her poverty, would have her children and grandchildren
milling all around as she labored. As if all that were not suffi-
cient, mother-in-law Liu also had to care for a "harsh and fussy
uncle" and her own widowed mother-in-law, a woman "so
short-tempered that even her own family members found it almost impossible to talk to her," even as they had to "appease her
in every way, and endure all her insults."

When Zhang Dai's wife finally gave birth to a son, this baby,
too, nearly died—from smallpox. Zhang Dai attributed his son's
survival to a remarkable local doctor in Shaoxing whom he had
known since he was a young man. Zhang Dai described this doctor, Lu Yungu, as being a self-taught eccentric with passions for
the finest tea and for playing the flute as well as an amazing skill
at growing rare orchids. Dr. Lu also had three phobias: he hated
people who smoked, he hated heavy drinkers and he could not
bear it if people hawked and spat out phlegm on the ground. But
most important, to Zhang Dai, Dr. Lu had a detailed knowledge
of the medicinal plants growing in the region, and apparently

deep and intuitive understanding of the workings of the body. Because Dr. Lu "never learned medicine from any teacher or classical compendium," Zhang wrote, "but relied almost totally on his own intelligence and observations, even though he often cured seemingly hopeless cases with his experimental methods, most people had little trust in him, and did not go to him unless absolutely desperate." But what truly mattered, wrote Zhang in a poem of thanks, was that Dr. Lu "used medicine as if commanding troops, attacking the dwellings of disease with reserve." And his skill was not merely intuitive: "In the blood and flesh from which the body is composed," Zhang added, "he could clearly trace all the interconnections; it was as if the inner organs could speak to him." Early in his career, Dr. Lu had begun to specialize in diseases afflicting babies and young children, and had a skill for treating smallpox that left the child unscarred. Thus it was that widow Liu ended up with a healthy grandson to carry on at least some of the family traditions.

In Zhang's mind, his mother-in-law's great strength had been that she was "both strong-willed and tolerant." However hard things were, she tried to keep those around her satisfied. In this lay her true obituary: "She does not depend on sons and daughters-in-law to mourn her, for there are many others who will do so; she does not need her kin to praise her, since travelers on the road will do the same; it is not just those who received her help that praise her, but even idly chattering strangers. So how can I, Zhang Dai, convey my respect for my mother-in-law? All I can say is that throughout her life as a daughter she was always dutiful; as a wife, chaste; as a daughter-in-law, respectful; as a mother, hardworking; as an aunt, generous. With all that being so, despite the countless sufferings she experienced in her life, she can still enter the underworld smiling."

Yet though widowed at twenty-seven, Zhang Dai's mother-in-law had certain things to be grateful for. There is no evidence that anyone in her own or the Zhang family pressured her to marry again, as was often the case in other lineages, and after her husband's death she seems to have been free to bring up her children the way she chose. The wealth of her own family and of the Zhangs undoubtedly helped, but so did her skill and patience in living the roles assigned to a woman of her station. When we place her story side by side with those of the women who married into the Zhang clan, such as great-great-grandfather's pessimistic Lady Liu, the protectively parsimonious Lady Wang, the tough-minded Granny Zhu and the unknown number of rejected concubines, we can better understand why Zhang's own mother would seek reassurance at the local Buddhist shrines and take her little son with her on her visits. And why, once there, she might draw out some of the money she had carefully stashed away, and pay those who had brought her and her child to the temple to spin the great case full of sutras, spin it round and round at ever increasing speed, until they lost their grip on the whirling mechanism and the countless prayers that it contained went streaming out from the sacred precincts, up into the Zhejiang sky and thence to the presence of the silently watchful gods.

CHAPTER FOUR

THE WORLD BEYOND

Zhang Dai was in his early thirties when he finally decided to leave his familiar comforts in the Yangzi delta region and to head into the unknown terrain of northern China. He was married now, and his mother and grandfather were both dead, so perhaps he felt the pull of a wider world. But the catalyst seems to have been his father's final success—after so many years of failure—in the provincial examinations. It was, to be sure, a limited success, which had led father to be named as an "alternate" candidate in the subsidiary listings for the year 1627, but by virtue of this rather tenuous ranking, at the age of fifty-three father received his first appointment, to one of the hereditary princely households of the Ming dynasty. The rulership of these fiefs was restricted to the direct male descendants of the children born to the Ming founding emperor back in the fourteenth century, but the administrative posts were open to outsiders. Father's title was "junior superintendent of the household to the prince of

Lu" and mandated his presence at the princely palace of Lu in southern Shandong province, in the prefectural township of Yanzhou. It was there that Zhang Dai traveled, on a birthday visit, in the autumn of 1629.

Father's situation at the princely court was an odd one: succession to the Lu fief had been troubled for many years, since a series of early deaths of some heirs, and the childlessness of others, had led to generations being skipped and younger brothers inheriting the title. Prince Xian, to whose court Zhang Dai's father was appointed in late 1627, was just such a younger brother of a younger brother, as well as the son of a lowly concubine, and had been enfeoffed as prince in 1601. (He was to die childless in 1636.) Father found that he and Prince Xian initially had a surprising affinity, since, as Zhang Dai noted, the prince was "an enthusiast of the Taoist way of immortality. Father himself was skilled at [Taoist] breath-control techniques, and thus ruler and minister followed the same path; father was constantly summoned to [the prince's] personal chambers in the palace, and kept there until well into the night. Thus everyone from the prince himself down to his senior staff and the residents of his fief all came to the office attached to the junior superintendent's residence to consult with him, and his house was always filled with people." The prince's ways were not always fathomable. For example, he often carried with him "a branch of cut gnarled pine, which he cradled in his arms and slept with; over time it became supple and smooth, and looked as if suffused with blood."

Based on his experiences in Shaoxing, Zhang Dai had confidently considered himself a connoisseur of lantern displays, but as he wrote of this 1629 visit, the lavishness of what he encountered in Yanzhou was on a scale beyond anything he had imagined or experienced before. In the open space in front of the main gates to Prince Xian's palace, eight sections of scaffolding had been erected, from which hung beaded curtains twenty feet high. On each curtain, in giant calligraphy, was written the character for one of the various exemplary moral traits: filial devotion, respect, loyalty, trustworthiness and so on, all sparkling in the light. Within this curtained amphitheater, large model animals—lions, elephants, camels—in wax and resin roamed apparently at will, but in fact were steered from within by concealed men who pushed the creatures along on rollers. On the creatures' backs rode other men, dressed as barbarian warriors, each shaking bowls of ivory, rhinoceros horn, coral and jade, from which jetted flowers of colored light, some appearing like wild geese in flight and others like yellow wasps in swarms. The smoke wreathed the southern face of the palace, "so that the moon could not be seen, nor could the dew settle on the ground." But it was not just the scale of the spectacle that moved Zhang Dai, for he knew how easily apparent grandeur could cross over into vulgarity. It was the intensity of the light that at last approximated what he had dreamed of finding, a form of perfection that upset one's basic expectations and equilibrium.

As he wrote of that experience: "Those of us here on earth who look at a lantern look at that lantern from the outside. Those of us watching fireworks also observe them from the outside. Never before had I realized that the watcher could enter the center of the lantern, could be in the center of the light itself, could enter into the shadowed areas and into the smoke, could enter into the fire, metamorphosed, not knowing if these were fireworks being set off in the prince's palace, or if this were a prince's palace composed of fireworks." It was, wrote Zhang, as if "the prince and his relatives, their female attendants and retainers, their dancers and their musicians, became *themselves*, amidst the lanterns, an element within the décor."

On a subsequent visit in 1631 to his father at the Prince of Lu's Shandong palace, Zhang Dai made a side trip to the famous sacred site at Mount Tai. The rich historical associations with China's past, and the profusion of Buddhist shrines and temples, gave to Mount Tai an especial fame among all ranks of people; the paths up the mountain were normally thronged with pilgrims, some eight or nine thousand each day by Zhang's estimate, with as many as twenty thousand at the height of the spring season. The view from the summit was reported to be one of the great experiences that life had to offer. But as Zhang Dai soon discovered, there was little chance on the Mount Tai pilgrimage for quiet spiritual concentration, since this was a large-scale commercial operation. It was not just that the Shandong provincial administration profited so handsomely from pilgrims thronging at the site, though that was a factor: Zhang noted that the "mountain ascent tax" was close to a fifth of a tael of silver per person, which, with thousands of pilgrims coming each day, easily generated two or even three hundred thousand taels a year. This income was divided between the officeholders in the provincial government and the three Ming princely families enfeoffed in the region. There was also the fact that the entire structure of each individual's pilgrimage was supervised by the half-dozen professional tour managers who were based in the sprawling inns clustered around the foot of the mountain, where the path to the summit began.

Even before reaching his chosen inn, Zhang had seen the outlying buildings allocated to actors and entertainers, to stabling for the pilgrims' horses and mules and to prostitutes. Around the temple compounds at the foot of the mountain sprawled a vast open area where dozens of entertainers competed with the sacred images for the pilgrims' attention: there were scores of stalls selling every kind of knickknack, geared mainly to the women and children, and here and there, amid the din from singing and from gongs and drums, one could see wrestlers, football players, horseback riders and storytellers as well as battles between fighting cocks and full-scale theatrical presentations.

Basic accommodation at the inns ran to around a third of a tael per person, and the extras at once started to add up. There were three different meal plans, for instance, of varying degrees of luxury for each of the three different meals that the inns provided: an early breakfast before departure, a lunch on the way to the summit and a "congratulatory banquet" when the pilgrims had made a safe return. Before the ascent, the meals were vegetarian, with fruit, nuts and some wine to accompany them. The most expensive of the congratulatory meals, however, were complex affairs, with up to ten meat dishes, sweets and cakes. As well as the level of the catering, meals were graded by the seating arrangements and the entertainment: the highest grade provided a separate table for each pilgrim and a choice of dramatic and musical entertainments; the middle grade sat two to a table; those paying the cheapest rate were crowded in three or more to a table and were regaled with music but not theatricals. The prostitutes were extra.

Zhang Dai was roused on a rainy dawn for the ascent to the summit. His tour manager had already hired a sedan chair with bearers for Zhang Dai, and he was carried up the steep steps balanced sideways between his carriers, who had fastened the curved carrying poles to their bodies with leather thongs. The route was jammed with beggars, to whom Zhang Dai's guides scattered, in profusion, special charity coins bearing the Buddha's name, coins that had also been provided for him as part of the packaged arrangements.

It was a long climb, and Zhang Dai was able to appreciate the surprising fact that between the inn and the summit he passed through what could literally be called seven "changes of weather." The downpour in which he left the inn gave way to an overcast sky by the time he reached Hongmen; at Chaoyang cave it was sunny, though it turned dark again by Yuzhang cliff; at Yitianmen ("first gate to heaven") a strong wind began to blow, at Santianmen ("third gate to heaven") there was mist and fog and on the summit there was snow and ice. "If Heaven itself cannot make up its own mind," wrote Zhang, "then how can we humans be expected to?"

By this time, Zhang's hands and feet were freezing, and his guide took him to a simple earth-walled shack he had erected there, and lit a small fire to thaw his client out. But by the time Zhang was warm and left the shelter, the dense mist had rolled in again, and every trace of the view had vanished. It was only by groping their way forward, "feeling the way out with hands so the feet could follow," that the group was able to reach the summit shrine known as the Bixia Palace, home to the guardian deity of the mountain, Yuanjun, known as the "Goddess of Green Clouds, the Heavenly Immortal, the Jade Maiden." Inside the shrine were three images of her: none of them was large, but each was believed to be powerful. The left-hand image was worshipped by those who hoped for sons, the right-hand image by those who had been threatened with the loss of their eyesight. The central image, marked by a special coin of gold, was for those who sought a variety of other blessings. The pilgrims threw copper coins and even small lumps of silver over the temple railings in the direction of the golden coin. If they managed to hit it, they would receive extra blessings. The result, wrote Zhang Dai, was that the offerings lay thick upon the ground, all around the images. Some pilgrims left silver tokens in thanks for favors the goddess had granted: little silver models of a boy child from those who had borne sons and little silver eyes from those whose sight was restored. Others left silks or embroidery, rugs, precious or semiprecious stones, even clothing and shoes. Each night, a squad of soldiers from the base camp at the foot of the mountain came to patrol the shrine and guard the offerings, which were collected at intervals and sold to supplement the income from the mountain ascent taxes.

Hoping that the clouds would lift, Zhang Dai wanted to linger on the summit, but his tour guides and bearers were adamant that they must return before conditions grew any colder or more perilous. Zhang could not dissuade them and had to agree since he could see no trace of paths or lodgings where they were. The rushed journey back to base was terrifying: "My bearers helped me into the chair and began a rapid descent from the South Heaven's gate. Their legs moved in a blur, making me feel I was in free-fall. If they were to miss but a single step, in my opinion certain death would follow. Closing my eyes, I tried to imagine the feeling of being smashed to pieces. Several times in my dreams I have felt like that again, falling freely through the air, cold sweat covering my body."

Back at his inn, Zhang's tour manager had prepared the welcome-home feast, complete with theatrical entertainments and wine. To the manager's satisfaction, Zhang had now completed his pilgrimage: fame, strong eyes, wealth or male heirs would all be his. But to Zhang, the pilgrimage so far had been frustrating, and he partook of the festivities only with reserve. Since the night sky was clear, and the stars shone brilliantly, he resolved to try again the next day. When he made his purpose known at dawn, the tour manager was resolutely opposed: no one ever made a second ascent; it would bring nothing but misfortune. Zhang was left to his own devices, and it took him a long time to find sedan chair carriers willing to convey him, while the local people who knew that he had been on the summit the previous day pointed at him and laughed at his folly. But this time the trip was worthwhile, the weather fine and the views spectacular. Zhang had time to visit a number of other shrines and temples on Mount Tai, to study the stone stelae of Buddhist sacred texts and a selection of inscriptions from Confucian classics and to understand—now that the weather let him see more clearly—how truly dangerous the headlong descent in the fog the day before had been.

Zhang's closing reflections on the whole experience were not positive. There were two aspects that were especially depressing to him: one was the incredible number of beggars at every stage of the ascent and the generally mercenary aura that clung to the whole enterprise. The other was the unsuitableness of the inscriptions carved into the rock faces or stored in the various shrines. Some visitors had simply obliterated earlier, more elegant inscriptions by superimposing their own clumsy calligraphy directly over the original renderings. Others, who presumably claimed some scholarly pretensions, wrote messages of mindnumbing banality. There were two that Zhang quoted with especial disdain: "Venerated for Ten-thousand Generations" and "Redolence Continuing for all Eternity." The beggars and the visitors between them, thought Zhang, "had desecrated every part of the once sacred soil of Mount Tai: their crimes are comparable to those who in their pursuit of fame and riches have defiled the world at large."

Such ambiguity over the significance of religious manifestations of any kind (as well as sacred or revered sites) echoes through Zhang Dai's writings. Few places in China were regarded as more awe inspiring in their historical and symbolic implications than the original home of Confucius in Shandong province in the town of Qufu, but Zhang treated the site without reverence. The curators at Confucius's home demanded an entrance fee when he visited there in 1629, and the entire site was filled with inappropriate or wildly unlikely labels of explanation prepared for gullible visitors, even though Zhang Dai seemed to accept the fact that the bent old juniper tree whose trunk he stroked and tapped was indeed the one originally planted by Confucius himself: "I felt its trunk. It was smooth, moist, firm and shiny. The pattern of its bark swirled to the left. When

struck it produced a sound like that of metal or stone." He noticed, too, that for fear of pilferers the ritual objects on the various altars were all nailed down.

Though Zhang Dai traveled far afield, and saw many shrines
and talked to many so-called sages, few of them really drew him
into their world. Some tried, but Zhang Dai chose not to follow
through. For instance, on a winter's day in 1638, he tells us, he
took a servant and a bamboo travel basket "and walked to a
shrine just southeast of Nanjing at the summit of a mountain.
Among strangely-shaped rocks and sharp peaks, and dense
and brushy shrubs, lived a mad monk—he spoke to me, with
wild and disordered words that were based on bizarre moral
principles—I was sorry not to have the time to really go into
things deeply with him." But that disappointment did not prevent two contrasting thoughts from occurring to Zhang Dai at
the same time: one, that this monk lived on a mountain where
every rock was already completely covered with carved images
of Buddha, so that, like the criminals found guilty under the old
legal code, every rock was either "tattooed or noseless." And yet,
at the same time, it was impossible for Zhang Dai to deny the
feeling of sublimity that welled up in him as he gazed down at
the shadows of the sails on the distant Yangzi River, which was
nothing less than a sense of "the silence, in which one could feel
the full immensity of mountains and lakes."

As Zhang Dai prepared to return to Nanjing on that day in
1638, a figure strolling in front of him turned out to be an old acquaintance, a scholar by the name of Xiao. Sitting down at another monastery nearby and drinking tea prepared for them by

one of the monks, the two friends talked of many things involving religious pilgrimages. Xiao was interested in the shrine on
Mount Putuo, out in the sea beyond Ningbo, one of the most sacred Buddhist sites in the whole of China. It happened that a few
months earlier, in late March and early April, Zhang Dai had
made the sea journey to the famous Putuo shrine and had written an essay about it; rummaging in his travel basket, he found a
copy, and he and Xiao pored over it together. Delighted by
Zhang Dai's essay, Xiao wrote an introductory preface. They
came back together by the light of flaming torches and spent the
whole night talking before they parted.

Putuo Island, seven miles long and two wide, lay in the ocean
about seventy miles east of the prosperous harbor city of Ningbo.
It owed its fame as a shrine to the claim that it had once been the
earthly home of the goddess of mercy, Guanyin, and as Ningbo
became famous as a commercial entrepôt, Putuo's fame increased
over the centuries along with the city's, spread by the ocean-
going junks that docked there, often transshipping their cargos
for entrance to the Grand Canal via Hangzhou or for the other
waterways linking the ocean trade to the Yangzi River.

Zhang Dai estimated that there were at least fifty-seven
monasteries of various sizes and two hundred small shrines or
temples on the island, and countless scenic spots. The peak time
for pilgrimages was on the nineteenth day of the second lunar
month, which was accepted as the exact date of Guanyin's birthday. In 1638, the year of Zhang Dai's journey there, that day fell
on the solar-month equivalent of April 3. To get to Putuo on
time for the major religious celebrations, Zhang took a ship on

March 31, having already noticed the wild commercial frenzy that occurred in Hangzhou as the solemn date approached: weeks before Guanyin's birthday, eager pilgrims converged on Hangzhou from all over China, especially from the north; and all the available empty spaces in the city and the temple court-yards were crammed with stalls selling everything under the sun. Zhang carefully itemized hairpins and makeup, lotions and ear-rings, elephant tusks and knives, religious tracts and wooden begging clappers, sacred images, toys and trinkets of every kind.

Zhang was no lover of ocean travel, and he noted that when he invited friends to make the journey with him they all declined with some excuse or other, except for his friend Qin Yisheng, with whom Zhang had previously visited several other shrines and temples in the Ningbo region. One earlier visitor to the is-land whom Zhang knew personally was his maternal grand-father Tao Lanfeng, whose calligraphy was still kept in one of the island's many temples. Zhang felt that people could not be blamed for shunning such a journey. Putuo had nothing to offer but its shrines and holy memories, with crowds of the faithful "bowing every three steps and prostrating themselves every five" as they "clasp their hands in prayer and chant their sutras."

Also, getting to Putuo was not half the pleasure. The seas were often rough, the winds fierce. The sailors were brusque and superstitious as they scattered paper money to propitiate the dragons of the deep and insisted on passenger silence lest the ocean spirits waken. Nor did Zhang approve of the accommoda-tions on the cheap tourist boats that ferried the ranks of the faith-ful to the island shrine. Supervised by monks known as the pilgrim leaders, these "pilgrim boats" were, he wrote, "a living hell on earth. The pilgrim boats have two decks, with the male faithful on the top deck and the women believers on the lower. Each boat is enclosed by cloth awnings which are drawn so tightly that no air can circulate. The hundreds of people crammed in the boats have nowhere to wash or rinse off, but still all have to urinate and relieve themselves." Any people seeking to go to Putuo, Zhang wrote, should only travel if they could get space on one of the government's naval craft called tiger boats. These provided a spacious passenger cabin where one could sit, sleep or stroll around, and had curtains that could be opened to let in the fresh air. Such boats were safer, too, manned by professionals in sea skirmishes, and had eighteen oars a side to supplement their sails. If Zhang did start his journey on a pilgrim boat, he seems to have changed to a tiger boat before too long, for he writes of donning warm clothes and sitting on the deck late at night, enjoying the breeze and the golden play of the moonbeams on the water.

Zhang Dai found no personal enlightenment on Putuo Island, but he did find signs of profound devotion. On the eve of Guanyin's birthday, he saw thousands of men and women "packed like fish" into the main and side halls of the main temple. They stayed there in a nightlong vigil, reciting the scriptures and also mortifying their flesh by burning incense on their heads or their arms. One could, literally, inhale the smell of singed flesh, even though Zhang wondered if that was the kind of offering a bodhisattva would welcome. He was not surprised that in their sleepless and pain-sharpened state many pilgrims saw the Guanyin image moving or emitting shafts of light; but when he asked a resident monk whether the monk himself had

seen a vision of Guanyin, the monk gravely replied that the goddess had moved during an earlier emperor's reign and hence
could no longer be seen in her previous haunts. Zhang mentions
that he had to stifle his desire to laugh at the naïvete of the
answer.

As at Mount Tai, so now at Putuo, Zhang Dai was impressed
by the feats of organization that the whole operation demon-
strated, by the thousands who were fed daily and by the scale of
the markets and other commercial operations. There were unexpected joys as well, like the chance to walk on Putuo's famous
beach, which stretched for more than a thousand paces between
two of the island's main temples. "The sea water had scoured
everything clean," wrote Zhang. "The sand was a kind of pur-
plish gold, and the sun reflected off it sharply. The strip of sand
was like a thoroughfare between two oceans; and no matter
whether the tide was high or low, the waters kept up their snort-
ing and inhaling. As I concentrated carefully, the sound became
indistinguishable from human breathing—we were beyond
dawn or night, beyond haste or gravity. The perils of the sea
ebbed and flowed in just such a way." Looking out to the east
from another mountain, Zhang Dai's eyes could just see, on the
very edge of the horizon when the clouds parted for an instant,
the hazy outlines of some distant lands: these, he was sure, must
be Korea and Japan. But there were always anomalous aspects:
the hundreds of thousands of fish caught and eaten each day by
the local fishermen hardly seemed to accord with the bodhisattva's religious principles, and though there was much
genuine charity, generosity and goodness there was also waste
and ostentation. As so often, Zhang Dai caught the broader prin-

ciple with a personal vignette. During the whole pilgrimage, which spanned most of a month, he wrote, he had followed a proper Buddhist regimen of strict vegetarian meals. When he landed at the harbor town of Dinghai, on Choushan Island, the pilgrimage ended, he hurried to the local market and ordered a meal of his own favorite "pebble fish." No sooner had he swallowed that longed-for treat than he vomited the whole thing up.

Drawing together his two different experiences on land and by sea in the world of faith and pilgrimage, Zhang Dai came up with his own personal synthesis: "When I climbed Mount Tai, the mountains rose and fell like furious waves, their appearance resembling water. When I traveled to the South Sea, I saw great waves like moving mountains, cliffs of ice, and boulders of snow, their appearance resembling mountains. Mountains and waters are connected, their shape different but their essence the same. The clouds of Mount Tai produce the world's rainfall, and are the origins of water; Putuo, on the other hand, is a land of mountains; therefore, water naturally cannot exist separate from mountains. Suppose the waters were infinitely broad and vast, yet without mountains to support their frame and secure their joints. The world, then, would have blood, but no bones. Should the world have blood but no bones, it would not even create mankind, far less the sea!"

Even though Zhang Dai did not make many of these lengthy journeys, they nevertheless let him meet and talk with a wide circle of Chinese travelers. Especially on the trips by water— whether on the inland Grand Canal running north from Hangzhou to Beijing, on the adjacent rivers or on the sea voyage to Putuo Island—there were long periods of waiting or tedium, in which casual conversation between complete strangers was a commonplace. Especially on the overnight ferries that operated in the Yangzi delta region, with their lower deck for bulk goods and their well-furbished upper deck for passengers, stops were few, and the passengers' level of education was comparatively high. This fact subsequently gave Zhang Dai the idea for a book, a kind of compendium of knowledge to be called *The Night Ferry*. As Zhang explained his motivations for this book in his preface: "Of all the forms of knowledge that exist under heaven, none is harder to handle than the kind one needs on the night ferry. For this reason, the rustics and simple folk all try to get themselves properly prepared before the journey, so that if there is a discussion of the 'eighteen scholars of Yingzhou' or the 'twenty-eight generals of Yuntai' they won't make the kind of simple errors over names that would make their listeners cover their mouths to hide their smiles. It seems that they don't realize that even if one forgets some of the names of the eighteen scholars or twenty-eight generals it is not proof of any lack of learning. Yet these voyagers feel that to make a mistake over just one of the names is somehow to be considered shameful."

It was also a sad fact, wrote Zhang, that many of those who claimed to be scholars had enormous gaps in their learning and often made glaring errors. He illuminated this with the tale of an alleged scholar and a simple Buddhist itinerant monk who found themselves in the same cabin on one of the ferries. Though the monk was curled up in a corner and trying to get some sleep, he remained courteous, while the scholar lectured him on a range of topics. But the monk was finally so startled by the scholar's many inaccuracies that he had to claim the need to "stretch his legs" in order to get out of the cabin and so bring the scholar's long monologue to an end.

What was at question here, to Zhang, was the whole nature of learning. In some townships around Shaoxing, he wrote, almost everyone was literate, and only when people reached the age of twenty were they sorted out, some to continue on with the scholars' life, while all the others went off to acquire "manual arts." In such areas even artisans and craftsmen might have extensive book learning and appear to be "book-cases with two legs." Yet their learning was not based on any deep or fundamental knowledge, and hence amounted to a kind of illiteracy. The pompous scholar was equally hollow in his learning.

What was the answer then? Not completely to give up studying the names of celebrated figures and important allusions from the past, wrote Zhang, but to be able to select from all the available texts those people whose lives or actions had truly been of significance, to draw the idea of quality out of the massive amounts of data. Hence Zhang Dai presented his selection of things that should be remembered from the past if one were to have an enlightened talk with one's ferry-riding companions. To help with this task, Zhang distilled from his own wide reading twenty categories—from astronomy and geography to antiquities and politics, from funeral rituals and soothsaying to foreign lands and medicine—and under each one he listed the things that he felt needed to be known. With this knowledge at one's disposal, the ferryboat journeys could proceed without embarrassments. The task would still not be too simple—Zhang's basic list ultimately included some four thousand names and items, each with a short passage of explication. But if Zhang managed "to prevent monks such as this one from having to stretch their legs," then his work would be justified.

In *The Night Ferry* Zhang Dai had whole sections dealing with foreign lands, ranging from nearby Korea and Japan to far-off Hormuz and other territories explored by the eunuch admiral Zheng He on the east coast of Africa in the 1420s. But interesting though the information might have been to his readers, nowhere in this book of over three hundred thousand words did Zhang mention the writings in Chinese of the Catholic missionaries from the West, who had made Hangzhou their major base in the 1620s after facing persecution in Beijing. In Hangzhou the Catholics had made new converts, and their supporters and their denigrators kept up a running debate on the significance of Christianity and the nature of the society from which it sprang.

Zhang Dai's grandfather had been one of those involved in these debates. It was typical of grandfather's scholarly eclecticism that around the year 1615 he had read one of the first books that the Jesuit missionary Matteo Ricci had written in Chinese (a composite tract on leading the moral life), had digested it down into a coherent summary and at the request of a prominent Chinese Christian in Hangzhou had composed a preface to introduce the work to a wider circle of Chinese readers. In this preface, grandfather pointed out how the Westerners' moral teachings stacked up against those of the Confucians and the Buddhists, ending with the tongue-in-cheek endorsement that this particular Western work "had the power to make stupid people more intelligent, but it could also make intelligent people more stupid." There was a certain redundancy and showiness about the Western scholar's writing, grandfather noted, as though "a blind man [was flashing] a golden scapular [to clear his sight], or a man returning home had a feather banner waving over his head." But perhaps some of this judgment sprang from the attempt to substitute a part for the whole, grandfather added charitably: "When eating a chicken some people just eat the tendons, when eating the *xun* fish some people just want the cheeks. How can one just take one little slice to stand for the whole sacrificial offering?"

Zhang Dai's townsman and close friend Qi Biaojia—who had written an affectionate preface for Zhang's *Profiles*—also had copies of various Catholic writings in his family library, which Zhang Dai could have consulted whenever he chose. An undated essay by Zhang Dai on Matteo Ricci—which he later incorporated in his history of the Ming—shows that Zhang had absorbed a good deal from the various Catholic writings in Chinese available to Chinese scholars in the 1620s: he knew, for instance, that the Jesuit father Diego de Pantoja had stayed on in Beijing after Ricci died there in 1610, while Alfonso Vagnoni had moved south to Nanjing and Hangzhou, making a large number of converts there. Zhang Dai also knew that several Chinese scholars in Nanjing regarded the Jesuits as troublemakers and had successfully petitioned the emperor to banish them to Guangzhou in the far south. Zhang knew, too, that despite this ban some of the missionaries had surreptitiously returned from the south to the Nanjing region and continued preaching as before.

Zhang Dai was impressed by the sheer duration of Ricci's journey to China in the 1580s and calculated that the missionary had covered more than twenty-five thousand miles and taken three years, as the huge ship capable of carrying fifteen hundred men "sailed on a vast and borderless sea, following only the direction of the wind." Zhang found many things of interest in what Ricci also wrote of the world he had left behind: people there used a solar calendar, rather than the lunar one common to China. Silver coins were the basic currency, and jade and precious stones were not much sought after. Crime of any kind was virtually unknown and aroused astonishment if it occurred. They had mechanical clocks that chimed with small bells every quarter of an hour and with a larger bell every hour—Ricci brought several with him to be presented as gifts. The Western people lived often in high towers to avoid the omnipresent damp. They made containers out of gold and tin. They even had a kind of horizontal zither or *qin,* noted Zhang Dai, and Ricci presented one of these to the imperial palace. Contained within a wooden box almost three feet wide and five deep, it had not less than seventy-two strings, made of some kind of refined metal, that ran the whole length of the *qin* to an exterior keyboard. They had a passion for astronomy and for geography, and brought with them various instruments related to those disciplines. They claimed that the Earth was floating within the firmament, so that if one kept going westward one passed the bottom of the Earth and was then going east. By the same token, if one kept going farther and farther to the north one finally ended up traveling south. Apparently they had no interests in divination, though it was rumored that Ricci himself dabbled in alchemy and may have dealt in medicine. There was also one surprising similarity: not only was the total area of the group of seventy countries that Ricci described "just the same size as China," but "to their north they also had alien peoples, against whom they had to protect themselves just as we in China have to defend ourselves against alien tribes: they fortify their cities, and use firearms as well as bows and arrows. There are also cities in the heartland of those countries, but they do not have to be protected so strongly."

Zhang Dai was impressed, too, by the determination with which Ricci applied himself to his Chinese language studies, so that he "could read the writings of Confucius and communicate with us." He noted that Ricci had not heard of Buddhism until he arrived in China, but had refused to take it seriously because the Buddhists did not recognize the guiding power of a transcendent god.

There were a number of other interesting facets to the lands from which Ricci came, wrote Zhang. Some seventy different rulers, all sovereign in their own territories, lived together in harmony, due to the guiding presence of a central figure, the pope, who was aided by the wisdom of some two thousand highly educated and moral churchmen. Their religion had three coexisting components: the original company of sages or saints, who wrote the texts that now gave counsel and comfort to the people; God himself; and the mother of God. (God, according to the Christians, had no father, Zhang Dai noted.) The distant society was so structured that their popes and religious leaders never married, thus avoiding much strife and expense; and even the rulers of the seventy territories never took concubines or secondary consorts: "Without multiple wives, how can there exist any perverted lust or coarseness?" Ricci himself had been chaste and celibate when he left his homeland at the age of twenty-five, and had remained so throughout the twenty-seven years he spent in China. And in his homeland, many women also never married at all, which in turn left many young men as unmarried bachelors. Though the months of textual preparation demanded from those aspiring to be scholars, the cost of books and the difficult examinations that they had to pass seemed to echo Chinese practice, there was in fact a fundamental difference: "According to their custom, all those engaged in academic pursuits never marry, and consider passing the examinations their only source of glory."

The essentials of their religious practices were simple: "Each morning the people of [Ricci's] country rise and worship Heaven. They pray that, for today, they may avoid evil thoughts, evil words, and evil actions; in the evenings they again worship, expressing their relief that during the day they avoided evil thoughts, evil words, and evil actions. After a time, they find themselves wishing to have a kind heart, kind words and kind actions every day from dawn to dusk. Making this their habit, they fill their books with fine sentiments." It was possible, Zhang Dai could see, to draw from this the conclusion that their texts enforced many of the teachings one could find in the work of Confucius, Mozi, the Taoists and the Buddhists, and then to draw positive conclusions about their culture as a whole: "If the pope gains authority by attending to the people, and yet exercises his authority only on behalf of the people, how can his rule not be fair?"

And yet, there were lingering doubts in Zhang Dai's mind, as there so often were when he pondered moral questions. As was his practice, he bunched them together at the end of his essay:

"This religion of the Lord of Heaven has spread across the world, yet its teachings are often both strange and shallow. As for [Ricci's] writings on world geography, the absurdity is often beyond question. His *qin* with its metallic strings, and his chiming clock, which he offered at court, are good only to arouse curiosity. As to his writings on western religions, they follow the language and argumentation used by our Confucians. If one can penetrate his difficult prose, and substitute common words for his abstruse diction, then his book offers nothing very new or exciting. Some people have praised his work as having a divine spirit to it; others have disparaged it as rank heresy. Neither such praise nor such contempt are warranted." The truth, for Zhang Dai, as with so many other areas of faith and practice, clearly lay somewhere in between.

Zhang Dai accepted the fact that the things that people believed, just like the things that frightened or excited them, were often bizarre and not susceptible to easy explanation. Like the flame at the heart of the firework experience, they had their own consuming force. In perhaps no case was this more true than the visit to the Asoka temple in Ningbo, which he made in 1638 enroute to Putuo Island with his friend Qin Yisheng. The temple was named in honor of the Indian ruler Asoka, one of Buddhism's greatest early patrons, who in the third century BC had ordered the creation of eighty-four thousand Buddhist reliquaries, some of which were believed to have reached China. This Ningbo temple housed one of these treasured reliquaries, which contained a bone of the Buddha. In a side chapel, next to a sandalwood sculpture of the Buddha, was another bronze reliquary donated by the empress dowager, mother of Emperor Wanli—

the ruler under whom three generations of Zhang Dai's forebears had won the highest degrees and served in the bureaucracy.
The main temple was especially beautiful to Zhang Dai: "A
misty light among the shady trees shines through the gate so that
one can look up at the sky and perceive a brilliance that is icy,
cold, crystal clear, and penetrating." Despite the beauty of the
setting, however, the empress dowager's relic carried a darker
message. As Zhang explained, "Whenever someone prays to the
relic, it produces all kinds of visions according to the person's
karma; but if it remains dark as ink and nothing is seen, the person will certainly die."

Zhang Dai's taut account of what transpired leaves the reader
unsure of Zhang's own religious feelings, though sure of the thin
line that he saw as separating illumination from perpetual darkness. The sun was just rising, writes Zhang, when a monk came
to fetch him and Qin from their rooms and escort them to the
Buddha hall. There he opened the bronze reliquary for the travelers. Inside, Zhang could see a miniature hexagonal pagoda en-
cased in sandalwood; it appeared to be made of some kind of
hide and was covered with complex ornamentation and lettering
Zhang recognized as Sanskrit. Inside this second casing was the
relic, hanging from a fixture within the pagoda and gently swaying. Staring intently, Zhang was sure he could see three pearls
strung together, as in the chain of pearls created by the historical
Buddha. They shone with a strange brilliance. Resting his eyes a
moment, Zhang Dai bowed down, requesting that a vision be
granted, and as he focused his gaze once more on the relic, the
sought-for vision appeared: it was a small image of Guanyin, the
goddess of mercy, "robed in white, so sharp that one could see

her eyes and eyebrows, even the ringlets at the side of her face."
But Zhang's friend Qin Yisheng was less fortunate: "He looked
at it again and again, but could see nothing. Seized with panic,
his face flushed, Qin wept and departed. And indeed Qin
Yisheng died that same year, in the eighth month."

When Zhang had finished his first book ten years before, his
friend Qi Biaojia had praised Zhang's extraordinary concision.
As Qi wrote in the preface he contributed to the volume, Zhang
was able to condense into twenty words or so thoughts and
events that would have taken Qi two hundred words or more.
From this, we can guess that Zhang's swift depiction of Qin's fate
after his temple visit was the kind of thing that Zhang's contemporaries found admirable. No one was really to blame for Qin's
death, and if there was a central contributing factor, surely it was
Qin's own failure of imagination. Even while being rushed down
the frozen steps of Mount Tai with his bearers, Zhang Dai had
been able to imagine the death that might await him and had
thus avoided it. Qin, on the other hand, could not force himself
to conjure up a vision when it was needed. That was why Zhang
Dai had lived to write the tale and Qin had had to die, why
Zhang was back at home and Qin was in the underworld.

CHAPTER FIVE

LEVELS OF SERVICE

Emperor Tianqi died in late September 1627. Normally, emperors came and went, and lesser lives continued on their course, but this particular death promised to have more resonance than most, for few reigns in China's history had been so corrupt and so vicious. Tianqi's father had been poisoned back in 1620, after reigning for less than a month, and Tianqi was not yet fifteen years of age when a group of officials hustled him to the throne room to take over the reins of government in person before an ambitious alliance of palace women and eunuchs was able to establish a regency in his name. But the officials had miscalculated, and young Tianqi was already completely dependent on the palace eunuch Wei Zhongxian, a thirty-year veteran of life in the palace, a skilled master of court intrigue and a confidant of both the new emperor's mother and his nurse.

The overriding passion of the teenage emperor Tianqi was

for fine carpentry, and he was more than willing to let Wei handle government matters as long as he could be left in peace in his workshop. In this strange situation, even the most senior officials in the state bureaucracy found it impossible to reach the emperor Tianqi in person, and thus were forced to seek permission from Wei and his acolytes if they wished to implement any policy decisions. As Wei assumed greater power over both national and palace finances, he assigned trusted eunuch agents to serve in several wealthy provincial cities, to funnel taxes thence back to the treasury in Beijing. Though China was facing internal bankruptcy and a growing number of popular uprisings, as well as threats by Mongol tribes to the northwest and powerful forces of Manchu warriors beyond the Great Wall to the northeast, the Chinese troops received few supplies or the cash with which to obtain them. Furthermore, venomous Beijing politics led to the execution or disgrace of many of China's finest generals on the northern frontier. Emboldened, the Manchu troops in 1626 had intensified their attacks on the Ming forces, a clear indication that they were contemplating an all-out assault on China south of the Great Wall.

During Emperor Tianqi's reign, so strong was Wei's faction— supported as it was by a network of high-security prisons in the capital, run by selected bodyguards—that Wei was able to have even senior officials killed at court if they criticized his person or his policies. In the most celebrated case, in 1625 six prominent officials, all holders of the senior examination degree, were arrested and tortured. The leader of the group, Yang Lian, a former senior censor who had dared to accuse Wei of twenty-four "great crimes," was falsely accused of bribery and beaten to death in prison; the other five all died from their beatings or from torture designed to make them confess to their own "crimes." Sycophantic officials further contributed to Wei Zhongxian's public image. The governor of Zhejiang, for example, petitioned in 1626 to have a temple with an honorific image of Wei erected overlooking Hangzhou's celebrated beauty spot of West Lake. The petition was granted and other temples soon followed in other provinces. Only Emperor Tianqi's death in 1627 brought a halt to Wei's dizzying career, and in December of that same year the new emperor—Tianqi's younger brother, for Tianqi's five children had all died in infancy—instructed Wei to retire and shortly after ordered his arrest. To escape the fate he had brought on so many others, Wei committed suicide. The new emperor had acted decisively and effectively, and seemed a harbinger of better times to come.

Such astonishing news would have traveled swiftly; one effect it had on Zhang Dai was to make him decide to write a detailed history of the Ming dynasty. By intriguing coincidence, when Emperor Tianqi died Zhang Dai was just finishing his first book, which he had started writing in 1618, shortly after his marriage to the young Lady Liu. That book was a collection of historical vignettes assembled from Zhang's careful culling through both official dynastic histories and unofficial popular chronicles, from the earliest reigns in the second millennium BC down to the collapse of the Mongol Yuan dynasty in the 1360s. Zhang Dai eventually assembled close to four hundred compact studies, which he wrote out carefully in his own hand. He titled this first collection *Profiles of Righteous and Honorable People through the Ages*. For each exemplar he gave a condensed biographical sketch and an accompanying commentary on that person's actions. Naturally there were the famous warriors, scholars, officials and rulers from China's long past, but there were also those from more humble stations: merchants, monks, beggars. What all the stories shared was the fact that they bound together both reader and writer. To further explain his motivation, Zhang evoked the great Song dynasty poet Su Dongpo, who used to assemble quantities of medicine even though he was not sick, and stockpile alcohol that he did not drink. As Zhang quoted Su, "When those who are really ill get my medicine, I can feel their relief; when the drinkers take my liquor, I can share their drunkenness." So with Zhang Dai himself: "It is my aim to make them have the same feelings that I do, and to read with the same exhilaration. If their eyes pop out, then my eyes will pop out; if they rub their hands together, then my hands rub together."

Zhang Dai's wish to become a history writer, he tells us, sprang from the excitement he felt as a reader when he encountered these inspiring figures from China's past. Reading about such moral and courageous people from earlier epochs swept him along on an emotional surge: he became "like a tiger or wolf who has just sighted meat, or a piece of ice that is placed next to a blazing cauldron. When I read these books my excitement reaches such a pitch that my face turns red and my ears burn, my eyes protrude and my hair bristles. I am like someone who has been tethered up out in the cold and has no way to control his shivering, or like a sick man sneezing, coughing, sweating, his tears flowing."

The kind of people who thrilled him in this special way were all around us in the past, wrote Zhang. They were the natural risk takers who at once could recognize those who shared their passions. "For in this world there are totally unrelated circumstances which, when we learn about them, cause us to clench our fists and discard our writing brushes, as if driven by a common urge for vigorous action: thus do strangers who have never met before pledge to each other that they will face death on the same day." These exemplars from the past could also help us understand the dramas of the present: "When I come across people like that, my spirits are charged up; every time this occurs and one comes across righteous scholars and martial followers, my emotions are moved by our contemporary situation." The more parlous the situation, Zhang wrote, and the more challenging the cure, the more exciting the events came to seem: "Why is this? If the things that happen to us in regular life are not painful, then they will not be exhilarating; if not intensely painful, then they will never be intensely exhilarating." Thus it was in our own daily lives as well, that drastic cures were often the best: after "using violent pressure to burst a boil, or taking a metal awl to dislodge a splinter, once the sharp pain is over, the soreness and swelling will swiftly fade. All our pent-up stresses vanish with a swift cut of the knife."

In a separate comment on the methodology for his volume of *Profiles*, Zhang Dai divided the people he chose to write about into more specific categories. In pride of place were two groups of figures whose actions sprang from sudden impulse and unthinking generosity. First came people whose "compassion for those in extreme peril, fleeing in panic or facing an apparently inevitable death, roared to life like a bolt of lightning or a tidal wave, completely unconquerable." Linked to such people, in moral grandeur, were those commoners who "gave their lives for their country without regret, out of personal compassion, even though under no obligation to do so." The spontaneous impulse behind their courage was what fascinated Zhang Dai: that was why, he added, he would not write about those who sacrificed their lives for a "benefactor," like the swordsman Jing Ke, or those in official positions who "had no virtuous choice but to die for their ruler." Nor would he write about those who died for totally unworthy masters or who gave their lives "out of weariness and exhaustion rather than in a burst of passionate loyalty."

In the concluding section of his comments Zhang Dai veered into potentially perilous territory: "I will record all those who, when wolves hold power and no justice can be sought through official channels, attempt to limit such men's influence through acts of personal bravery, or to humiliate them through wit and intelligence. I only wish to preserve such acts of resistance in my empty words, but do not care about their success or failure." If the issues from the past that he was presenting seemed to have relevance to "current affairs," Zhang continued, he would not drop them from his book, even if people accused him of irresponsibility or of drawing undocumented conclusions, for it was his hope that his words might "strengthen the morale and honor of today's society." His model here would be the ancient historian Dong Hu, who had been praised by Confucius for his integrity and refusal to conceal harsh truths. In a final sarcastic flourish, Zhang ended his comments by noting that even horses, dogs, birds and monkeys have been known for their virtuous deeds such as saving their riders from drowning or warning of approaching robbers and therefore he would give them the coverage they deserved: "I reserve a space in my book for them, in order to shame those men who cannot even be compared with monkeys and horses."

During 1628 and much of the year following, Zhang Dai was preoccupied with arranging for the publication of his *Profiles* and encouraging friends and local scholars to write prefaces. Their comments were glowing, with several writers equating his achievement with that of the great early historian Sima Qian, and it was with their praises still fresh in his ears that in the autumn of 1629 Zhang Dai set off to visit his father in the north. Their enthusiasm may have been exaggerated, but it undoubtedly helped to firm up Zhang's embryonic plans to write a book that would begin with the Ming founding in 1368 and continue through the fifteen emperors who had ruled China from that time until Tianqi's death. Common prudence mandated that Zhang end his story there and not attempt to pass any judgment on Tianqi's younger brother, China's new ruler, who had so swiftly struck down the eunuch Wei Zhongxian.

Zhang saw the dramatic implications of Wei's story, and even as the events were unfolding he seems to have begun work on an operatic play, entitled *Ice Mountain*, about Wei's rise and fall. The initial response was gratifying, and when he offered public performances of *Ice Mountain* in Shaoxing a year or so after Wei's fall, Zhang tells us, crowds jammed the theater and all the space in front of the gates: they identified so strongly with the courageous censor Yang Lian that when the actor playing Yang appeared on stage and announced, "I am Yang Lian," the whole crowd began to chant in unison, "Yang Lian, Yang Lian." The result, wrote Zhang, was that "the sound of their voices spread to

the area outside like a breaking wave." As other heroic characters appeared—like the town laborer Yan Peiwei, who struck
back at the corrupt local officials loyal to Wei—the crowd
"roared their approval at his courage and stamped their feet in
rhythm, shaking the foundations of the theater."

When Zhang Dai made a second journey to Shandong, this
one in 1631, he took one of his own opera troupes north with him
so he could perform *Ice Mountain* for his father. He tells us that
while giving performances of the play in Shandong, he updated
the script by adding various episodes that were told to him by the
sophisticated audience assembled there, many of whom had
lived through the most critical events while serving at the Beijing
court in the 1620s. By drawing on their memories, wrote Zhang,
he was able to amaze other audiences with the extent of his own
knowledge.

Despite this apparently firm moral stance in the face of Wei's
enormities, Zhang Dai remained tolerant of other people's aber-
rations as long as they showed the fixity of purpose he had celebrated in his *Profiles*. Especially of his own family's bizarre
financial and political dealings, he wrote a series of sketches with
what appears to be carefully calibrated candor, starting with his
own immediate ancestors. For instance, in Zhang Dai's estimation great-great-grandfather Tianfu ruined his career because
he would not make the adjustments that greased the wheels of
society in the far southwest. Appointed to a prestigious post in
Yunnan, he found himself immersed in local politics and the intricacies of a regional rebellion. The local strongman, Mu, ran
the territory and was willing to pay handsomely to keep it that
way. All great-great-grandfather need have done was to keep

Mu's money and share the honors of suppressing the rebels. He was offered over ten thousand ounces of gold by Mu simply to share the glory. When he refused absolutely, on the grounds of personal integrity, he lost both the money and the honor. Mu used the money to buy other members of the bureaucracy, to have men criticize great-great-grandfather's handling of the crisis and then to back their criticisms with impeachment memorials to Beijing. Only because Wengong, Tianfu's son, interrupted his studies to hurry home to Yunnan and bend the law almost to the breaking point did the old man survive and win a partial reprieve—and even so the cost was high and his career was ruined.

Great-grandfather Wengong's own career, despite his examination triumph, sputtered in Beijing due to his refusal to woo the great or even to be polite to those who had corrected his examination books, normally a common bond of patronage and loyalty. Thus instead of making the most of the fact that the chief examiner, who was responsible in 1571 for ensuring Wengong was placed first in the country, was also the most powerful of the grand secretaries, great-grandfather spurned that heaven-sent chance of patronage and made a point of insisting that he be considered the disciple of Luo Wanhua, once his own former study mate on Dragon Mountain. The grand secretary, according to the version of Zhang Dai, responded curtly when great-grandfather's name was mentioned by saying, "The man is crazy." Great-grandfather Wengong's only answer was an adamant refusal to join the sycophants who clustered round the grand secretary if he was ill and dutifully attended every funeral in the great man's family. Instead Wengong opted for early retirement and a chance to revise the local histories of the Shaoxing region where he had been born. Great-grandfather, wrote Zhang Dai, "was both virtuous and candid, and took the welfare of the whole country as his personal responsibility. People often considered him a lifesaver of the country. Yet fortune did not favor him, and left him a worried old man."

Grandfather Rulin seems to have been equally impractical, allowing his focus on his studies—and perhaps his attempts to emulate his father Wengong's stellar examination successes—to completely deflect him from attending to the family's broader economic priorities. Zhang Dai's account is terse, but despite some of the stock phrases on the life of a recluse, it fills in some details about grandfather's student years: "When [great-grandfather] Wengong died [in April 1588] the family began to fall on hard times. The local magistrate altered the old system of land registration, and was unsparing in the way he did it. Grandfather pursued his studies in the Dragon-bright tower, climbing up to the top and having his meals sent up on a pulley; for three years he never left the tower. Much of the land and property that the family had accumulated was now appropriated by others and [grandfather] did not dare stop them, but just resigned himself to the situation." Perhaps grandfather was wise to stay away from the world of practical affairs if he wanted to triumph in his exams—but one can also see how his refusal to get involved in worldly business might have brought grave damage to the family fortunes.

Zhang describes in somewhat more detail how, when grandfather had finished his studies, passed the exams and received an appointment as a magistrate in Jiangxi province, he was not without administrative flair. He could see right away that a new mining tax imposed by Beijing had such a damaging effect on the local economy that many local miners fled into the mountains; to curb this loss of revenue, grandfather was able to get several magistrates from neighboring counties to collaborate and jointly to face down the new tax commissioner. He was similarly successful, wrote an admiring local historian, in calming the disorders caused by a eunuch commissioner who had been demanding impossible amounts of medicinal plants. Yet, there is no evidence that such actions brought any profit to the Zhang family. As one of the county histories put it, "Thrift was the custom of our county: Zhang Rulin came from a family that had been influential for generations, but he was content with a simple life."

In contrast to these somewhat moralistic actions by earlier Zhang relatives, Zhang Dai's own father seems to have behaved, while employed in Lu, with a breezy insouciance. Shortly after father's arrival, wrote Zhang, in late 1627, "Seditious rebels rose up in Shandong province, and completely encircled the city of Yanzhou. Father was put in charge of the city's defenses, and by his surprise moves he routed the insurgents." The senior officials in the region—including Financial Commissioner Liu, for whom in 1631 Zhang Dai performed his opera on the evils of the eunuch Wei Zhongxian—"All honored and saluted father, and gave him the name 'The Rebel Pacifier.' "

Sometime later, when ordered to check the records of recently condemned criminals in Lu, father used his own private funds to bail out the families of subordinates who could not collect taxes owed to the fief, providing coffins for the deceased and travel expenses for those returning home. Father also turned the local

jails upside down in his quest to have all people released from
what he termed the "living hells," and redesignated the crimes of
condemned criminals by the use of euphemisms, so that their
crimes could be pardoned if they came up for review: thus in
Zhang's father's words, convicted murderers became "fighters
for justice," thieves became "knights errant," violent avengers
became "filial sons." Either because of these eccentric actions or
for other reasons of which we are ignorant, late in 1631 father
was dismissed from his post in Lu. Zhang's only hint about the
reason for dismissal was that after father had redefined these
criminals and returned to his service with the prince, "Father intensified his quest for the art of cultivating the mind and clearing
it of all attachments: in conversations with others he became increasingly absurd and flighty, so that people made fun of him."

If criticism was intended in Zhang's analysis of his ancestors,
it remained muted. Yet the same is not true of two longer tales
told by Zhang of two more distant relatives: great-uncle Rufang
and third uncle Sanshu. This great-uncle Rufang was a few years
older than Zhang Dai's grandfather and so was considered
within the Zhang family to be a member of grandfather's generation. Yet he seems to have had none of grandfather's family
wealth, scholarly training or any distinguished forebears. Perhaps Rufang was born to a junior consort or concubine or one of
great-grandfather's older cousins—Zhang Dai does not give us
the details. He contents himself with launching straight into Rufang's story with no preamble, sure that the story will carry itself.
"Great-uncle Rufang was some years older than my grandfather,
but he was not successful at his studies, and left school. He tried
working as a dealer in various handicrafts, but did not succeed at

those ventures either. His poverty was so extreme that he could not make a success of anything. He got married to someone, but was unable to look after her; by doing the washing, sewing and mending for wealthy families they just barely got by."

One morning, according to Zhang Dai's narrative, Rufang was sitting on the ground, holding his first-born son Shouzheng, and discovered that he had no food to give the child. Weeping, he said to his wife: "I am completely poverty-stricken, and if I cling to the comforts of home any longer I will surely end up dead in some ditch. I'd like to go up north, to try my luck there for a few years, but unless I can get some money to cover my travel expenses I'll have to give up the idea. Things have reached such a pass! If I go, I'll die. If I don't go, I'll die. But given the choice, I think it is better to go and die, rather than not to go and die. I have no possessions of any value, but I can see that on the collar of your jacket there are still two silver clasps. Will you let me sell them?" His wife took the scissors and cut the clasps off for Rufang. He immediately hurried off to the pawnshop and was given three *qian* worth of cash for them. Rufang divided the money in half with his wife, saying: "This will give you enough food for several days. But after about ten days you'll have to go to some wealthy family and try to get by. I will take my share as travel money and will set off tomorrow." Both of them wept at the need to part.

The most that "three *qian*" can have meant in the currency of the time was "three-tenths of an ounce of silver," enough for a few days' food for his wife, as Rufang observed, but certainly not enough for him to get all the way to Beijing. The best hope of getting to the north with only a few coins in one's pocket would be to leave Shaoxing, cross the Qiantang River to the north and make one's way to the provincial capital of Hangzhou. Hangzhou, as well as being one of China's great cultural and entertainment centers, was a commercial hub for the southeast in the days before Shanghai's spectacular growth. Most important, it was the southern terminus of the Grand Canal, along which traveled much of China's rice and the other foodstuffs that fueled the voracious appetites of the northern garrisons along with the court and the bureaucracy in Beijing. Towing the heavily laden barges up the canal gave tough but regular work to thousands of men, who would get their keep and a minuscule daily wage. Rufang decided to take that opportunity, and Zhang Dai described how his great-uncle "put on his rain hat and left home, crossing the Qiantang River until he got to the junction for the northern shipping. There he bought a towing rope and signed on for work as one of the haulers on a grain boat. After several months, he reached Beijing."

For a southerner with no contacts, limited education and high ambitions, getting a job in Beijing could not have been easy. Again, Rufang's solution was practical: to work as a copyist in the office of the *Capital Gazette*, the Beijing official news sheet that recorded the key decisions and documents of the court and bureaucracy, and circulated them via the courier system to all the administrative offices across China. The wages were miserable—according to Zhang Dai, after paying for food and lodging his great-uncle earned only a few copper coins each day. But by living at the poorest possible level for twenty years, he was able to save up around one hundred taels (equivalent to as many ounces) of silver. With these hundred taels in hand, Rufang could have returned home with dignity, maybe investing in a small business or buying a decent-sized plot of land—sale contracts from the later Ming show sizable pieces of land changing hands for anywhere from three to twenty taels. But as Zhang Dai noted, his great-uncle chose to use the money to advance a step up the Beijing bureaucratic ladder, even though to most observers the move must have looked like swapping one dead-end job for another. "What great-uncle Rufang did was to use the money to procure a job with the personnel ministry, as a minor clerk in the registry for princely families." Most of the offices in the personnel ministry were known to work their staffs at full pressure, but the registry for princely families, wrote Zhang Dai, "was so quiet you could catch sparrows in the doorway." Most of the clerks who had jobs in this office only came in for a few days each month. The rest of the time they left their office doors closed and attended to their other interests. Usually there was no one else around at all so Rufang was alone, with nothing to do, but since he had no home to go to, he spent every day there, lazing around the office. "So passed more than ten years," wrote Zhang Dai, "and he was promoted to chief clerk."

Then came the once-in-a-lifetime chance: "One morning, as [Rufang] was dozing away, he heard the sound of rats up in the rafters, pushing the papers around. The scuttling sound was unnerving, and highly agitated he yelled at the rats to drive them away. One roll of papers tumbled to the ground, and picking it up he took a look at it, and saw that it was the official document registering the births in the Chu princely clan. Rufang hid it away underneath a box."

As a Beijing bureaucratic habitué, even at a lowly level, Rufang

was not merely eccentric in so doing. It reflected his knowledge—
widely shared in the capital around the year 1603—that there
was a major confrontation taking place within the Chu princely
clan. This eminent family, descended directly from the Ming dynastic founder, had been enfeoffed in a parallel way to the Lu
family with whom Zhang's father was to work some twenty-five
years later, but the Chu fiefdom had its enormous estates in Hunan and Hubei provinces, focused around the city of Wuchang.
The complex financial and legal case hinged around whether the
current princely Chu incumbent was indeed the legitimate heir
to the fief or whether—as his enemies claimed—he had been
smuggled into the palace from the outside as a baby by scheming
palace women and their male confidants, so that they could claim
a new prince had been born to keep the faltering line extant. The
story was an intensely tangled one, involving charges and coun-
tercharges from different factions among the Chu princes and
their hangers-on. At least two senior ministers in Beijing had
been directly involved in the confidential investigations, and the
emperor himself knew the scale of the alleged conspiracy.

The initial accusation had been made years before by the father of a previous prince's concubine, who claimed that as part of
his contacts with the Chu house he had made available to them
several hundred thousand silver taels, which had then disappeared. The money had never been found despite extensive
searches of the Chu estates, and the emperor had allowed the incumbent prince to stay on in his position with his lavish stipend.
In gratitude, the young man had sent twenty thousand taels to
the emperor, ostensibly to refurbish three of the palaces in the
Forbidden City that had been damaged by fire a few years be-

fore. This gift was followed by several other massive payments, some of which were seized by members of the imperial clan and also disappeared. Eventually, with the Chu fief on the edge of open rebellion, the emperor ordered a series of harshly conducted investigations in the year 1605. Two members of the imperial clan were decapitated, four were permitted to commit suicide (considered a less harsh punishment than beheading) and forty-five other people were imprisoned. This last purge took place in May 1605 and "From that time on, none dared to speak of this Chu affair."

According to Zhang Dai—who may have either fabricated the dialogue or heard it in person from his own relatives—great-uncle's instinct that he might have had a potential fortune thrust into his hands was swiftly borne out: "Some days later, when great-uncle was once again lazing around with nothing to do, a group of people came and rapped on the door; when he nervously asked what they wanted, they said they wished the registry clerk to show them the archival materials. Rufang went out to meet them, and they said, 'Where has the registry clerk gone?' Rufang replied, 'That's me.' The visitors said: 'We have all come from the offices of the Chu princely estate [in Wuchang city]; because of the problems concerning the prince's succession to this fiefdom, we have been to the imperial clan court [in the Forbidden City], but they have lost the birth registration documents [for the Chu princes]. So we have come to your esteemed bureau to search for them. We beg the clerk to use all of his energies to look through his documents in search of them. If you can find the original document, we will be happy to offer you eight thousand taels as a mark of our gratitude.' Rufang answered, 'I've seen it around somewhere, but can't quite remember where. And the amount of money offered is rather small, and does not exactly meet what I had in mind.' The visitors responded, 'If you can find the original document, we'll double our offer.' Rufang let a little time go by, then gave a shrug, and a slight shake of his head. The visitors said, 'If you still think our offer too small, we'll bring it up to twenty thousand.' Rufang was secretly pleased, looked all around and whispered, 'Don't spread the word around, but if you bring the money tomorrow to such-and-such a place, I'll give you the original document.' The visitors thanked him and left. Next day, Rufang secretly took the original document out [to the agreed place] and gave it to them; he received his twenty thousand taels."

So, at least, Zhang Dai chose to record the story for posterity, and there is no doubt that the sequel reinforces the advice Lady Liu had given to Zhang Dai's great-great-grandfather back in the 1570s, namely that one should retire when one is ahead, lest too much good fortune breed its opposite through the jealousy of others. For, as Zhang Dai wrote, though various people in Beijing had been urging great-uncle for years to use his savings to apply for more senior positions, now that he had the money he had been seeking for so long Rufang became suitably cautious. Zhang records that Rufang sighed and answered: "Human suffering comes from not knowing when enough is enough. How long it has been since I saw those silver clasps on my wife's dress, and we parted. I am going home to live as an old farmer, and if I can get warmth and a full belly, that will be enough for me, that will be enough!" So Rufang procured an official transit pass from the Beijing garrison command, put on his official hat and came back home in his official robes.

Zhang Dai closed his account on an elegiac note. "It was now more than thirty years since [Rufang's] wife had borne him a son, and that son now sported a scholar's sash, was married, and had produced a grandson. When father and son came face to face, they did not recognize each other. Rufang bought land and property, and lived in his home for over twenty years; certainly one could now say his was a wealthy household. Until they were both in their eighties husband and wife lived together happily as a married couple."

As Zhang Dai wrote in a final summary, his great-uncle Rufang was initially as poor as it was possible to be, incapable of even obtaining handouts to stuff in his mouth, but his obsession with obtaining enough money to return home and care for his family kept him going: "Empty-handed he traveled to the capital, enduring a hard life there for over thirty years, until from the middle of a pile of old pieces of paper he pulled out twenty thousand taels, as easily as turning over the palm of his hand. In former days, dressed in coarse and filthy clothes, he sat opposite [his wife], both of them weeping. But now he had grown rich as Fan Li. His name had entered the roster of the famous and the rich and who can say that he had not become larger than life, a true man of talent? With this huge fortune fallen into his hands, he created his own version of the ballad 'I'm Coming Home.' Carefree as a seagull, and with the income from his orange groves, he lived many years as a member of the 'untitled nobility of wealth.' Once he had come home to Yue, he never sought office again."

Yet Zhang Dai was not content to stop there. In his "broad-mindedness and far-sightedness," he added, "it was only fair to place great-uncle Rufang one grade higher than even Fan Li himself."

The references that Zhang Dai made to Fan Li and to the poem "I'm Coming Home" would have been familiar to all his readers. They were Zhang's gracious way of saluting the curious achievement of his long-suffering great-uncle Rufang, who seized the chance to sell the enfeoffment of Chu documents—even though they were not his to sell—and thus made his fortune. Fan Li was a real character from the distant past who had been brilliantly analyzed by the great early historian Sima Qian. Fan Li had been for many years the political adviser to the ruler of the Yue region, whose capital later became the city of Shaoxing. But one day, when he saw catastrophic political changes coming, Fan Li sailed away from his lord on a boat, changed his name and in the second stage of his life became one of China's greatest merchants and financiers, leaving his entire family rich and secure members of the financial elite, the select group that Sima Qian called the "untitled nobility of wealth."

Written in the year 405, some twelve hundred years before great-uncle Rufang's financial windfall, Tao Qian's ballad "I'm Coming Home" was a central reference point in the literature of those Chinese who over the centuries had traded in an official life for the peace of life at home. Though the historical Tao Qian received no sudden windfall and had served in office only intermittently, for around eight years in total, his determination to live at home with his family came to transcend in his mind all the possible advantages to be drawn from a scholarly or bureaucratic career. Like Rufang, Tao Qian claimed to seek contentment in leading the life of a farmer. Like Rufang, he wanted to see his son again and, like Rufang, he was granted twenty years (in Tao Qian's case twenty-two, from 405 to 427) back in the home he loved.

All of Zhang Dai's relatives would have known the famous lines of the ballad by Tao Qian to which he referred:

I'm going home.
Fields and garden overrun with weeds,
How can I not go home!
It was I who made my mind the body's slave.
Why live on in sadness and in grief?
I know the past can't be corrected,
And know my hope lies in the future.
I have not gone far on the wrong road,
And understand today is right where yesterday was wrong.
The boat sways in the gentle breeze.
The wind puffs out my travel gown.
I ask another traveler, "How far still to go?"
Sad I can't yet see in dawn's pale light.
Then I glimpse my cottage gate—
Filled with joy I run. . . .

Rufang remains a mystery in Zhang's account, dishonest yet loyal, a gambler when he had the chance, a patient watcher the rest of the time. Zhang Dai let him sit on the family's edge, a name without a real context, a man who could have served any emperor who let down his guard. But in the case of third uncle

Sanshu, born around 1578, Zhang Dai took more care to isolate the character traits and habits that helped explain how Sanshu also managed to acquire a fortune—and also in Beijing. In each case Beijing was the magnet; but in uncle Sanshu's case, success was speedier and more tied to his own advance planning as well as to the active practice of corruption.

As Zhang Dai observed, this third uncle of his was "quick and versatile" when young and had an invaluable trait: "Once he got to know someone, he could get right into his inner thoughts and talk about things that were right on the mark; everyone gravitated willingly towards him." Perhaps it was this combination of traits that had made this same uncle such a good companion for the young Zhang Dai when they were experimenting together with their Snow Orchid tea. In Shaoxing, Zhang Dai elaborated, his third uncle had understood how to make himself an all-purpose helper, both to the local gentry families and to the incumbent officials: in the first two decades of the 1600s, for instance, Sanshu helped the local gentry when they were building their mansions, and whether it was a matter of landscaping or supervising elegant workmanship, "Even if the expenses ran into tens of thousands, he would see to everything with his own bare hands, and never found such things burdensome."

By the early 1620s, Sanshu had shifted his focus away from the local gentry to the local officials in Shaoxing, who were always appointed (according to the law of the time) from outside the province they were to administer. Sanshu volunteered his services as private secretary to several of these powerful men and proved so effective in his knowledge of local conditions and had such a widespread acquaintance that unless the officials "had discussed a particular matter with him first, they did not dare to tackle any aspect of official business in their jurisdiction."

In 1627, just as great-uncle Rufang had done in the 1570s, uncle Sanshu set out for Beijing "without taking any store of cash with him." But unlike great-uncle Rufang, Sanshu glided easily toward the center of power by mixing in the right circles. Zhang Dai describes his uncle's swift rise to a position of influence in these terms: "In Beijing, after a single social conversation he obtained a post as a private secretary in the Grand Secretariat, just as if it was no more than finding a room to rent. Once Sanshu said to Dai [me], 'If you can be of help to the three senior ministers it will be worth seven thousand taels.' That is truly what he said."

According to Zhang Dai, his third uncle was a remarkable-looking man: "His beard and eyebrows stuck out like lances, his hair and eyes were all topsy-turvy: he never looked straight at other people, and so people never dared to look straight back at him!" But clearly that did not get in the way of his effectiveness in the Beijing bureaucracy: "Sanshu was quick and alert, and good at adapting to circumstances. When he saw something he at once remembered every detail of it and forgot nothing. All those in the provincial and central government offices, if they submitted a memorial [to the throne] in the morning, that same evening they would have to gather outside Sanshu's door to find out about the latest news. The carriages and horses all crowded outside [his door] so that those on some errand could not even get past. If at night he wanted to go home and see his own guests, it could never be before the fourth watch. If an edict was issued, and the news was good, he would announce it on a small placard;

the people of the time all called him 'Magpie Zhang.' On the days that he went in person to the palace, there would be a respite for all those in their various offices. As soon as he came back out, people clustered around him like flies or bees, it was impossible to brush them away."

Sixty years before, to prove his own integrity, great-grand-father Wengong had declined to toady to the powerful grand secretary Zhang Juzheng. But uncle Sanshu had no such inhibitions with the grand secretary Zhou Yanru, who dominated the court between 1630 and 1633 and was widely recognized as the most corrupt member of a spectacularly corrupt group of senior court officials who, to the disappointment of the reformists, had established a power base with the successor to Emperor Tianqi. Third uncle seems to have rapidly made himself indispensable with this powerful man, especially as a go-between with the senior provincial officials receiving their new assignments. In Shaoxing, back in the mid-1620s, one of the men uncle Sanshu had served as confidential secretary was a rising official called Xu Fanggu, from Hefei. Now in Beijing, Sanshu was ready to build on that relationship as Xu was promoted to a governorship.

Always fascinated by both bureaucratic jockeyings and the ruthlessness of power, Zhang Dai gave his own version of his third uncle's spectacular coup: even though all the details are not precise, the general idea of what transpired seems clear enough. As Zhang Dai explained, when Xu Fanggu was promoted to governor of Guangxi province in 1630, he sent a payment of ten thousand taels to grand secretary Zhou and commissioned third uncle Sanshu to act as the intermediary. Sanshu had indicated his agreement to this arrangement with a nod of his head, but the money did not reach its destination. Governor Xu's special messenger felt that the response time had been too slow, so, being an impatient man, the messenger went directly in person to ask Grand Secretary Zhou about it. Zhou thanked the impulsive man but said the money had not arrived yet. Zhou thereupon asked the messenger for the name of the intermediary. The messenger replied, "Secretary Zhang in the Grand Secretariat." So Zhou summoned Sanshu, who came at once. After greeting him, Zhou asked, "Is the business with the Guangxi governor on or not?" Sanshu replied, "It's on." Zhou held up one thumb, and Sanshu repeated "It's on." "Then why has it not reached me?" said Zhou. Sanshu asked him to wait for a moment while the various attendants were sent out of the room and then replied: "Why did your excellency mention this so brashly? The governor's messenger is a man without any discretion, and the [eunuch] secret police and guards are on the alert; once things loosened up a little, I was going to return the gift to him and send him away." Zhou nodded his head emphatically, saying, "Excellent!" And as he brought the meeting to a close he added, "I can see that you really have my best interests at heart."

Zhang Dai explained that his uncle Sanshu, after leaving the grand secretary, summoned the messenger and chided him: "Such transactions should be done under cover of night, and yet you want his Excellency to expose it to all in the middle of his office? What possible point is there in that? There will be no acknowledgment letter, but I will give you a letter of my own to convey to your master post haste." The messenger hastened back to Guangxi, but because he had botched the job so badly Governor Xu had his messenger executed right away. "After this,"

Zhang Dai added, "whenever other people had money to send in, they left the matter in Sanshu's hands, and no one ever again dared to ask any questions."

Clearly, if Zhang Dai's account is even partly accurate, Sanshu played for high stakes in Beijing. Later, in the 1630s, according to Zhang Dai, Sanshu added a more dangerous aspect to his work by using his position to alert officials if they were being impeached for some dereliction and even to delay impeachment charges being leveled against certain officials if those officials were willing to make him substantial payments for his services. Finally Sanshu overreached himself and was brought down by his inability to work himself free from his own coils of deceit. It happened in 1638, when third uncle's own cousin (who happened to be Zhang Dai's ninth uncle) was newly appointed to a financial audit post in Nanjing and impeached the director general of grain transport, a man called Shi Fan, for inefficiency. As he had often done in the past, third uncle warned Shi Fan about the accusations and blocked the charges from being forwarded to the court. As was expected, Shi Fan paid him handsomely for this service. But unexpectedly, ninth uncle forwarded a second, and even harsher, impeachment, which third uncle was unable to block. Shi Fan was imprisoned and launched a counteraccusation of graft against Sanshu, effectively ending his career. After this debacle, Zhang Dai noted, his two uncles became implacably hostile to each other and could do nothing but yell in fury whenever they happened to meet.

What Sanshu's habitual cut in such transactions might have been is left unspecified by Zhang Dai, but clearly playing around with such enormous sums as ten or twenty thousand taels was not something foreign to many senior officials. Nor were such sums unknown to other members of the Zhang clan, the art dealers and collectors of the family, of whom Zhang Dai's second uncle Zhongshu was a prominent example, along with Yanke, Shanmin and Zhang Dai himself.

The term Zhang Dai chose to use for his third uncle, "Magpie Zhang" (the genius at insinuating himself into court politics through his carefully honed words), implied someone very different from Fan Li, as Zhang Dai knew: "Was my paternal third uncle Sanshu the Cai Ze of our day?" Zhang asked rhetorically, invoking yet another celebrated figure from early Chinese history. "With empty hands he went to the north, and after just one conversation secured high office for himself. Even when he was with a senior minister he could turn [the truth] upside down and insult [the messenger]." Zhang Dai's favorite historian, Sima Qian, who seventeen hundred years before chronicled the rise of China's first centralized empire, had written an extended biography of Cai Ze, citing Cai as an example of a man with intense rhetorical subtlety who was able to take over the senior minister's job of his day by the shrewdness of his talk. Sima Qian's own judgment on Cai and Fan Ju, a man with similar skills, was of course known to Zhang Dai: There was no doubt that both Cai Ze and Fan Ju were men of superlative eloquence, wrote Sima Qian, and their initial slow start in politics was "not because their schemes were inept but because the persons they addressed wielded little power." But as soon as they encountered someone with real power, they "accomplished deeds that were known to the world. . . . And yet," Sima Qian added, "there is also an element of luck in such situations. There are many men who were as worthy as these two, but who never had an opportunity of fully expounding their ideas—too many, in fact, to finish describing! Nevertheless, if these two men had not met with adversity, they might never have been inspired to such efforts." By the simple act of implying that Sanshu had acted in a "worthy" way, Zhang Dai brought the full force of his sarcasm to play upon the politics of the day and the lessons to be drawn from them.

After his dismissal by the prince of Lu, father returned to Shaoxing in early 1632 just before the region was smitten with a prolonged drought, which badly damaged crops and led to the threat of famine. For both father and son the ordinary fabric of life was starting to unravel. Zhang Dai, as one might expect, had been busy giving to the disorder the aura he thought it needed. In the absence of effective administrators who could help curb the famine, he tells us that he followed the townspeople in their decision to summon to their aid the characters from one of China's most flamboyant and exciting novels, published around the time Zhang Dai was born. This was the novel *The Outlaws of the Marsh*, whose watery title promised, the townspeople hoped, to stimulate the local gods to end the drought. As was true for the courageous men who had faced down the eunuch henchmen of Wei Zhongxian, so the characters of *The Outlaws of the Marsh* stood for the determination of those who chose to defy the leaders of the state. The band of 108 bravados who lived long before in that lakeside marsh that gave the novel its title had the power to threaten the rulers of China as well as to offer their own services to shore up a state they despised. Zhang Dai, like many of his contemporaries, was drawn to these erratic heroes and had used the characters from *The Outlaws of the Marsh* in unusual ways. He wrote a series of aphoristic couplets on the main characters in the novel and also treasured the painted depictions of the work's heroes that were made by his close friend the painter Chen Hongshou. Both of them sought to catch the elusive quality of these outlaws' natures and Chen achieved levels of true brilliance in his own renderings, which Zhang Dai likened in achievement to the works of the celebrated painter Wu Daozi in conjuring up the images of Hell.

In the threatened villages around Shaoxing, the local farmers had been competing with each other to see who could plead with the gods for rain most effectively. Since, only four years before, high winds and freakishly high tides had smashed houses, uprooted trees and brought flood waters surging through the streets of the city, in the year 1632 each day villagers dressed up as the gods of the tides or the spirit of the sea, and spat as often as they could to imitate the water that they hoped would soon fall from the sky. In Shaoxing itself, the people decided to dress up as characters from *The Outlaws of the Marsh*, believing the title of the book to be auspicious, given the circumstances. To encourage them in their endeavors, Zhang Dai tells us, he went beyond these earlier depictions of the novel's main characters in verse or paint, and instead sent his friends and servants to comb Shaoxing city and the nearby villages and hills for people who looked exactly like the fictional images envisioned by the novelist. Without a precise similitude, Zhang Dai argued, without the exact kind of blackened faces, luxuriantly bristling whiskers, helmets with streamers and weapons like tree trunks as well as authentic delivery and cadences, the performers would only catch a portion of the full possibilities of the narrative. So slowly, over weeks of effort, and with the expenditure of large sums of money, one by one Zhang and his teams of searchers located thirty-six people to represent the key figures from the novel—a dark-skinned dwarf, a powerful fighter, a portly monk, a tall seductress, a man with a twisted head, a man with florid face and bushy beard—and gave them the means to come to the city. As the chosen thirty-six made their measured approach along the roads that led to the city, the crowds of watchers grew ever larger, threatening to drive the newfound denizens of the outlaws' fictional march to share the fate of the celebrated male beauty Wei Jie, who had been killed by the sheer concentrated force of the public's staring eyes.

Zhang Dai tells us that his relatives were divided over the efficacy of this planned appeal to the gods. His fifth uncle, recently returned from an official posting in Guangling, where he had accumulated several bolts of brocades and satins, was so much in favor of the project that he gave a large quantity of the material to decorate eight covered stages on which the impersonators could act out their parts. Six stages were in honor of the thunder god; one was for the god of war and one for the dragon god. Banners hanging beside or in front of the stages bore exemplary mottoes: "The rain that is needed," "The Imperial Orders bring peace," "Balmy winds and calming rain," "With the outlaws at rest the people are peaceful." The effect was seen by the crowds as being spectacular, though still on too small a scale to be truly effective. But a great-uncle of Zhang Dai's (the younger brother of his late grandfather) expressed skepticism over the whole venture, bluntly asking what on earth the criminal gangs from *The Outlaws of the Marsh* had to contribute to the pressing search for rain? Zhang Dai explained that his 36 chosen personages fitted in with the scheme at the heart of the novel itself, in which the grand total of 108 figures who populate the novel's band of comrades divide symbolically into a group of 36, representing the pole stars of Heaven, and a group of 72 representing the stars that are tied to the rhythms of the Earth.

Father died early in 1633. During January, Zhang noted, father had shown no signs of illness, but suddenly announced that he would be "leaving" on February the fifth. On February 2 he invited all his friends to come by and say farewell, and he died on the fifth, exactly as he had said he would, at noon. Zhang Dai never tells us if, before he died, father had a chance to salute the extraordinary company of simulacra as they entered Shaoxing amid the excited crowd. As son and father, they had not always seen things eye to eye. But they had shared an affinity for the odd and the occult, to which one should add a fascination with words and their meanings. Now, with grandfather and father both gone, it was Zhang Dai who would have to bring order to the jumbled images from the past that pressed upon him.

CHAPTER SIX

OVER THE EDGE

In a world where men such as Rufang and Sanshu were identified primarily by their specialized functions, how did Zhang Dai fare? Poorly, in his own sardonic estimation, as he analyzed himself in later life, using the third-person form to distance himself further from his own center. "Zhang Dai worked away at his books, but got nowhere," wrote Zhang. "He studied swordsmanship, but got nowhere; he tried to follow the norms of good conduct, and got nowhere; he tried to be a writer and got nowhere; he studied magical arts and studied Buddhism, he studied agriculture and studied horticulture, but all to no avail. He let the world call him a squanderer, a good-for-nothing, a stubborn commoner, a low-grade scholar, a somnambulist, a long-dead demon." How you interpreted all that was up to you, Zhang Dai explained, for he knew full well that this character was a sea of paradoxes, which he himself lacked the skill or insight to disentangle: "If you wanted to call him rich and well-born, then you could go ahead. If you wanted to call him poor and lowly, that was fine, too. If you wanted to call him wise, that was fine, but it was also fine if you called him an imbecile. You could call him aggressive and competitive, or call him gentle and weak. You could call him anxious and impatient, too, or else call him lazy and disrespectful."

On the subject of writing, at least, the self-denigratory list of failures was at best a half-truth. For from the moment that he had begun writing his first book of *Profiles* in the early 1620s, Zhang Dai seemed to take pleasure in pursuing several writing projects at once. From 1628 onward, he was collecting the material and writing the draft for his history of the Ming dynasty as it had manifested itself up to that date in fifteen reigns. He was developing the idea of giving a structure to the rubrics under which to organize essential human knowledge for the riders of the night ferry. He was expanding on his teenage readings of the Four Books and developing a series of his own commentaries to help students comprehend the text in its full richness—clearly, he anticipated that his own comments would be intensely personal, thus sustaining both grandfather's and his own expressed contempt for the orthodox and unimaginative commentaries that passed for "received wisdom" in the examination halls. And he was playing with another idea for historical writing, one that he believed would bring a deeper level of meaning to our knowledge of the past. This was the filling in of *Historical Gaps*, as he titled the work, so as to create a deeper and more evocative level of the past than currently surviving records could provide.

Zhang Dai framed his discussion in broad terms. Historians of olden days, he wrote, faced similar problems to those faced by historians of his own time. If an event had been deeply troubling, one could simply leave it out altogether; the more such gaps there were, the easier it became to add one more. But, as Confucius had said, "The meaning of an event can be grasped indirectly." To Zhang, this showed that "even if the exact meaning of a certain document is not written down, it can be not written down in such a way that we know what has not been written." A parallel could be adduced from astronomy: "If something is not written down at all, that is like having gaps missing from the moon. If it is not written down and yet we grasp what has not been written, then that is like an eclipse of the moon. If it is a lunar eclipse that caused those gaps in the moon, then the true spirit cannot be said to be really missing; and if you continue seeking that true spirit, then the moon will appear in whole form once again."

To give more specificity to his argument, Zhang Dai chose a dramatic moment in earlier history that was known as the Xuanwu Gate Incident. In the year 626 an aspirant to the Tang dynasty throne killed the heir apparent, imprisoned his father, the ruling emperor, and watched as his henchmen killed another of his brothers at the Xuanwu Gate. Enthroned as Emperor Taizong, the usurping ruler urged his court historians to "write the truth about the incident." Naturally they had to be careful in what they wrote, but to Zhang such a situation was equivalent to an eclipse that would allow the whole moon to shine once again: "The whole truth was eclipsed but *not* hidden, and so the impetus for reform was present. Because it was not totally hidden, people could point to the truth; by pointing it out, they became encouraged; once encouraged, they could gallop away; at a gallop, they headed forward; heading forward they could save the situation and bring about reform." Hence Taizong should be praised for his stance.

Other kinds of gaps in history were simpler to deal with: A parallel here was the kind of "shadow picture" one could draw from a profile illuminated by lamplight, where the addition of a salient detail—the eyes, the eyebrows—might not be necessary for the sitter's identity to be obvious. At other times, however, the need to fill in the details became urgent. As Zhang wrote: "I have become disappointed with the orthodox histories' lack of comprehensiveness, and have dedicated myself to the collection of historical materials that can fill in the holes within those histories. With the addition of one word, an entire record becomes more convincing; with the addition of one incident, an entire history becomes more compelling."

Zhang explained the procedure of "gap filling" as he had conceptualized it, with two other examples drawn from the life of the Tang dynasty emperor Taizong, one of which showed how to expand and the other how to cut. Zhang drew his first example of gap filling from an unofficial history that recounted the emperor's mode of acquiring for himself the most admired example of early calligraphy to be found in China. The official accounts were cautious and evasive on the subject, but the unofficial history, Zhang noted, explained the emperor's action by creating details specifically designed to highlight the emperor's canniness, greed and duplicity. In the second case, that of a prominent minister's ability to dominate the emperor, one needed to clear away the hundreds of banal examples of the minister's prowess that could be found in the orthodox histories and to substitute just four words to highlight the emperor's shyness and guilt: the four words were simple ones: *sparrow-hawk/dead/chest/within*. But those four single words could fully illuminate how the emperor was surprised by his minister while playing with his favorite bird, and then, trying to conceal it by pressing it against his chest until the minister had left, accidentally suffocated it. "The key to capturing the spirit of someone," wrote Zhang, "is to identify the salient characteristics." In this particular case, "With thousands of words there were gaps, yet with those four characters there were no gaps." Surely, Zhang remarked, the informed readers of history would rather have the gapless four-character version than the gap-enhancing thousands of words.

Could this somehow be linked to the idea of "exhilaration" that Zhang had cited in his *Profiles* as a way of catching the excitement of the moment? The two were not necessarily incompatible, even though the exhilaration had sprung in part from the moral stances of the historical protagonists, whereas the concept of a gap was morally neutral. As Zhang Dai thought more about which of his family members deserved biographies, he was drawn to those who behaved in extreme rather than merely devious ways, and thus helped to highlight the dislocation of the times. In writing down his own informal commentaries on the book of *Analects* by Confucius, Zhang had saluted the sage for his insight that it was a fine line indeed that separated the wisest of men from the most irresponsible. Now the focus shifted away from those who were admirable to those one would prefer to be with. As Zhang Dai put it, "If a person has no strong passions, you cannot be tied together in friendship, for that person will have no deep feeling; if a person has no major flaws, you cannot be tied together in friendship, for that person will have no true center."

With one's own relatives, he reflected: "There are those who have admirable traits and those who have blemishes. When we speak of admirable traits, then [perhaps] there is no need to write their biographies; when we speak of their blemishes, then [perhaps] there are certain things that could be in a biography." To support this idea, Zhang quoted the early-fourteenth-century biographer Xie Jin, who had written: "If there is a blemish in the piece of jade, then the entire rock of jade cannot be without a blemish. Yet when people have blemishes, they can still be like a jade: How could I dare to cover up their blemishes and end up losing their jade-like qualities?" When Zhang linked such thoughts to the broader category of family biographies, it struck him that "The strong passions spring from their deep feelings: when young, the major flaws were dominant; as they grew older, the strong passions took over." Such people as these "may not be suitable for biographies and yet if the passions were as strong as they appear to have been, then it is not possible not to record the detail of their lives."

Such surely was the case with seventh uncle Jishu, whose whims seemed to have guided his entire life. According to Zhang Dai, Jishu was recalcitrant from the moment of his birth and showed no pleasure in book learning. Instead, "He gathered around himself the village adventurers and wastrels, and together they flew whistling kites and played at football, gambled with dice and dominoes, adorned themselves with make-up and acted on stage, gathered for cock-fights and horse-races, inviting fifty or sixty people for banquets. Sometimes he would steam an entire boar to feed his guests, and they would eat till they could eat no more, and then recline on the beds and make merry." The excess here could lead to a kind of unwitting sadism, for Zhang Dai recorded that this seventh uncle "had a passion for the taste of oranges, and when the oranges were ripe he piled them up all over the beds and furniture, there was no place that was not filled with oranges. He would finish them himself without giving any away, abruptly giving orders to his serving boys to stand in a circle and peel them for him. In the winter months, the servant-boys' hands became all rough and mottled, and frostbite stripped off layers of their skin."

Absolute carelessness was another of seventh uncle's traits: according to his nephew, "His greatest passion was for raising fine horses, and once he paid three hundred taels for a horse called Daqing [Great Grey]. One of his friends took this horse out on the weaving maid's festival [the seventh day of the seventh month] in early autumn, to race it against some other horses. The track was a sea of mud and the horses were slipping all around; Daqing's four hooves got torn apart, and the horse died. When uncle heard about this, he had the horse wrapped in a shroud and buried. Not wishing to hurt his friend's feelings, he didn't even ask him anything about it."

Seventh uncle's recklessness and generosity led him into bizarre areas of duplicity and vengeance. Zhang Dai wrote that in his uncle's neighborhood there was "a young thug" who called himself "the King." This man was constantly pushing uncle to join up with his group, but uncle would never do it, for he was not the kind of man to submit to the will of others. That truth was brought violently home to a man Zhang Dai called "Wang-something, a bully and a tough, who messed around with one of uncle's favorite boys." Learning of this, seventh uncle swore that he would see the man dead. Wang fled across a nearby river and tried to hide out in a riverfront inn. In the same inn there happened to be "a large group of fierce and brawny men," who carried in their hands a placard identifying them as being on the staff of the provincial governor. Uncle, who was in hot pursuit of Wang, told the governor's retainers Wang was a famous bandit who had just escaped from jail: "So they all raised their clubs and beat the man to death. Thereupon seventh uncle departed."

As far as the examinations were concerned, seventh uncle's only goal here seems to have been to prove that he could do whatever he chose to do. Apparently he never had any intention of sitting for the examinations or seeking a regular career. Instead, "Clasping the books under his arm, he set off on his travels around the country, and all the well-known scholars within the four seas were enchanted by him."

So seventh uncle, having built himself a country retreat while maintaining a house in the city, drew together his two contrasting worlds: those of the "wastrels" and those of "the well-known older scholars from all around who also came to the mountains to visit him." In Zhang Dai's telling, seventh uncle's death was typical of the man in both its randomness and its self-indulgence. One day in 1615, two of uncle's friends came to the mountain, and the three men set off together on an excursion—in the pouring rain—to a well-known beauty spot. The rivers were swollen, but seventh uncle stripped and walked through the cold gorges, with the water sometimes surging over his head. This led to some kind of swelling in his ankles, and in the ninth month he finally took some medicine, which made him a bit better. The doctor who was treating him told seventh uncle, " 'This particular medicine contains a poisonous ingredient, so just take one little pinch of it every day; this whole package of medicine is designed to last you for one hundred days.' Uncle said to himself, 'Who can wait that long?' and he emptied out all the medicine from the package and consumed the whole lot in one evening. The poison had its effect, and he died."

What drove seventh uncle Jishu in Zhang Dai's account was a strange willfulness that could be unfeeling or casual in its cruelty as well as literally self-destructive. But seventh uncle's extraordinary abilities led him to also explore the world of the local scholars and to fit into it comfortably. Zhang wrote that the finest scholars of the region came to his uncle's funeral and left poems of homage. In the summary that he appended to this particular biographical sketch, Zhang Dai tried to get at those levels of character by using seventh uncle Jishu's racehorse as the central image: "There is an expression: The thousand-mile horse loves to kick and gnaw at people. If it does not kick and gnaw, there is no way that it can be a thousand-mile horse. When uncle Jishu was a youngster he kicked and gnawed to an extreme extent. But after he was twenty, just on seeing the shadow of a whip he was ready to gallop away. And in just a flash he could cover a thousand miles. How can it be that this horse was so quick to change? It was because he was so good at kicking and gnawing, and also had the ability to cover one thousand miles, that he was able successfully to become a thousand-mile horse. Seventh uncle had a fondness for adventurers and wastrels, so the adventurers and

wastrels came to him. He had a fondness for scholarly men of
fame, so the scholarly men of fame came to him. With one
thought, he was able to transform himself, and also to change his
whole set of friends. If one did not know this man, then just examine his friends. As for me, I have taken a close look at my seventh uncle Jishu."

Seventh uncle died when Zhang Dai was only eighteen, but he
left what Zhang thought to be a trenchant comment on the intersections of theater and life. The comment came in the form of two
matching hanging scrolls, which seventh uncle composed and
hung on either side of the stage that he had just constructed for
one of his opera troupes. Zhang Dai transcribed them both in full.

SCROLL NUMBER ONE:

Retribution links the dead and the living:
See how the finest and the vilest are forced to answer.
In the end, who can escape?
The way unfolds day and night:
The newborn and the dead take on new names.
But once off-stage they return to their old existence.

SCROLL NUMBER TWO:

Some adorned like gods, others disguised as demons:
How the simple locals squirm in panic,
Fearing that reality is just like this.
The perfect Buddha, the ancient patriarchs,
Leave the intelligentsia unmoved.
When their time is come what can they expect?

"Truly," wrote Zhang, "that is the way in theatrical terms to elucidate the Buddhist dharma."

It was to his cousin Yanke that Zhang Dai ascribed the wildest range of behavior. In no one else did the different facets of life flow together in such complex and inharmonious ways, and presumably in recognition of that fact, Yanke was the only family member about whom Zhang Dai wrote at length on three occasions. Yanke was probably the wealthiest among Zhang Dai's own generation of brothers and cousins, being the adored only son of the principal wife of second uncle Zhongshu, the celebrated collector of art. His bonds to Zhang Dai were especially close, since Yanke's mother was related by marriage to Zhang's closest friend Qi Biaojia. Uncle Zhongshu had been trained in connoisseurship by the members of the powerful Zhu clan, and Zhang Dai knew his branch of the family well. Nowhere else in his writings did Zhang Dai plunge into an intimate family biographical sketch with such abrupt intensity: "My younger cousin Yanke's father was the well-known Zhang Baosheng [Zhongshu, second uncle]. His mother, Lady Wang, only bore this one son, and loved him to distraction. He grew up to have a nature that was temperamental and cruel, irritable and obstinate. With a nature such as that, his teachers could not correct him, his father could not comprehend him, tigers and wolves could not check him, knives and axes could not cut him down, ghosts and spirits could not alarm him, thunder and storms instilled in him no fear. When he was six years old he found some sweet-tasting wine and secretly drank several pints (*sheng*); he collapsed dead-drunk underneath the crock, and only on the following day after he had been dunked in water did he begin to return to consciousness."

Despite such inauspicious beginnings, there was no doubting Yanke's intelligence: "At seven, he entered the children's school and was able to comprehend completely every book that he recited from. As he grew older, his intelligence was superior to anyone else's: after a single reading he could commit all the classics and histories perfectly to memory." But Yanke's mental energy could not be so easily channeled, and he explored even more routes to pleasure than seventh uncle. "He developed a mastery of virtually every form of diversion and pastime: poetry in all its metrical forms; calligraphy and painting, music and chess; musical instruments, whether pipe or reed, plucked or bowed; kicking a football and playing at 'go'; gambling with dice and competing in card games; handling a firearm or jousting with staves; archery and horseback riding; playing drums and singing; applying the makeup and performing on stage; reciting ballads and telling funny stories; thrumming the guitar and pitching arrows into a jar—at all of these his skills and understanding were so great that they seemed to be at a divine level." Even at something as simple as a game of cards Yanke tried to encapsulate every known form and remake them into one of his own liking.

Yanke's father was usually away from home, either traveling to search out news about acquisitions for his swelling art collection or working in various official posts in Beijing and the provinces. At intervals, he gave Yanke large sums of money and also land and art objects, which Yanke speedily converted into cash and just as speedily spent. Yanke's money and lifestyle attracted many spongers, just as they enabled him to get away with

OVER THE EDGE 181

acts of random violence and—in at least one case—even murder. "To his home came all kind of frauds and manipulators, loafers and cheats, but if they were not careful, with no warning he might ridicule and abuse them and chase them away. Today we have no knowledge of the fates of those whom once he favored." Yanke kept up the same violent and erratic pattern with his concubines and his personal attendants, his maidservants and his male slaves. Once he bought a woman to be his concubine for several hundred taels, but after spending a single night with her he drove her out, because she failed to please him. "It was the immediacy of something that brought him joy, not the repetition of the experience," wrote Zhang. "Yanke took little care when choosing his companions, nor did he bother about the cost of something. He never considered it a waste, no matter how much he lavished on those who came to his home, or whatever he gave to his servants. If any of those within his power aroused his anger, he might suddenly give them hundreds of lashes, till the bloodied flesh was falling off them, yet even this sight did not arouse his pity. People of the time likened him to Li Kuangda." (Li was a figure from earlier history, known for boasting that he constructed drums from the flesh of his enemies.)

Zhang wrote that after Yanke's wife, Lady Shang, had died, the young man's nature became even more uncontrollable. "Once he beat one of his maidservants way beyond the limits of the law and drove her out of the house. The woman took poison and died. Her clansmen picked up her body and forced their way through the gate, placing her corpse in the middle of the magistrate's courtyard. Yanke remained unmoved. Several thousand people came to take a look, and when they saw this woman with her skin all torn open and the flesh hanging out, their cries of anger echoed like thunder, and they were on the verge of burning down his house. Again, he showed no emotion." Yanke's father-in-law, Shang Dengxian, together with Zhang's friend Qi Biaojia, jointly acted as his mediators. "The whole region was in an uproar, which almost burst out into open insurrection, but my cousin remained as vile-tempered as before, and none of this changed his behavior. Those people he had violated felt compelled to bring lawsuits against him, and if they invoked the law, then of course they were determined to win. But he did not tire even if the suit dragged on for one or two years, and even if the cost rose into the thousands of taels, he did not begrudge paying it."

Nor did Yanke worry about the money he lavished on his garden estate. Zhang Dai was experienced enough to know that not all gardens offered the fecund perfection of the Happiness Garden on Dragon Mountain. He knew, too, that not all passionate gardeners were like his friend Jin Rusheng, who had made a lifetime battle zone out of a little rectangle of fertile soil, with its small stream and single miniature mountain artfully concealed behind a bamboo fence and eastern wall. Every inch of space was used, with flowers blooming for every season of the year. But the cost of Jin's dream was ceaseless vigilance. As Zhang described his old friend, "Jin Rusheng himself was weak and often sick, yet he always rose early; before he had even washed or dressed his hair one could see him spreading out a mat at the foot of the steps, removing the killer-insects from under the petals, chasing down the earthworms at the roots. He spent each day patrolling all his thousands of plants, in search of the fire ants that destroyed the maturing shoots, black millipedes that attacked the spiny stems, the worms and slugs that damaged the roots, the inchworms and caterpillars that laid waste the leaves." Jin's only recourse was total war with no quarter given: "To lure out the fire ants he scattered cuttlefish bones or tortoise shells near their holes; he deflected the black millipedes with a stick wrapped in hemp; holding a lantern high, he killed the slugs in the depth of night; and the earthworms were flushed out with running water mixed with lime. The caterpillars were killed with liquid horse manure; the snouted beetles were driven from their holes with thin iron wires. All of this he did in person, even when the ice caused his hands to crack, or the sun burned his forehead."

But the tenor of Yanke's obsession was on an unimaginably different scale. Zhang Dai recalled that in 1631 his cousin Yanke decided to move an unusual rock that lay in the western part of his estate. So he collected together several hundred workmen to excavate around the rock and scrub it clean, creating a rock face dozens of feet high whose precipitous appearance delighted him. But it so happened that someone said to him that if the rock face were reflected in a deep pool beneath it, then it would be even lovelier; accordingly, below the rock face Yanke had the earth dug out to create a large pool. Since the rock was too hard to be penetrated by crowbars, he hired rock experts to chisel into the rock to a depth of several feet, to store up the water that he had tinted with indigo dye for visual effect. Then someone else said that the pavilions and the pond were indeed beautiful, but it was a shame that there were no fully grown flowering trees around. "So Yanke sent out for flowering plum trees, for cone-bearing pines, for choice tea shrubs, flowering pear, and other such trees, all of which had to be the tallest and the thickest, even though it meant dismantling part of the garden wall to bring them in, and hiring dozens of men to plant them. After planting, they did not thrive, and within a few days they began to wither; so he sent out for even more large trees to fill in the gaps. At first, this made the whole garden look lushly beautiful, but once again after a few days they dried out and were good only as fuel for the cooking stove. In olden days, some people used to cut down osmanthus trees to use as firewood, but my cousin's excesses were several times greater than theirs."

Yanke now had new regrets, especially that the rock face looked so newly cleared and had no moss growing on it, so, according to Zhang Dai, his cousin bought large quantities of green mineral pigments, summoning those among his houseguests who were good painters to brush in the colors. "When the rain washed it all away, Yanke had them color it all in again, just as before."

As he had in some of his other family vignettes, Zhang Dai explored the theme of waste as it was exemplified by Yanke's actions. In this instance, the impatience with the garden could now be seen in the wider context of the art world. As Zhang Dai had written in a commentary on Yanke's gardening methods, "When the trees he transplanted died, he sought to replace them with other large trees. Just planting trees that could not die was not enough for him. If they died, he had to plant more. That is why the trees had no choice but to die. Even if they did not wish for it, they ended up dying." The same apparently was true with other rare species: "Whenever Yanke chanced to see something that caught his fancy, he would do absolutely anything to obtain it, caring nothing at all about this cost. Once, when he was in Wulin, he saw dozens of gold fish, and paid thirty taels for them. He put them into a small container and on his way home, if any of them turned white, he scooped them out and threw them away. By the time he crossed the river not one fish was left, but he continued laughing and joking just as he had before."

Yanke was also crazy about antiques, Zhang Dai noted, but if they had the slightest flaw or blemish, he would insist on having them repaired. Once he bought a two-hundred-year-old Xuan-era bronze censer for about fifty taels, but since the patina was not very lustrous, he placed it in a blazing fire to bring out the beauty. "Yanke took a whole basket of charcoal and used the bellows to build up such a fierce flame that in only a few moments it started to melt. But all he did was cry out 'Ya.' "

Yet another anecdote made a similar kind of point. At a local temple, Yanke bought a particularly rare kind of inkstone for thirty silver taels. The surface drew its texture from what seemed to be little hills in strange shapes, with flecks of translucent white running through them. It had been given the name "Green mountains, white clouds." "The stone shimmered as if it had been oiled," wrote Zhang Dai. "It was truly several hundred years old. Yanke looked it all over carefully, and finding that there was an extra protuberance on the base of the stone he decided to trim it off. Taking a large metal spike he chipped away at it, and the whole thing split in two. Furious, Yanke took a metal hammer and smashed the whole thing to bits—not forgetting the mahogany base—and threw the fragments into West Lake. He told his boy attendants not to tell anyone about the incident."

Certainly, such a life rejected all rules and erased all normal flows of cause and effect. It was Zhang Dai's way of showing what happened when the obsessions lost their function and became nothing more than flawed behavior, as damaging to the objects of affection as to the wider world that harbored them. Zhang Dai noted that the name Yanke had been chosen by his young cousin in a sardonic moment, after reading the story "Yao Chong Dreams of His Visit to Hell." In this tale a Ming traveler dreamed he entered into Hell and saw great mounds of precious metals there being melted in giant forges by thousands of demons on behalf of their master, the prince of Yan. In the same dream, the Ming traveler saw another forge, this one grown almost cold, where two dejected demons lethargically watched over backup reserves of that same prince of Yan. On awakening, the Ming traveler observed that "Master Yan was a spender to the bitter end, perhaps that was why Heaven tolerated him." His cousin loved the story, said Zhang Dai, and, in homage to the dreamer, named himself Yanke, the "guest of Master Yan."

So, how then could one neatly categorize someone like that? Zhang Dai wrote that contemporaries likened Yanke to Yuhong, an officer of the Liang dynasty, famous for his wild extravagances, his hundreds of concubines and his ruthless exploitation of all living creatures, whether animal or human. But, that was not quite right, thought Zhang Dai. Yanke may have had the passions of his celebrated precursor, but he lacked the patience—whatever he went for, he ruined by haste so that "he never tasted anything to the full." It was for this reason that Zhang Dai gave his cousin a special private nickname that he could keep all to himself: "the Emperor who lost it all."

It was a powerfully evocative name to confer on a mere wastrel, but of course Yanke was more than that. He had a powerful intelligence and was a valued member of several scholarly circles in Shaoxing and far beyond, including the group that orbited around the sophisticated official Qi Biaojia, the close friend of Zhang Dai. It is not hard to see the nickname bestowed by Zhang on his cousin as an augury for the fate of China as a whole, now that the reigning Emperor Chongzhen had proven to be an inept ruler rather than the providential savior so many had been hoping for. The country was sick, with bandits and rebels south of the Wall plus a threatening Manchu confederation to its north along the River Liao in the area known as Liaodong. At the same time there were real epidemics in China that needed real physicians, and metaphor and diagnosis became echoes of each other and could no longer be disentangled. Qi Biaojia, who had passed the highest level of the state examinations and whose official career flourished, was at the same time spending many of his own funds trying to obtain and circulate medicines. Acknowledging Qi's generosity in a formal poem of thanks dated 1637, Zhang Dai implies that the polity was infected now at every level:

Last year, during the closing days of winter, the sky was
    not clouded;
With the rolling of thunder, evils were dispersed.
Summer came, and clouds of disease filled villages and
    towns,
Menacing the poor like greedy merchants do.
Swarms of insects fly around the dimly lit room,

While the entire family lies dying, calling to the heavens
    for help.
Earning no salary by daytime, having not even a bamboo
    mat to lie upon at night,
They can only dream of obtaining medicine. . . .
Yet the great official doctor [Qi Biaojia] cares for them,
    analyzing their illnesses,
Gathering enough herbs to form a mountain.
The aroma of his medicine, of even his mere fame,
Can raise the almost dead from their beds.
He cures several thousands in no time at all,
Winning the admiration of all kind-hearted men.
Upon reflection, I find that the entire world has come to be
    like this:
Dead soldiers, dead bandits, death spread everywhere.
The defeat in Liaodong is like a piece of rotting flesh,
The poison spread by hostile spears more powerful than
    the plague.
Heavy exploitation of the people is like an ulcer,
Weakening our spirit and eating away at our strength.
How I wish for the curing hand of the great official doctor,
So that the state's spirit might yet be revived.

    The war had brought these new realities home to the south: Zhang wrote that he himself saw the bodies of northern refugees dead from famine stacked up on the streets of Hangzhou, awaiting burial. The obsessive and destructive worlds of seventh uncle and Yanke had begun to merge with the agonizing problems of the dynasty.

At the tomb of the founding Ming emperor in the hills above Nanjing, the same sense of imbalance prevailed. Though the site had been chosen for the best geomantic reasons by the wisest of men, and was protected by the bodies and spirits of two great former figures, one a warrior and the other a saintly monk, it had fallen on shaky days. On a visit to Nanjing in 1638, while staying at a temple on the shores of the Yangzi River, Zhang Dai rose one night and saw the dark cloud that had been hovering above the imperial tomb for a hundred days, preventing the view of certain constellations—and sure enough, he wrote, from that time onward bandits began to make their raids ever bolder, presaging the fall of the dynasty itself. Four years later, incompetent court officials, ordered to restore the emperor's tomb to its former glories, as if echoing the crazed behavior of cousin Yanke, had bungled the job in a hideous way. Zhang described them ripping up and burning irreplaceable old trees, gouging out the soil to a depth of ten feet or more and wrecking the flow of favorable currents that had hitherto protected the deceased emperor's powerful spirit-force. That same summer of 1642, Zhang Dai tells us he was permitted to visit the temple to watch the sacrifices held in the deceased emperor's honor. He was surprised to see how cursory the ceremonies were and how commonplace the ritual vessels. As if that were not enough to dispel any sense of solemnity, the severed carcasses of the sacrificial animals—a cow and a sheep—left to lie on the altar in the torrid heat of July filled the whole tomb site with "an unbearable smell of rotting flesh." One needed no special priestly skills to read those omens.

CHAPTER SEVEN

COURT ON THE RUN

Zhang Dai made no claims to be a war hero. Indeed, until he was in his late forties, Zhang never saw the bleakness of war up close. Strangely enough, the nearest he ever came before the Ming fall seems to have been on his Buddhist pilgrimage to Putuo Island in 1638. There, one evening, as he was drinking his tea at a mountain temple, he heard the distant sound of cannon fire; hurrying outside, he could see a confused blur of torches and fires shining on the churning waters. Only later did he learn that a group of pirates had attacked the local fishing boats as they returned to harbor after their day's work, seizing or burning several boats and killing a number of the seafaring villagers.

But that was a rare experience, and war most often entered his life as play. The spectacle of battle, the ingenuity of maneuvers, the vibrancy of music, the courage of the aerobatic actor-warriors, the wild haze of lanterns and fireworks—those were Zhang Dai's joys. Zhang's seventh uncle had purchased a former military training ground and converted it into a private theater space and Zhang remembered as a boy watching forty actors present the opera *Mulian* based on the tale of Buddha's disciple who descended into Hell to release his mother from her suffering. The performance extended across three days and three nights before a hundred or more guests seated at their ease along the ramparts: marches and countermarches in file, balancing acts on stilts and stools, acrobatics with jars and stone wheels, leaps with ropes and hoops, the belching of fire and swallowing of swords. And the story of the descent to Hell allowed every kind of terrifying tableau: demons of every shape and color, tortures with saws and tridents, "frozen mountains with sharpened blades, impenetrable forests of swords, iron walls and lakes of blood." Here once again was the world of Wu Daozi's "images of Hell," but this time "with décor and accessories that cost over a thousand taels." Even while the audience shook with fear at the spectacle, under the flickering lanterns their own faces appeared demonic. At last the noise from the crowds and performers was so intense that the prefect of Shaoxing, believing that pirates must be on the attack (as they had been so often in the past), sent his staff to check. Only when seventh uncle went to the prefect's office and explained that it was a performance was the official's heart at peace.

For martial spectacle on the river, there was nothing to surpass the dragon boat races, and for Zhang Dai the finest racing boats that he saw were in 1631 when he stayed with his second uncle, the art collector Zhongshu, in Yangzhou. This spectacle, to Zhang, had all one could require to replicate the martial spirit: the dragon heads and tails of the twenty or so boats conjured up

a world of rage; the twenty oarsmen in their ordered rows suggested arrogance; the colored awnings, the standards and the
banners offered splendor; the banging of the gongs and drums
set the rhythm; the racks of armaments at the stern of the boats
promised violence; the men standing erect and balanced on the
dragon head of every prow augured danger; the child dangling
from the dragon's tail on every boat aroused people's anxieties.

But for naval spectacle on a grander scale, it was best to go to
Dinghai, the harbor town off the northeast coast of Zhejiang, on
a rocky island with its defensive walls erected back in 1530 near
the shore and on the hill above the town. The watcher there
could see the countless warships as they assembled in the port,
the massive war junks, the gunboats and the oar-propelled assault craft protected by their tautly stretched coverings of water
buffalo hide. And around them scurried the little boats of the
fishermen and other small pleasure craft, seeming like the
threads that held the bolder patterning of the tapestry in place.
Too far apart from one another to hear shouted commands, the
naval officers communicated by means of flags and drums; up in
the mastheads, bold lads scanned the horizon for those designated as the "enemy" in the maneuvers. When they spotted an
interloper, they would dive effortlessly from the masts, soaring
through the air for a moment before disappearing beneath the
waves, and swimming swiftly to the shore, where they delivered
their breathless messages to the commodore. At night the naval
vessels communicated by means of lanterns hanging from their
mastheads or flagpoles. The lanterns doubled in number from
being reflected in the ocean, and for Zhang Dai or others watching from the comfort of a nearby mountain terrace, it was as if

"the constellations were frying in hot oil, or a soup made from stars was bubbling in a cauldron."

The most flamboyant military spectacles Zhang Dai witnessed were in the early autumn of 1631, when he paid his second visit to his father in Shandong, in the fief of the prince of Lu. This time there was an imperial inspector of senior rank on the reviewing stand, and the army—at least at first—was (or seemed to be) a real one: three thousand cavalry troops and seven thousand infantry moving swiftly and decisively at each command, marching and countermarching and trading positions with neighboring battalions as the imperial inspector had signs held aloft ordering the troops into new formations. "In the distance, a hundred horsemen appeared in the role of the enemy, stirring up a storm of smoke and dust. A patrol of horsemen, first no more than black dots in the distance, came galloping through the garrison gate to raise the alarm: assembling his forces by flag and by drum, the general planned his skillful ambush." Within moments the enemy were snared and taken prisoner.

But, with Zhang Dai, the grounding of a setting could change in a moment, upsetting one's preconceptions and presenting new ideas to digest: "At this point out rode thirty or forty horsemen, handsome boys dressed as women, red banners fastened to their backs, fur capes, embroidered sleeves, and hair in a tight chignon." As a choir massed in front of the imperial inspector began to chant regional folk songs in their unmistakable northern accents, and stringed instruments played in accompaniment, the boy-women performed acrobatics on horseback, "spinning in all directions, vertically and horizontally, flexible as if they had no bones in their bodies." Who or what were these people who possessed such talents and such charm? "The imperial inspector that year was a man named Zuo," Zhang gravely explained, "and these performers were all his young songsters or his concubines. That was why they were so beguiling. Others, performing in their place, could certainly never have done so well."

Despite the force of Zhang Dai's colorful memories, the realities of violence were now thrusting their way to the fore. The small group of bandits routed by Zhang Dai's father in Yanzhou in the late 1620s was just a local example of the far larger roving groups of bandits who were spreading over northern China. Such bandits came from a wide mix of occupations: there were unemployed soldiers and clerks, laid-off couriers, miners, landless laborers driven out of the desiccated farms, refugees from the Manchu-dominated areas north of the Great Wall, Muslim and other traders who had lost their money as the Silk Road trade faltered. Initially restricted more to the northwest or to parts of Shandong province, the unrest spread into the centrally located and strategically crucial province of Henan by 1631 and was exacerbated by fiercely cold weather that froze the Yellow River solid in 1634.

As Zhang later wrote in a chapter he called "Biographies of Various Bandits in the Central Provinces," knowledge of history helped in understanding what happened during that decade: the government lacked the foresight to open the state granaries to feed the starving commoners. Had they done so, it would not have been hard to persuade the rebels "to doff their armor and return to their farms, to sell their swords and to buy a calf." But the sheer numbers of rebel groups proved unmanageable: "Our central provinces became a wasteland. The buds and shoots were not trimmed so they extended wildly. The skin disease was not treated and became a lesion." Certainly, Zhang pointed out, the bandits made things hard to anticipate by their practice of constantly switching sides as the battles ebbed and flowed. Nor did the government ever concentrate its forces properly: "While the front door was resisting tigers, wolves were breaking in the back door." Gradually, though, the balance tilted further: "As the weaker half of the bandit forces surrendered to the government, the stronger ones began to render allegiance to the peasant leader Li Zicheng," and "both country and people were trampled like mud and ashes."

Though Zhang's history of the Ming was only in the initial drafting stage, and his family biographies were not yet written down in final form, the extant versions of his writings suggest how he once again linked Zhang family tales to the broader fate of the country. Second uncle Zhongshu, for instance, was in combat several times once he embarked on his official career. While serving in the Henan county of Chenzhou during 1633 he was assigned to defend the neighboring township of Wanshui and did so, though in a way that reflected his own love of art. In Zhang's words, "At that time bandits were pressing in upon Wanshui, cutting the people down like hemp. Zhongshu climbed up to the ramparts, to defend the town to the last. By day he lodged in the guard tower, and at night he had the lamps lighted as he painted for his friends: layer upon layer of mountain peaks, barring the way. The brush and ink seemed composed, but the will and the inner force were lively; all those who witnessed this were in awe of his courage."

Second uncle also showed the logistical skills and practicality he learned as a youth on his far-flung travels. When in 1634 he was promoted to be magistrate of Mengjin (in Henan-fu), "Mengjin had a wall but no moat," wrote Zhang Dai, "and after Zhongshu arrived he had a moat dug. In just a short time, the work was finished. A local scholar, Wang Duo, wrote an account of this moat building."

In 1642, the fighting grew fiercer still. A force of Manchu troops attacked Yanzhou and the prince of Lu, nephew of the prince under whom Zhang Dai's father had served, took his own life. The dead prince's younger brother inherited the title to the fiefdom. Signs of dynastic collapse were visible everywhere, and Zhang's family members got sucked ever deeper into the crisis. Second uncle Zhongshu, now promoted to be the military coordinator in the major Grand Canal city of Yangzhou, was assigned to supervise all transport and defense along the Grand Canal, with his base in the strategic Canal and Yellow River junction at the city of Huaian. Zhang Dai's comment was laconic but clear: "Second uncle had a separate office in Huaian [on the Grand Canal] from which he supervised the administration of the boat traffic. [Regional Commander] Shi Kefa praised second uncle's abilities, for in all the ups and downs of grain transport matters, no matter what [uncle Zhongshu] was assigned to do, there was nothing that he did not handle right away." Shi Kefa was one of the most able and respected military commanders in China, so his views had weight. But things were still not controllable: "In 1643, roaming bandits laid waste Henan, and the alarm was given in Huaian. Zhongshu drilled the local troops, and went to hold [the key river junction of] Qingjiangpu. The constant stress led to an illness from which he did not recover." In 1644 second uncle died.

Overlapping with second uncle's ordeals, in the autumn of 1642 ninth uncle was ordered to defend Linqing, another strategic riverine and canal town farther north. He was killed by enemy forces in November of that same year. Zhang Dai knew the military context of these times in detail, but he chose to present ninth uncle's death as proof of the posthumous power of third uncle Sanshu, the Beijing manipulator of careers and information control, who had died still convinced that ninth uncle had deliberately ruined him. As Zhang Dai described what had transpired, Sanshu's own death came from his rage and frustration: "Sanshu's fury was so intense that finally he could not even speak, but just uttered loud cries. Once back home, he became all bloated from an illness, and within less than two months he was dead." But just before Sanshu died, he assembled his sons and said to them, "When I am in my coffin I will write to you all at length, and once underground I'll tell you everything that you should know."

Many officials would have known that in 1642 ninth uncle was summoned by the court to take up a new position in Linqing. Zhang Dai connects this promotion to the fact that the recently deceased Sanshu appeared in a dream to his son Zhenzi and said: "When I and ninth uncle were involved in a case at Linqing, we did a grave injustice to the military official Wang Eyun. Tomorrow evening I want you to set out a banquet in our home, and to burn a large amount of paper carriages, horses and attendants; then my spirit will be set free." Zhang Dai records that Zhenzi did as he was instructed, prepared the animals and the wine for a feast, assembled the guests and saw that they all dined together as they had when Sanshu was still alive. "When the service was over and the libations had been poured, a great wind started to blow beneath the table, the oil lamps and lanterns grew faint, and there came the sound of marching men and of hoof beats, as if truly carriages and horses were passing by." In death, third uncle Sanshu had reasserted his right to dominate his younger cousin. As Zhang Dai succinctly observed, "Ninth uncle lost his life [fighting the Manchus] in Linqing. So those words about 'being involved in a case at Linqing,' which had first appeared in that dream, were settled in this way by [Sanshu's] fierce and angry ghost." Zhang Dai reasserted the connection in a concluding comment: "When Sanshu hated someone in his heart, his strength was great enough to drive that person to his death. He could even cause his angry ghost to be seen in the light of day, so as to cleanse away a past injustice. Thus his awesome force [qi] was both dark and profound, and truly something that could not be violated."

In a somewhat similar fashion, Zhang Dai used dreams to link second uncle Zhongshu to Zhang Dai's wild seventh uncle, owner of the celebrated "thousand-mile horse" Great Grey. It was seventh uncle who had died in 1615 after consuming one hundred days' worth of medicine in one evening. "Six days after seventh uncle had died," Zhang Dai tells us, "second uncle, who was then living in Beijing, dreamed that seventh uncle came riding up on his horse Great Grey; he was dressed in a horn cap and robes of reddish fur, attended by five or six retainers. His appearance was really strange. Second uncle asked him, 'Why are you here?' and he replied, 'I am here to serve my older brother; I have written a "Poem on My Crossing Over" that I would like to recite to you:

> With a serious countenance, and in formal clothes, I face
>   my friends.
> All my life gathering then discarding, what a toil it has
>   been.
> And yet today here we are, still in touch with each other.
> In front of Nine Mile Mountain, the yellow birds are
>   calling.' "

Second uncle, still caught up in the dream, suspected this must be a bad omen, so he pulled himself free by tugging on the sleeve of his robe. Seventh uncle mounted his horse and rode off. "Second uncle rode up behind him in pursuit, but [seventh uncle] raising his whip in the air called out to him from the distance, 'I miss my elder brother so much, yet elder brother is in such a hurry to get home!' He kept on riding, and so was lost to sight." Upon awakening, second uncle wrote down the poem, and when he later came home he found that it was the same as a "Poem on My Crossing Over" that seventh uncle had composed three days before his death. In this case it took almost thirty years for the fates to round out their message, but it was at the Qingjiangpu River crossing that second uncle finally met his death and was ready at last to be reunited with his younger cousin.

In Zhang Dai's telling, second uncle was also an unwilling witness to the death of yet another of his cousins. This was Zhang Dai's tenth and youngest uncle, Shishu, one more talented but reckless member of the family. To Zhang Dai, tenth uncle's entire existence was defined by his excess of *qi* (vital energy). *Qi* was most often seen as a positive trait, but to Zhang Dai tenth uncle Shishu was taken over by his *qi,* which thus became a kind of daemon, a driving force manifested by vile temper and calculated cruelty. In the last years of his life, during the early 1640s, this same tenth uncle became an official in Beijing, working in the ministry of justice. According to Zhang Dai, he devoted much of his energy to the hunt for weaklings within official ranks, constantly trying to toughen up their spirit, "with the result that he was feared by all his subordinates"; tenth uncle even shouted abuse at the minister of justice if he felt that eminent official was being "indecisive." With prisoners in the ministry's jail he was ruthless, adding extra beatings to their other punishments, demanding harsher punishments for degree holders and even tightening up supervision of the prison visitors, insisting on meticulous records of their comings and goings. But when tenth uncle began suggesting that some of his own staff deserved the death penalty for dereliction of duty, they decided on joint preventive action and managed to get him impeached and fired.

Tenth uncle's end was in consonance with the life he had lived. After his dismissal, wrote Zhang Dai, tenth uncle "was so intensely angry that he got a bloating disease, his belly swelled up like a bushel basket." He set off for his home back in Shaoxing, but by the time he reached Huaian, the illness had reached an extreme stage. By coincidence, second uncle was stationed in Huaian, in charge of boat traffic, and he found lodgings for Shishu nearby in the Qingjiangpu temple and engaged a doctor to look after him. But Zhang Dai explained: "When tenth uncle saw the doctor, he cursed the doctor. When he saw the medicine, he cursed the medicine. When he was sent firewood and food, he cursed the firewood and food. When he was offered meats and fruit, he cursed the meats and fruit. When nurses and attendants were assigned to look after him, he cursed the nurses and attendants. . . . All those assigned to care for him ran away, so he forced second uncle to take their place. Things went on like this for two months. Then one day the sickness worsened, and though with his mouth he was still cursing at people, the curses gradually became just a murmur, and he died."

Half a month before he died, tenth uncle learned there was an expert in ceramic making who was carrying out some work on assignment in Huaian. So tenth uncle summoned the craftsman and ordered him to make a coffin of the finest Yixing ceramic tiles. At the same time, he instructed second uncle to buy a large supply of pine resin. As tenth uncle explained the logic behind these unusual requests: "When I die, make sure that I have the right burial clothes and cap. Melt the resin and pour it into the tile coffin. After a thousand years, the resin will be transformed into amber, and inside people will see me just like they see the forms of the flies and termites that have been fixed in amber. To be like a crystallized picture—is that not lovely?" Commenting on this parting vision, Zhang Dai observed of his tenth uncle that "his imagination had gone quite out of control—most of the time it was like that!"

For all the surviving members of the Zhang family, as for those throughout China, the culmination of the rising levels of violence and death came in 1644: Li Zicheng and his peasant rebels seized Beijing in early April and occupied the Forbidden City; the last Ming emperor, Chongzhen, abandoned by most of his troops and his ministers, took his own life in the garden of the Beijing palace. That summer, Manchu troops aided by Chinese collaborators marched into Beijing, ousting the peasant rebels and declaring their own new dynasty, the Qing.

With their emperor dead and the enemy in control of the Forbidden City, the former Ming forces were demoralized and lacking centralized leadership. In the absence of a designated heir apparent, different factions suggested different candidates to take over the legacy of the Ming ruling house. In the swiftly changing political world after the last emperor's death, the scholar-bureaucrat Ruan Dacheng—greatly admired by Zhang Dai for his operas—emerged as a leading political force in the newly designated resistance capital of Nanjing. After much maneuvering, Ruan supported an imperial descendant, the prince of Fu, as the resistance leader in Nanjing. The current prince of Lu, Zhu Yihai, had already fled to the south, after enemy forces had seized his fiefdom of Yanzhou. As the prince of Lu made a base for his motley forces south of Shaoxing, other imperial princes and powerful generals jockeyed for position and influence in north and central China. Few men were more highly regarded than Shi Kefa, a formidable military officer and administrator, who was named by the prince of Fu and his senior advisers to be coordinator of the defenses at Yangzhou on the Grand Canal, and to the north. And it was General Shi himself who gave Zhang Dai's prematurely born younger brother Shanmin a chance for combat action.

Zhang Dai explained briefly how this came about and how his brother responded: "My younger brother Shanmin was simple and sincere in getting at the heart of a matter, and he had

a remarkable capacity for making practical decisions. As an example, the Huaiyang defense coordinator Shi Kefa heard about
his abilities, and sent an official with gifts to invite him to accept
a military planning position; [Shi] also instructed the county
magistrate to put pressure [on my brother] to make him come.
My brother was aware that the times were full of troubles, and
was not willing to accept without good reason. So he moved
away deep into the mountains, and sent a letter [to Shi] declining
the gifts." As had been the case with earlier examples of his
brother's canniness, Zhang Dai added, "I just cannot understand
how he found the time to get the feel for the context of a situation, and yet to attain a lofty vision as good as this!"

Shi Kefa's attempted last ditch defense of Yangzhou ended on
May 20, 1645, when the city walls were breached by cannon fire,
followed by a massacre of almost all the city's residents and the
capture and summary execution of Shi himself. In one sense,
Shanmin had clearly made a well-calibrated decision. Thousands
of other Ming intellectuals and officials, however, answered variants of the call to duty, even though they knew that the risks
were high and that the Ming claimants and their accompanying
warlord generals might be not worth serving and might even be
regarded with contempt. Zhang Dai's close friend of many years
and fellow Shaoxing native Qi Biaojia was a spearhead of these
uneasy loyalists and tried to bolster the resistance to the Manchus
in the Yangzi delta region. Zhang had often traveled with Qi and
talked about books with him, for the Qi family library was one of
Shaoxing's finest. Qi had brought order and a measure of coordi-
nation to the defense of the Suzhou region, where he was a senior official, but even though some members of Ruan Dacheng's

faction supported him, he was forced to resign. On June 8, 1645, the great city of Nanjing, where many Chinese had hoped to consolidate the anti-Manchu resistance, was surrendered to the Manchus by the ruling elite without a fight. A week later, the prince of Fu was captured by the Manchu forces and taken to Beijing, where he died soon after. The alleged leader of the Ming loyalists Ma Shiying fled to the area south of Shaoxing to investigate the chances of joining the fugitive prince of Lu.

Like everyone else in the region, Qi Biaojia would have heard this grim news and been forced to decide what action to take. In his case the options narrowed after emissaries from the Manchu regional commander sent him gifts and a message asking him to join the new regime they were in the process of establishing. For Qi, as for millions of other Chinese loyal to the old ways and the old regime, the Manchu order, issued on July 21, 1645, that henceforth all Chinese men must shave their foreheads and braid their hair in emulation of the Manchus, so as to prove their loyalty to the conquerors, was an agonizing extra decision that could not be avoided: all those not obeying the order within ten days were faced with immediate execution.

Qi talked things over with his wife, put his affairs in order as well as he could, arranged for a large plot of family land to be given to the Buddhist monastery nearby and wrote the last entries in the diary that he had kept meticulously for the previous fourteen years. On July 25, he had his son warm several cups of wine, and he invited a number of relatives and friends to visit. Then, as they departed, he summoned an old friend called Zhu Shanren to talk with him. Zhang Dai gave his own affectionate rendering of how the rest of the night passed: "Later, when most

of his relatives and friends had left, Qi called Zhu Shanren to a
secluded room and discussed at length the history of ancient heroes and loyal subjects. He asked Shanren to burn some incense
and open the window. Looking towards the southern mountains,
he laughed: 'The people who roam these mountains are all but
vain shadows. The mountains are changeless but another lifetime has passed.' He then sat down on the bed, his eyes closed
and his breathing slow. After a while, he suddenly opened his
eyes, saying: 'If you want to know what death is like, this is it.'
He then urged Shanren to get some sleep."

Qi himself, however, walked to the Baqiu Pavilion and wrote
a farewell letter in the great hall of his ancestors there. He then
wrote a short will, which read: "My loyalty as a subject demands
my death. For fifteen years, I have served the Ming ruling family
with great loyalty. Those who have attained higher intelligence
than I might not wish to end their lives in this lowly fashion but
I, a dull scholar, can find no alternative." He wrote these words
in red ink, and then threw himself into a nearby river. When
Zhu Shanren woke up early the next morning, he could not find
Qi Biaojia anywhere and raised the alarm. Qi's son, Lisun, "wak-
ened from his dreams," immediately gathered several boats and
searched the river, though without any result. Zhang recorded
the sequel: "Soon, the east began to brighten and revealed a hair
strap fluttering in the shadow of the willow trees on the bank.
When they hurried over, they found Biaojia sitting in the water,
his head submerged. His clothes were still tidy, his hair and
beard orderly. He was smiling."

Less than a month later, on August 19, 1645, a number of

leading families in the Shaoxing region, still determined to keep resistance to the Manchus alive, persuaded the prince of Lu to take the title "protector of the realm." This prince was a nephew of the earlier immortality-seeking prince of Lu for whom Zhang Dai's father had worked in the late 1620s; following the suicide of his elder brother and the sacking of the family palaces in Shandong, this new prince of Lu had fled to the south and been ordered by the Ming pretender in Nanjing to oversee the defenses of Zhejiang province from a base near the coast seventy miles southeast of Shaoxing, in the township of Taizhou. The political situation was volatile. Only one day earlier, on August 18 and initially unknown to the prince of Lu, another Ming prince had been declared emperor at his base farther south in Fujian province and insisted that the prince of Lu accede to his prior claims. But the prince of Lu, acting on his supporters' recommendations, spurned the advice and kept his own new title as "protector." Other Ming princes were also jostling for power and imperial titles with the backing of their supporters. The powerful and corrupt political figure Ma Shiying, who had dominated the Nanjing fugitive court from mid-1644 until he fled the city in the summer of 1645, was also encamped in Zhejiang with the remnants of his armies, in the town of Dongyang, only about fifty miles from the prince of Lu's base.

That same summer, Ma moved with his surviving troops— some three hundred in all, both cavalry and infantry—to Qingpi village, just a few miles from the prince of Lu's base. Rumors began flying that the prince of Lu, protector of the realm, was being courted by Ma Shiying, even though many in the region saw

Ma as a corrupt traitor, and a coward to boot, who had betrayed the Ming ruling house twice already: once in Beijing and once in Nanjing.

Zhang Dai was one of those who heard the rumors about Ma and was horrified. In shock and anger, he wrote a letter to the prince of Lu in a style that was at once courteous and critical, begging him in the strongest possible terms not to be beguiled by Ma Shiying, but to try to install a government of honest and courageous men. Since Zhang had never passed the advanced examinations or held any official position in the Ming bureaucracy, and thus had no formal titles to invoke, he identified himself as merely "the cotton robed Zhang Dai, from Zhejiang." The modesty did not stop him from plunging at once to the heart of the matter:

"To: The Prince of Lu:

"Your subject Dai respectfully presents a petition concerning how the recently named Protector of the Realm, with all eyes upon him, for the appeasement of the people and the morale of the army, should immediately execute the most treacherous subject who dared to kill the emperor and betray his country." As so often with Zhang Dai, the historical context was part of the story: "I have heard that when Emperor Shun received his title from Emperor Yao, he harshly punished four evil men, winning the respect of all; when Confucius first became the minister of Lu, his execution of Shao Zhengmao gave Lu peace and prosperity. Even in those prosperous times, executions were still made with the swiftness of winds; in these times of great turmoil and change, then, when stars and constellations alter their positions, swift and just actions are even more needed! The laws of the worlds are no longer respected and followed, while men have become ignorant and shameless. They see serving their enemies as common sense and honor, surrendering to thieves as wisdom. Given this, the common behavior of learned men has indeed lost all its integrity. If no actions are taken to punish and reverse such trends, then this senseless world will soon crash into ruin. Then, how will we even speak of restoring the empire? You, my lord, have won the affection of both gods and men, rising as protector of the realm. Whether the bloodline of the revered [Ming founder] Tai Zu lives on for but a single day, or whether the relics of the Imperial house survive for but an hour, it is all up to you."

For the remainder of his lengthy letter, Zhang gave a detailed list of historical allusions to demonstrate that, try as one might, one could find no one in previous Chinese history who had the complex mix of deceitful and treacherous motives displayed by Ma Shiying. Dropping all reticence about names, Zhang Dai called him "Ma Shiying, renegade official, blue-faced demon, with flesh that cuts like knives." Even the Manchu invaders distrusted Ma so much that they sought to kill him rather than win him over to their cause, wrote Zhang. And "if even weak rulers, when their country was in danger, could execute dangerous subjects and extend their rule for a few more years, then what is there to prevent your highness, whose great reign has only just begun, from doing the same? How can you allow Ma Shiying to disrupt the order of your court?" Offering himself as the avenger of the Nanjing ruler, who was now a Manchu captive, Zhang Dai asked for a "small force of troops" so that he could capture and execute Ma, which all would see as "the first beneficial policy of my lord's revival of the empire. When news of this spreads, our people and soldiers will surely feel exalted, and become a hundred times more courageous." And Zhang begged for execution for himself as well should his action not startle and awe the northern forces.

According to Zhang, the prince of Lu read the letter and summoned him to an audience in Taizhou, suggesting that Zhang "kill first and report afterwards." Entrusted with a small force, Zhang tried to corner Ma Shiying in the nearby village where he was camped. But Ma eluded Zhang by withdrawing into an area protected by two friends, both generals favored by the prince of Lu. These two cleverly assigned to Ma Shiying the task of holding a forward defensive line along the Qiantang River north of Shaoxing and then blocked any access to Ma's base with their own troops. Zhang Dai's rhetoric, however powerful, could do nothing to break through such an array of military force.

In September 1645, even though Hangzhou was now occupied by Manchu forces and their allies, the prince of Lu moved his base from Taizhou to Shaoxing City. Zhang Dai, however frustrated he may have been by his failure to curb Ma Shiying, felt obligated by filial duty and gratitude to offer his support to the fugitive prince. But when Zhang Dai came to write an account of his Shaoxing meeting with the prince, he did so in a bantering style and tone that had nothing at all in common with his letter written a few months before: "Since my late father had served as an official to the former prince of Lu, when the [new] prince of Lu transferred his base to Shaoxing, it was natural for him and his entourage to visit the residence of his former official.

It fell to me to welcome [the prince], even though I had had no chance to study up on the etiquette of such a reception, and just had to do the best that I could."

Zhang's preparations included rearranging the main reception areas of his home, constructing a raised dais reached by a short flight of steps, finding carpet and seating mats and preparing a banquet of seven courses composed of "the best foods from land and sea." The prince arrived with only a small entourage of staff and bodyguards; he was attired grandly in a feather headdress and black robe decorated with twining dragons. Rich jades adorned his belt and sash. Zhang writes that the spectators crowded densely around the prince, eager for a glimpse of him, some pressed so closely around him that he could barely walk, others balanced precariously on footstools or even on ladders. Commanded to draw nearer, Zhang Dai approached the prince and performed the ritual greetings and prostrations "appropriate to an official in the presence of his ruler." Zhang offered tea and food, though he writes that he initially did not proffer the teacup or the chopsticks so as to show that he did not dare to claim the title of "host" to such an august visitor. When the wine had been heated in silver flagons, three of the Lu prince's own staff were in charge of pouring it into goblets. The meats and soups were offered in similar style, the silver serving dishes all kept clean under cloths of three shades of imperial yellow. And as the prince ate, his own staff celebrated the importance of the occasion with seven rounds of ritual dances and musical pieces.

For Zhang, this was all just elegant preamble to the operatic spectacle. With his deep knowledge of opera and his experience in staging plays of many kinds, Zhang Dai knew just what to

choose for this unusual occasion: a scene from *The Oil Seller*. At a
basic level, *The Oil Seller* was a fairly conventional romantic tale,
adapted into a popular drama, in which a poor seller of lamp oil
woos and wins the heart of the most beautiful and accomplished
courtesan in the capital. But its context was the important thing:
the action was set in the dark days of the fall of the Northern
Song dynasty in the late 1120s, as the armies of the powerful Jin
marauders attacked and seized the northern capital of Kaifeng,
capturing the emperor and most of his sons, and forcing hundreds of thousands of panic-stricken refugees and leaderless government troops to jam the roads to the south, in a helter-skelter
flight to cross the Yangzi River for the comparative safety that lay
beyond. The Jin invaders of that time were of the same stock as
the Manchu invaders of the 1640s; the fates of the twelfth-century
capital city Kaifeng and the Song imperial family were similar in
many ways to what had happened to the Ming in 1644 and 1645.

This appeared clearly in the scene in the opera that Zhang
Dai chose to emphasize by remarking that "it fitted the current
situation exactly right." Titled "Prince Kang Crosses the River
with His Terracotta Horse," it told how just one of the captured
emperor's sons had been able to escape the Jin conquerors' net in
1127, and, by dint of guile, speed, courage and luck, had crossed
the Yangzi just ahead of the Jin forces and established his capital
first in Hangzhou, then out to sea in the Choushan Islands and
subsequently in Shaoxing before returning to Hangzhou as a
permanent base. Despite the desperate danger of the situation,
the fugitive Prince Kang had survived and ruled the whole of
southern China until he chose to abdicate in 1162, while the
Southern Song regime he established endured until 1278. To re-

inforce the apposite nature of the parallel, the historical Prince
Kang had taken the Chinese archaic term for Shaoxing City as
that of his official reign designation. Apparently the prince of Lu
appreciated the optimism of this historical echo, for, as Zhang
Dai added, during the performance the prince's face "showed his
intense delight."

The play ended, and as evening drew into night, Zhang Dai
moved the party to a more intimate setting, that of Zhang's
"plum blossom library" in the "one-of-a-kind studio" initially
built by great-grandfather, where another meal was served.
Sprawled on Zhang's own reading couch in the library, drinking
steadily, the prince of Lu talked opera and summoned Zhang
Dai and the painter Chen Hongshou to sit beside him, "bantering and laughing with us as if we were old friends." "The ruler
had a huge capacity for alcohol," wrote Zhang, "and had already
drunk at least half a gallon. Taking a large horn goblet, he finished it off in one gulp. Chen Hongshou, who was not good at
holding his liquor, threw up next to the ruler's seat." The prince
took no notice, but ordered a small table brought, and told Chen
to do some calligraphy for him. Too drunk to comply, Chen
dropped the brush and had to stop. But the festivities continued,
with more scenes from plays, another move to a different set of
rooms and further drinking. Only after the prince had absorbed
another half gallon or so, Zhang noted, "did the imperial counte-
nance become somewhat flushed." Zhang Dai does not say at
what hour the party ended—just that, when the sedan chairs
were called for at last, the prince of Lu had to be held up under
the arms by two of his attendants, since he could no longer walk.
But when Zhang Dai said his formal farewells at the outer gate,

the prince was not too far gone to order his attendants to deliver a final message to Zhang: "Old master says he had a grand time today. Old master says he had a tremendous time today." "Strange indeed," added Zhang, "for ruler and official to be so harmonious together, so completely unrestrained."

For a short period, like many other educated residents of Shaoxing who had welcomed the prince of Lu to their city with genuine enthusiasm, Zhang Dai tried to be a part of the new order and accepted an official post in the prince of Lu's nominal government. But the office was an insignificant one, as an "administrative secretary" in one of the subdistricts of Shaoxing, and Zhang grew restless at the impossibility of getting anything done. Zhang's friend Chen Hongshou was also given a position by the prince of Lu, who seems to have borne no grudge against the painter for having thrown up in the royal presence and been unable to hold his brush. Chen, who had passed the lower-level examinations long before, was named by the prince of Lu to be "an academician awaiting orders." This post was within the study center that the prince had established in Shaoxing in obvious emulation of the similar academy in Beijing now occupied by the Manchus.

While Zhang Dai wavered, the prince of Lu picked up an even more unlikely ally, Zhang Dai's reckless and extravagant cousin Yanke—only son to the great art collector, second uncle Zhongshu. After Zhongshu died in the fighting to the north during 1644, Yanke inherited all his father's estates and collections; according to Zhang, Yanke had sold them all immediately and had managed to spend all the money he got for them—about fifty thousand taels or more—within less than six months. By

1645 Yanke, who—like Zhang Dai—had never held any administrative positions, seems to have decided that serving the prince
of Lu in the name of a Ming restoration was a worthwhile goal,
and his family's connections with the princedom of Lu gave him
the opportunity to pursue it. As Zhang Dai wrote in some be-
musement: "It was in 1645, as the need to defend the line of the
Qiantang River from the attacking armies became of absolute
urgency, that Yanke devised strategies for the prince of Lu, hoping to be given an official position. Yanke was [like the man who]
wore straw sandals but hoped for the jade emblem for his belt.
The ruler [the prince of Lu] stalled. Yanke was furious that he
had not been given office. By using prior contacts with members
of the prince's family he managed to break through the rules and
obtain a commission as a local military commander."

To aid him in his military endeavors, Yanke reached out to
another member of the family, his blind cousin Pei, whose abilities and resourcefulness Zhang Dai admired so much. After becoming totally blind, Pei had made his name as a physician, but
he had an extraordinary range of other abilities, none of which
were affected by his blindness. Zhang Dai had written glowingly
of Pei's abilities in the local community: "Pei saw to the restoration of all the family's ancestral temples, as well as banking up
and repairing the family graves. He acted as a negotiator in all legal cases [involving family members], evaluating what was true
and what was not. He carefully analyzed the productivity of the
family's farmland, and saved those who were in trouble from
dire calamities. And in any matters at all that involved unfair-
ness, or injustice, or else were frightening, or startling, when
brought to Pei's attention he was able to set them to rights. And

so Pei's house was always full of activity. He responded to every-one who needed help, and no one went away dissatisfied."

Clearly for Pei it was no problem to help his cousin Yanke in this moment of dynastic catastrophe. As Zhang Dai wrote ad-miringly: "When his young cousin Yanke was supervising the troops along the river, Pei helped him get food supplies, gave in-structions in the use of firearms and spears, drilled military for-mations, and talked over battle plans. Truly he was a man 'with three heads and six arms, a thousand hands and a thousand eyes.' Whenever someone could not finish the job they were doing then Pei, despite being blind, would get into motion and do it. There was nothing that he could not handle successfully in a flash. So although both eyes had indeed been made useless he had no need for all five senses in order to be complete."

The newly purposeful life of cousin Yanke had no apparent effect on Zhang Dai. "It was in the late autumn of 1645," he wrote, "that I realized the business of everyday life was getting more hopeless every day. So I said farewell to my Lord of Lu, and went to hide in seclusion in the mountains." Perhaps Zhang was influenced here by any one of a number of friends and rela-tives who had sought shelter through withdrawal. Chen Hong-shou, swiftly realizing that service with the Lu regime made no sense in these circumstances, had at about this time left his post as an academician, shaved his head like a Buddhist monk and withdrawn into the Cloud Gate monastery, even though he ad-mitted the decision was opportunistic, prompted by the desire to be sheltered from the fighting and from demonstrating whether or not he accepted the Manchu hairstyle. The year before, younger brother Shanmin had refused Shi Kefa's pressing invitation to help with logistical planning in the Yangzhou campaign. And a cousin of Zhang's, surviving the surrender of Nanjing, had moved to the hills outside Hangzhou and become a monk.

But for Zhang Dai, things were not destined to be so easy. The resistance came from General Fang Guo'an, an illiterate self-made soldier-general, who had fought in different parts of China in the late 1630s and 1640s and accumulated a private army of several thousand veteran troops before throwing in his lot with the prince of Lu. Fang was a fellow townsman of Ma Shiying, and had, according to Zhang, been a crucial factor in saving Ma from death and assigning him to help guard the defense line on the Qiantang River. Fang was as famous for his greed as for his toughness, and his reach was considerable. Fang's troops had ravaged the Shaoxing region so thoroughly and interdicted all river traffic so steadily in the name of local defense that even the most treasured local festivals—such as those to sweep the graves of the dead in springtime—came to a halt. With no merchant or fishing boats allowed on the river, and private craft forbidden, the male mourners had to walk the long distances to the grave sites, carrying their offerings of food and spirit money on their backs, while the womenfolk were made to stay at home, within the city walls.

As Zhang Dai wrote, his first attempt to beat a retreat from the world was speedily interrupted, and by February 1646 his self-chosen exile appeared to be over. "Fang Guo'an sent people with honorific gifts to urge me to come out from the mountains and to be a consultant on military matters. He also sent local officials to come to my door and put pressure on me. So I felt I had no choice left."

And so Zhang Dai might have been forced to rejoin the small group of officials shoring up the prince of Lu, had not his dead friend Qi Biaojia intervened. "On February 26, 1646, I headed for the Beishan pass [thirty miles east of Shaoxing] and had reached the peak at Tangyuan, when I found a room at the Han Inn in Pingshui. I had a bad running sore on my back and was moaning with pain. Reclining on a pillow, I must have fallen asleep. I saw a green-clad attendant holding a calling card which he presented to me, with the words 'Qi Biaojia presents his respects.' I jumped up in alarm, and saw Qi Biaojia push open the door and enter. He was wearing white [burial] clothes and white cap. I welcomed him in, and we both sat upright in our chairs. In my dream, I knew he was already dead, so I said to him, 'Biaojia, you died like a martyr for our country, and have added luster to our generation.' Biaojia smiled slightly and said, 'My worthy friend, at such a time as this why are you not hiding your name and all traces of yourself? What's the point of leaving your mountain retreat?' I replied, 'I wanted to help Lu, protector of the realm.' Prompted by his questions I talked this way and that, and had everything worked out. Biaojia smiled: 'Is this your decision, or is someone making it for you? The only reason must be that someone is forcing you to do this. Within the next ten days, someone is going to demand a ransom from you.' I responded, '[General] Fang Guo'an has sincerely invited me to work along with him, he would not bully me.' And Biaojia answered, 'You know best. When the world is in such a state, there is nothing one can do about it. Why don't you try taking a look at what the heavens have to say!'

"He pulled me up by the hand and we went down the steps

together. As we looked out towards the southwest, I could see stars both large and small falling together like rain, and hear the sound of explosions. Biaojia said, 'If the heavens give signs like these, what can one do, what can one do? My old friend, return quickly to your mountain, and follow your talents where they lead. In the times that are to come, the best thing for you will be to follow what I suggested here.' He rose, and as he passed through the gate he whispered in my ear, 'Finish your history of the Ming Dynasty.' And with measured pace, he was gone.

"I heard the sound of dogs barking like leopards, they startled me awake; sweat ran down my back. The barking of the dogs outside my door became an extension of the sound of the barking of dogs I had been hearing in my dream. I woke up my son and told him about the dream. The next day we reached home, and within ten days my son was kidnapped and I was forced to pay the ransom. Such is the integrity of a martyred man: even in spirit form it remains like this!"

Zhang Dai's decision to flee again, after this sudden crisis, was precipitous. "I only took a few bamboo baskets with me," he wrote. He left the bulk of his possessions and almost the whole of his thirty thousand volumes of books in his Shaoxing home. The books that he had had to leave behind, he continued, "were all taken by General Fang's troops, who ripped them apart day by day, either to light their fires with, or to take them down to the bank of the river, and use them as wadding in their armor to ward off arrows. Thus, the collection I had accumulated for the span of forty years was all lost in a matter of days."

Strangely, it was Yanke who stayed behind as Zhang fled, Yanke who gave his life, of his own choice, for the prince of Lu.

The frail defensive perimeter along the south bank of the Qiantang River gave way in the early summer of 1646: two years of drought had so dried out the riverbed that the Manchu cavalry were able to ride across, and Ma Shiying and General Fang both fled, along with the prince of Lu. Yet filled with a quixotic sense of loyalty to the ruler he had been allowed—even if grudgingly—to serve, Yanke seems to have stayed at his post, where he either fell seriously ill or was wounded. Full of wild ardor and excess to the last, just before he died Yanke told his servants that after his death they should wrap his body in an old wineskin rather than in a horse's hide and toss the bundle into the waters of the Qiantang River. The gesture was elaborate, textual, ironic. In earlier times, those killed fighting bravely in battle would be buried in a horse's hide, while those who had suffered shame would be wrapped in old wineskins. Zhang Dai had little to add to such a death: "It happened just as [Yanke] said" was his only comment. As for Zhang Dai, he abandoned what remained of his property to the mercies of the armies and sent his surviving children and his two concubines to a safe spot in the hills east of the city, while he himself pulled back deeper into the high wooded hills to the southwest of Shaoxing, where the rugged terrain made it almost impossible for invading armies to penetrate. And, heedful of the voice of his dead friend Qi Biaojia whispering in his ear, he took with him the draft manuscript of his still uncompleted history of the Ming dynasty.

CHAPTER EIGHT

LIVING THE FALL

There is no sign that Zhang Dai had planned his flight from General Fang and the Lu court with any care, nor did he leave any systematic account of what happened during the three years in which he was in hiding some forty miles or so to the southwest of Shaoxing. The hills in that region are rugged and inaccessible; it was an area of isolated villages, dense vegetation and scattered temples. In one poem Zhang describes himself as hiding out in a mountain shrine for a few months in 1646 with just one of his children and a single servant to give him company, keeping his identity secret, while he tried to focus again on the draft of his Ming history. After a month or more, he was recognized and forced to take refuge in another temple, where he concealed his identity again, for a while, by living with the monks. He was so hungry, he writes, with no grain and no chance to even find a cooking fire, that he realized how far from the truth were the famous Chinese historical tales that told of loyal recluses who starved themselves to death in the mountains rather than live to serve an unworthy lord; now Zhang Dai understood that those men—so often praised for their morality—simply died because they could find nothing to eat.

Zhang had refused to cut and braid his hair in the Manchu style, and knew that he presented an astonishing sight: with "his hair hanging wild and in tattered clothes," Zhang wrote of himself, he looked like some "frightening man of the wilderness" whom those he met shunned "as if he were a poison or some wild beast." The possibility of suicide was often with him—but he pushed it away with the thought that his greatest task, the history of the Ming, was still uncompleted.

Zhang was now forty-nine, and during 1646 as he fled from place to place images from the past years of life circled aimlessly in his head. Memories came to him in flashes. They came to him at dawn, Zhang wrote, when the night air grew less sharp and the cocks crowed. At such times, he tells us, "I saw in my mind all the splendor and frivolous beauty of my life, passing before my eyes." Writing down those memories was not something he had planned to do, but it became an unexpected diversion from the rigors of life: "While living in constant hunger, I liked to amuse myself with brush and ink." For Zhang Dai the shimmer of serried lanterns in the night, the sounds of the *qin*, the rancid smell of sacrificial meat, the reflective silence of a courtesan, the wild expenditures on art and antiques, the murmur of his mother's prayers, young actors struggling with their parts, journeys by boat and sedan chair, conversations with old friends—these along with a hundred other moments all had their tallies and their tolls. Yet even as he began to write down what he called his *Dream Recollections* Zhang emphasized that the items stayed in their own space, defying formal organization: "They are not arranged by years and months, and thus they differ from a conventional biography. They are not divided up by categories and are thus unlike a collection of anecdotes. Just by accident I'll take hold of a certain item, and it's like visiting former scenes or seeing old friends." By the end of the year he found that he had written down over 120 of the past moments that came to him in this way. Even though he deliberately kept each record brief, from a paragraph or so to two pages at most, there were enough of these *Dream Recollections* to fill a short book.

In a preface that he drafted to go with the accumulated images, Zhang emphasized the random nature of the experiences and sensations he recollected, and yet he suggested that his quest for the past had developed its conscious goals as well: "As I remember them, I write them down, and bring them before the Buddha, so that I can beg pardon for every one." The entire exercise, in Zhang's mind, had developed an expiatory quality, as he explained in the same preface: every hardship that he was now forced to endure was in retribution for some casually accepted luxury or pleasure from the past. As Zhang wrote of himself, "This bamboo rain hat is retribution for his head and these straw sandals are retribution for his heels—dues paid for the hairpins and fine slippers of those days. This patched robe is retribution for his furs and this coarse cloth retribution for good silk— dues for all that warmth and lightness. Coarse greens are retribution for his meat and gritty grains are retribution for his rice— dues paid for all those treats. This grass mat is retribution for his bed and this stone is retribution for his pillow—dues paid for the gentle and the soft. This piece of rope is retribution for his door latch and a jar's mouth is retribution for his windows—dues paid for the easy lifestyle. Smoke acts as retribution for his eyes and dung as retribution for his nose—dues paid for the voluptuous fragrances. The road is retribution for his feet and the sack is retribution for his shoulders—dues paid to those who carried him. For every possible case of sin one will find a matching kind of retribution."

Yet if there was some sense in Zhang's mind that he deserved to face punishment from the Buddha for the wasteful life he had lived, that still did not weaken the power of his recollections to transcend time or conscious motive. Perhaps Zhang Dai did indeed in some sense bring each prose passage before the Buddha, so that he could "beg pardon for them, every one." Yet those past moments of his own and other people's lives had become his enduring creation, an "attachment," as he wrote in the last sentence of his preface to the *Dream Recollections* that "will be as hard and firm as the Buddhists' jewel of life which, no matter how hot the fire blazing around it, can never be destroyed."

Especially in the first year of his flight, Zhang Dai seems to have drawn solace from China's most esteemed recluse and poet, Tao Qian. Some years before, Zhang adopted the Tao of Tao Qian's name to be his own literary or "studio" name, a resonance deepened by the fact that Tao was also his mother's maiden name. But invoking Tao Qian as a poetic model was not just an idle fancy: Tao Qian's poems, written around twelve hundred years earlier, had become rooted in the country's consciousness, as catching the layers and mood of the educated scholar who out of inner necessity gave up all ambitions and career in order to return home, to work his little piece of land, to write, to reflect on the passing whims and fancies of life and in Tao's case—whenever it was possible—to drink. Tao Qian was celebrated for his love of wine and his willingness to go to any lengths to obtain it, even when that meant taking the rice money from his wife or shamelessly cadging off friends. In 1650 Zhang's friend Chen Hongshou was to celebrate this side of Tao Qian's nature with a witty and emotional series of paintings that illustrated anecdotes about drinking culled from Tao's own poems. But in 1646 Zhang Dai, who was not so dedicated a drinker, chose to write matching poems to different aspects of Tao's work: Tao's seven-poem cycle "In Praise of Impoverished Gentlemen," his political poems about regicide and usurpation, his "funeral-bearer's songs" and the realistic adjustment to poverty of Tao's famous "Inspired by Events." As Tao Qian had written in that poem:

> When I was young, my family fell on hard times;
> As old age comes on, I am always hungry.
> All I want in truth is wheat and beans,
> With no pretensions to the sweet and fat.

In his prose preface to the poem, Tao gave a moving summary of the difficulties of surviving on one's own: "The old grain is gone, and the new is not yet harvested. I have got to be pretty much an old hand at farming, but running into bad years with days and months to go has been a never-ending worry. Since nothing can be expected from this year's harvest, and a day's provisions scarcely supply a single meal, for over a week now I have been concerned about starving. As the year draws to a close, I am filled with constant care. If I do not set down my thoughts, how is posterity to know?"

One of Tao Qian's most celebrated poems was the opening one in the cycle of seven on the "Impoverished Gentlemen." This dealt with the loneliness that can suffuse such a rural retreat, and Tao's own sense of helplessness, which was best caught in one fleeting couplet:

> Slowly from the woods a bird emerges
> To return again before the close of day.

Learned commentators across the ages had written that Tao referred here both to himself and to the dynastic collapse of AD 420 that he had just lived through. Zhang Dai, in a cycle of seven poems echoing Tao's, written during a fierce storm of wind and rain, specifically noted that he wanted his own poems from the autumn of 1646 shared with all his "younger brothers and cousins, and with the children" who were still in the hills to the east, where Zhang had sent them to what he hoped was safety.

Tao's first poem in his cycle ran as follows:

> All the myriad creatures have their refuge,
> The lonely cloud alone has no support
> But vanishes darkling in the empty sky—
> Will ever any afterglow survive?
> The morning sun disperses last night's mist
> And flocks of birds all fly away together.
> Slowly from the woods a bird emerges
> To return again before the close of day.

Having taken stock, he stays at home
Where there is no avoiding cold and hunger.
Since none today is left who understands,
It's finished now—I have no complaint.

Zhang Dai's matching poem echoes Tao's but shifts the key metaphors: Tao's ominous cloud becomes Zhang's glowworm, whose light is finally extinguished under the steady rain. In Zhang's words:

When the season for harvest comes, all have hope,
But the autumn glowworm alone has no home.
It flashes through the air, in and out of sight,
Among the high grass, leaving trails of light.
When the mountain rain falls, gentle but relentless,
Its wings are dampened, and can no longer fly.
The mountains are deep and gigantic,
The road is long and twisted, and I cannot return.
When the evening wind starts to blow,
How can I avoid cold and hunger?
I silently think of my former home,
And suddenly I feel sad, even as I plow along.

Whether or not Zhang had exaggerated his plight—after his flight from Shaoxing, he said, all that was left to the family was "a broken bed and a rickety table, a broken tripod for rituals and an ailing lute, along with partially destroyed books, fragments of documents, and one cracked inkstone"—he inevitably felt the pull of his old world. He does not share details of his life in the late 1640s, but it is clear that by 1649 he had made the decision to return to the Shaoxing area.

He returned to a different universe from the one he had left. Whether it had been General Fang and his troops, local looters or officials of the victorious new Qing dynasty who penalized him for his two brief periods of support for the prince of Lu, Zhang Dai now had no family estates to return to. Instead, in October 1649 he rented a piece of land in Shaoxing, on the back slope of that same Dragon Mountain where once he lived and studied and watched the lanterns shine and the snow fall. The rented property was in that same Happiness Garden he had often visited with grandfather. In those days of his childhood and youth it seemed a paradise, one that earned its name from the joy of the man who had studied there: with the groves of fruit trees, a broad pond, flower gardens and the background walls, the landscape seemed to open like a scroll as one walked the grounds. It was also, in its glory days before the Ming fall, a garden that could make a handsome investment return to its owner. Zhang wrote of the fish that used to grow plump in the three-acre pond, of the fresh oranges one could trade for silk, of the cabbages and melons and of the peach and plum trees that could yield fruit for sale at a rate of 150 *qian* a day—"It was indeed like a market, even with its doors closed to the outside world." But by the time Zhang rented it, it was in disrepair. The once happy scholar was gone and his family had scattered. Zhang Dai claimed that he had to mend the thatched roofs of the pavilions himself, and that one could no longer tell what sense of order the earlier ornamental trees and rocks had been meant to convey. The Happiness Garden's very name, he told an old friend in a bantering conversation, was proof of the Chinese adage that "the name and reality usually do not match in this world of ours." Just as "Confucius who lacked nothing lived in Lack-All Village, and the man who stank lived near Fragrance Bridge, so did the man whose sufferings were extreme dwell in his Happiness Garden."

In a subsequent poem, Zhang Dai acknowledged that in a numerical sense his family had managed to come together again, but that he could in no way be described as in command:

I am not yet in my old age,
Nor has my fall in the world been for very long.
Yet though only a few blurred years have passed,
I look now like an old man.
After the chaotic warfare began,
The family collapsed, leaving me nothing but my bare
    hands.
I lament having so many offspring,
Especially after losing my wife at middle age.
Of my ten daughters, three have married,
Of my six sons, two have found wives.
They have added four grandchildren for me,
And the family now numbers eighteen or nineteen.
Even if we have only porridge two out of three meals
    a day,
We would still consume one *Dou* of wheat.
My fields of old used to be plentiful,
Not even half a *Mu* remains today.
Only two or three shabby buildings survive,
With a single willow tree standing before them.

That "single willow," as readers knew, was the symbol of the poet Tao Qian's constancy in the face of hardship. The trouble was that numbers were not necessarily equal to strength:

> I compare our family's current state
> To that of people in a shipwreck,

wrote Zhang. And continuing the metaphor:

> Only by a combination of individual efforts,
> Can we avoid sinking.
> Yet should you hope for my help,
> And all hang onto my clothes.
> We would become tangled,
> And not one will survive.

Zhang Dai could complain, like anyone else, but he was never rooted in his misery. Slowly, over the years, old friends had been surfacing, and there were sometimes unexpected blessings—such as the loving attention Zhang Dai always received from Lady Chen, the compassionate and affectionate wife of his younger brother Shanmin, whom he often visited. Though she herself was already fifty, she always served Zhang delicacies with her own hand when he came to call, and treated him with all the ritual attention due to an elder relation. Some who had served the prince of Lu had died as martyrs. The painter Chen Hong-shou had died from illness in 1652 and could drink no more. But Qi Zhixiang, stalwart friend from long before and elder brother of Qi Biaojia, had served the prince of Lu in Taizhou after his

brother's suicide and lived to tell the tale, walking back to Shaoxing for two weeks through the marauding troops and bandit
gangs with his pet songbird Treasure tucked under his arm.

One thing the Happiness Garden was still good for was conversation. Zhang wrote what a pleasure it was to sit there on late
summer afternoons with the youngsters—whether his own children or those of the neighbors he does not say—and talk about
former times. Especially on hot days one could sit under the
stone bridge in the shade by the water and conjure up old memories. After a while, when the memories had piled up, said Zhang,
"he would ask those youths to leave and then would write down
the conversations they had just had. After some time, this became a habit." Some of the conversations that Zhang wrote
down in the Happiness Garden have survived, and many of
them developed themes about Zhang's family that had been entered among the *Dream Recollections*. Stories often mentioned
grandfather's quickness and cleverness as well as the precocity or
wit of many members of the family, including Zhang Dai himself, along with close family friends like Xu Wei and Qi Biaojia.
He was seeking, Zhang told his readers, a way to combine the
lighthearted with the serious that would enlighten without being
ponderous—30 percent humor would be a helpful way to induce
70 percent of advice, in Zhang's calculation, and would keep the
young listeners awake: jokes, puns, word games, conundrums,
all could be useful in holding the attention of the young. Some of
Zhang's vignettes contained helpful hints for conceiving children, for holding one's liquor, for urinating in the correct order
of precedence. The point was to grasp the humor and the intensity of life.

In the 1650s Zhang Dai took another studio name, "Old Man with Six Satisfactions," and he discussed them with his garden audience: "Be satisfied when you can alleviate your hunger with plain food. Be satisfied when you can keep warm in patched clothes. Be satisfied if you enjoy an old, damaged house. Be satisfied to get tipsy with watered-down or cheap wine. Be satisfied to save with an almost empty purse. Be satisfied if you can avoid the evil people when they seem to prevail." Zhang Dai had clearly moved beyond the concept of retribution to something altogether less grand and more banal—an ordinary acceptance of an ordinary existence. Furthermore, it seems as if the pulsing memories of family that Zhang Dai during his flight entered as items in his *Dream Recollections*—especially rich on grandfather and father, on second uncle and Yanke—received elaboration and further thought in the Happiness Garden conversations.

From these varied background elements sprang Zhang Dai's considered decision to write three blocks of condensed yet detailed biographies of his family: one dealing with the direct paternal line, from great-great-grandfather down to father (who died in 1633); a second group dealing with three uncles; the third looking at five other relatives' lives across the generations, from great-uncles to young cousins.

Zhang's only hint as to when he wrote these three collections comes in a brief preface he appended to the second group of biographies, the collection on three of his uncles. He writes there: "Second uncle has been dead for seven years, third uncle for ten, and seventh uncle for thirty-six, and if none of them get a biography [soon], they will end with no biographies at all. There certainly exist people who are silent after they die, and never have any biographies. But it would be a great pity if that were the case for my three uncles, for all three of their lives deserve to be recorded." Good corroborating evidence that second uncle died in 1644 fixes the composition date in 1651, and using that date as a marker point, one can place the manipulator Sanshu's death in 1641 and the brilliant but wild seventh uncle's death in 1615.

Zhang Dai continued that these three uncles "had both strengths and shortcomings. Their strengths may not deserve biographies, but their shortcomings certainly do. Xie Jin once wrote: 'I would prefer to be an imperfect piece of jade, rather than a perfect rock.' It is precisely because the jade has imperfections that it is validated as jade. So how dare I hide my three uncles' imperfections, and thus disqualify them from being perceived as jade?"

Zhang justified his decision to add five more family members in roughly similar terms: "I once said that you should not take a person without obsessions as your friend, for such a person will lack deep feelings; a person without flaws also should not be made a friend, for he will lack true life. In my family, Zhang Rufang was obsessed by money, Zhang the Beard by drinking, tenth uncle by anger, Yanke by landscaping projects, and Pei by books and histories. Their unreserved passions for these things were [considered] flaws when they were little, and became obsessions when they grew up. None of these five had any interest in having their biographies written, yet because all five had obsessions that were so extreme, I felt I had no choice but to write out their biographies. Therefore, I have written *The Biographies of Five Unusual People*."

In these eight cases, the family members chosen by Zhang

were outside the direct descent line, the one linking Zhang Dai back through his father to the originators of the family's prominence. In accounts of the paternal line itself, a greater degree of caution was necessary in order not to break certain basic premises of filial piety, while the distance in time between the subjects' lives and the life of Zhang Dai himself was also a factor he needed to take into account. But these problems could be surmounted.

In discussing some of the challenges he faced in creating these central family biographies, Zhang Dai put himself in the company of two celebrated Ming political figures and prolific authors (both famous for their stylistic purism) whom he might have chosen as models had he wanted to, or whose equivalents in his own time he might have commissioned to do the work for him—only to reject the suggestion out of hand. "There are writers such as Li Mengyang, author of the 'genealogy,' and Zhong Xing, author of the 'family record,' and one could have waited for a Li or a Zhong to write these biographies. In the case of my own great-great-grandfather and great-grandfather, they were fully able to be their own biographers, and others have also already written biographies of them, so there is no need for them to wait for Zhang Dai to write their biographies. As for my grandfather, he too was fully able to be his own biographer. And since I was born late [in his life], I only saw grandfather when he was already an aging man, and thus know little about his earlier life; even if I wanted to write his biography there would still be some things that I would not be able to record completely. As for my father, I knew him truly, and garnered my knowledge of him over a long period; thus I am able to write a biography of him, even though I am not yet equal to catching his fullness. Thus as far as my writing biographies of my various ancestors goes, it is hard for me to be a Li or a Zhong."

But reflecting back to the other writings he had done—such as the *Profiles* and the *Historical Gaps*, both collections that he had expanded by including figures from the Ming dynasty itself—Zhang sought to strengthen his justification: "Even so, how is that any reason for me not to write their biographies at all? If I were not to write their biographies at all, that would be like saying I can write the biographies of the people who spent their lives under the fifteen different emperors who have ruled the Ming dynasty and yet am unable to write the biographies of my own various ancestors—and in that case I would really be the guilty party."

With each of these biographical ventures into his own ancestry, Zhang explained, he would be playing a different role. In writing about his own great-great-grandfather and great-grandfather, the need would be mainly to clear distortions that had formed part of the state's record of these men who had served years as senior officials, and suffered their political ups and downs: drawing on the metaphor he had developed in his study of gaps in history, Zhang described his role in those two cases as being similar to that of an astronomer "who is able to mend the moon after an eclipse, so that those gazing upwards can see it whole again." In writing about grandfather, said Zhang, "I will be like someone who sketches in half the likeness, so that the complete picture will come into view." With father, he would be like the fisherman "who first sees the large size of the fish in his net, and because of that is able to see all the smaller ones as well."

Zhang added: "I myself have little talent, and lack the skill to reveal a completely fresh face for any of these four ancestors. All I can do is strive not to lose sight of their original faces, not to lose sight of their true faces, and to be able to present each of them with half his face in laughter and half his face in tears."

Zhang Dai closed his brief preface to the Zhang family biographies with an image borrowed from the ancient Taoist philosopher Zhuangzi and now applied to the art of biography itself: "When a leper woman gives birth to her baby in the middle of the night, she at once snatches up a light so she can examine it, trembling with the fear that the infant may look just like she does." By good fortune, Zhang continued, "none of my four direct ancestors had leprosy; and yet in my biographies of them I could not catch their exact likeness. Thus if in the middle of the night I were to get a light and examine what I am writing, I would be both fearful that I had caught their exact likeness, and yet fearful that I had failed to do so. I would have both feelings at the same time."

Twelve hundred years before, Tao Qian had also used this image of the leper woman in a poem written for his newborn son:

> The leper woman whose child is born in the night,
> Rushes out to find a lamp.
> All of us have such an impulse,
> It's not just me alone.

As he had done with Tao Qian's poetry of escape to a bucolic world, after his initial flight into the hills, Zhang was not just writing in homage—he had taken the image used by Tao and shifted it to a new direction, where the fear of family disfigurement became the writer's fear for the integrity of his work as a whole. Zhang directed this message specifically to his own children, who brought no harmony to his home; the anxiety of the writer was not just in reassuring the ancestors, but lay in using the images of the ancestors to hold the family together at the moment it seemed near disintegration.

In such a world, the strife that Zhang knew also existed at the heart of his family in the Happiness Garden might be a warning of the ravages that one could find on a once-beloved face. To make this point, Zhang inserted a special "message to his children" at the close of the biographies of the three uncles and the paternal ancestors, and just before *The Biographies of Five Unusual People*. "In passing on these biographies of my ancestors to all my children I will say this: 'My forebears are present here; my descendants are also present here.' My children do not understand this. That is why I say that to understand the fundamental nature of our forebears, there is no need to look any further than how they relate to each other as brothers, older and younger. Great-great-grandfather served his older brother Zhang Tianqu as he served his own father. Great-grandfather, with his own hands, took charge of the two little brothers born to [his father's] secondary consorts and looked after them like his own sons. Grandfather and great-uncle Zhiru were as close to each other as are hands and feet, while father and my various uncles never lost their mutual regard for each other. But from that time onward, brothers in our family have treated each other like passing strangers, or even like enemies. As time has gone by, the members of our family have also fallen into decline.

"If my sons and grandsons can model themselves after their forefathers, and give especial value to filiality and friendship, then they can build a foundation for our family line. If they continue these excesses, and are incapable of change, then the benevolence from those wise ancestors will end after the fifth generation, and my own descendants will also come to an end. So I say this [again]: 'My forebears are present here. My descendants are also present here.' " It was indeed a difficult challenge that Zhang Dai had set for himself: through the reach of his own writing brush, in the tangle of his rented garden, in the span of his own skull and guided by his emotions and his memory, he had somehow to ensure that his own family was spared the harsh separation between the past and the future that had so shattered his country as a whole.

Near the beginning of his strongly personal preface to the *Dream Recollections* Zhang wrote that after the series of catastrophes that had struck him so closely together—"country destroyed, family routed, no home left to go to"—he had composed a farewell "coffin-pullers dirge" (as Tao Qian had also done before him) and had thought of suicide. His decision to live on, even in hunger and poverty, was not because of any intrinsic merits in his *Dream Recollections*. Rather, it was "because the *Stone Casket* history was not yet finished." Zhang chose the term *Stone Casket* for the title of his history of the Ming dynasty as an act of homage to Sima Qian, whom Zhang so often cited as the great precursor of all historians: the stone caskets were where the collections of sources that Sima had relied on for his own great work of seventeen hundred years before had been stored for safety. Sima Qian, who had suffered the terrible punishment of castration for daring to cast doubt on his emperor's judgment, was celebrated for his subsequent decision not to commit suicide despite his shame and humiliation, but to strive to live on, so that he could complete his own great study of the unification of China's first empire.

Just as he had with the preface to the *Dream Recollections* and to the family biographies, Zhang Dai used the *Stone Casket* preface to give some hints as to the book's dating and development: "I began to write this book in 1628," Zhang noted. "Seventeen years later, as the country endured its huge upheaval, I brought a draft with me into the mountains. I worked for another ten years before the book was completely finished. Luckily, I did not enter the world of politics, and had neither friend nor foe; and having no worldly concerns or forbidden topics, I could seek the truth in all matters, and strive to use precise language: five times I revised my draft, and nine times I corrected its mistakes." Thus his *Stone Casket* history—or at least the complete first draft—must have been completed in or around 1655.

It had been his initial decision, Zhang also wrote in the *Stone Casket* preface, to stop the story in the year 1628, when the new emperor, Chongzhen, ascended the throne. But though Zhang Dai stuck to that decision as far as the coverage of his Ming history went, he knew that the collapse of the Ming had changed the whole rationale of the intellectual adventure. To understand the Ming, one would now have to understand its ending, and to find room not only for the suicide of Emperor Chongzhen, but also for the regime of the prince of Fu in Nanjing and even the prince of Lu in Shaoxing. Zhang's dream of the meeting with his dead friend Qi Biaojia began with the nagging pain from the sore on his back and ended with Qi's whispered comment that he must finish his history rather than continue fighting. That pain may well have stayed with him in the mountains and later in the rented Happiness Garden, as he asked himself what it was that had gone so wrong, and how it was that the obvious symptoms of decay had been for so long unnoticed.

The "thing about history," wrote Zhang Dai, in the same *Stone Casket* preface, "is that those who really could write it, don't; while those who should not be writing it, do." To illustrate his point he chose two well-known figures from previous centuries: Wang Shizhen and Su Dongpo. A celebrated Ming scholar, Wang Shizhen was, to Zhang, the perfect exemplar of someone who should not be writing history and yet insisted on doing so. As Zhang put it, Wang "had his eyes rolled upwards, he had an endless flow of words, his brush was always swollen with ink, he cared only for what was right in front of him. It was his conviction that if he were not the one to be writing history then there was no one else who should be writing it, and he kept this idea clutched to his chest. Such a person is one who should not be writing history; and if he does go ahead and write history, it won't be good."

The Song dynasty writer and official Su Dongpo, who died in the year 1101, was the perfect counterexample to someone like Wang. A truly great poet and essayist, Su had steadfastly refused to write history, even when urged to do so by some of the most influential figures of his time. Su remained stubbornly attached to his conviction that "history was never easy to write, and that he was not the person to try to write it." Alas, wrote Zhang, Su's stubbornness in sticking to this decision made things all the harder for those who came later. But though Zhang knew that he himself was one of those "who could not write history" and lacked even a fraction of the talents of Wang (let alone of Su), he decided to press ahead. For he knew that "the world was not lacking in those who were truly able to write history but had not so far done so. And he would hold his brush in expectation of their coming."

To give a fuller sense of the issues at stake, Zhang Dai presented the case of Sima Qian (c. 145–85 BC), regarded by Chinese scholars of Zhang's time as the finest historian the country had ever had. In contrast to Wang, Sima Qian had been brilliant because "when he applied his energies to biography he always wrote without self-consciousness, never seized on a word inappropriately, and would never take lightly the writing of a single stroke." The result was that Sima Qian's histories had "both grace and strength. His subtlety of expression came from its simplicity. His own comments on history were always sketched in sparingly—if not three fine hairs on a cheek then one light dot on the eye would suffice; even if given a gallon of ink, he would use every drop exactly right."

Zhang did, as far as we can tell, literally carry with him the working draft of his manuscript on the Ming when he fled Shaoxing, and though it is impossible to chart exactly when he wrote which sections, the basic structure must have been well set before his flight. The format Zhang used was one that had been hallowed in China ever since Sima Qian's own day, and had proved so enduring because it was both flexible and comprehensive. In such long histories of a dynasty or dynasties, the work customarily started with annals of each reign, arranged chronologically.

The annals were followed by monographic chapters that focused on specific topics or concepts, such as economics, the law, transportation, public works, astronomy, music, climate and agriculture, philosophy and examinations. Much the largest section came last: the individual biographies of all those people who, the historians figured, had contributed to the history of their times, whether for good or for ill, in public life or private capacities. The biographies were bunched in categories, based on the nature of the achievements or shortcomings being described. Though the contents of the annalistic chapters were moderately predictable, the same was by no means true of the topical or biographical sections, where the historians were free to focus on whatever they chose, inventing entirely new categories when that seemed appropriate. The historians could show their own political or aesthetic opinions both by the material they selected for inclusion and by what they omitted. They also could append a short "judgment" or "discussion" of every topic tackled, including the individual rulers themselves. The level of detail was intricate and intense, and thousands of individuals might be featured within a specific study.

Furthermore, many of China's historians followed the example set by Sima Qian and traveled great distances either to view the sites of past battles or to interview those who were present at key events. Despite the poverty to which he was reduced after the Ming fall, Zhang Dai followed just that path. It was in autumn 1653, he wrote, that he combined a visit to his cousin Dengzi, who had settled in western Zhejiang province, with an exploration of the areas in Jiangxi where the recent fighting had been heaviest. Zhang was awed by what he found there: "I passed through several counties, and saw how in the townships only a few thatch-roofed buildings were still standing amongst the dense underbrush and the thorns. The sight made me weep. I asked some of the surviving elders about this, and they told me in detail how the armies ravaged and burned these communities, in some cases returning several times." The group of Jiangxi prominent families who rallied the resistance "were eventually wiped out. Words cannot describe it. When I got to Xinzhou, I saw that in dozens of places the local people had erected stockades they would defend to the death. But in the smaller rural villages over half the common folk had shaved their foreheads and adopted the queue. Among the upper gentry who were still alive, most had gone to hide out in the hills and forests, and refused to serve the new government. There were also many well-known local scholars who refused to sit for the examinations. In the ten years that have passed since the former dynasty fell, there were so many people who still stayed loyal to their former ruler." In exploring the historical roots of such events, concluded Zhang, "is it not perfectly natural to become emotional?"

In the context of this kind of social and military disintegration, one of the challenges Zhang faced in writing his history of the Ming was to work out when the dynasty had passed its zenith. In emulation of his hero Sima Qian, Zhang appended his own personal evaluation to the annals of each individual reign covered in the *Stone Casket*. Though he was critical of several earlier rulers, his conclusion was that it was really in the long reign of Emperor Wanli, which lasted from 1572 to 1620 (and thus spanned all Zhang's own childhood and youth) that one could see the major signs of decay first appearing. As Zhang wrote in his history, though Wanli started off as a young ruler in glory, "wise and resolute" and guided by fine advisers, that situation did not last. "After 1592, Wanli secluded himself in the imperial residence and avoided holding court. He had no general vision and could see nothing but trivialities, and he developed into a morbidly disinterested and idle person. Moreover, he was insatiably greedy. Eunuch commissioners were sent everywhere to collect commercial taxes and supervise mining operations, and they ravished the people of its resources. To draw a comparison, [the eunuchs] were like a neglected lesion that would later become the bane of the patient's life, except that at this point the lesion was yet to fester." Thus a firm historiographical judgment was possible: "The last years of Wanli already portended the fall of our Ming dynasty. Because his reign was quiet and generally uneventful, people called him a ruler who brought good fortune. Yet, how on the earth could a ruler who had a myriad state affairs to attend to every day simply use things being 'generally uneventful' as evidence of the reign being a fortunate one?"

Pursuing the same medical metaphor a stage further, into the reign of Wanli's grandson Tianqi, who ruled from 1621 to 1627, Zhang saw the fatal illness the eunuchs had given rise to as truly taking hold. In earlier reigns, including Wanli's, "The lesions were on the back of the head and on the spine. Since [the patient] was in his prime and his body was still robust, the toxin did not invade the body and the patient was saved from death. But in Tianqi's reign, the illness penetrated into the region of the kidneys: since [the patient] was running out of physical strength, malignant lesions developed in the bones. Shortly, those lesions festered and seeped with pus, and the life was gone." Not even the most famous doctors could achieve a cure in such circumstances, Zhang concluded, and that was why the last Ming emperor, Chongzhen, could not check the impending catastrophe.

As a practicing historian, Zhang knew that more had to be said about the Ming fall itself. Yet in a way he was trapped by his own structural decision to stop the *Stone Casket* story with Tianqi's death in 1627. The reasoning had been impeccable at the time, but now it made little sense; so it was after the conquest but well before the final draft of the main *Stone Casket* history was finished that Zhang Dai realized he could only make sense of the end of the Ming by writing a *Sequel* ("Afterthought") to the *Stone Casket*, in which later material could be analyzed. From this time onward Zhang Dai worked on the two projects together, shifting some material back and forth, while occasionally duplicating sections or biographies as the need arose.

So it was in the *Sequel* volume that Zhang completed the anatomy of the Ming fall by linking the fate of the dynasty to the person of Chongzhen, who ruled from 1628 until his suicide in 1644. "Since ancient times," Zhang wrote, "emperors have lost the country for a variety of reasons: because of wine, because of sex, because of tyranny, because of extravagance, or because of military expansionism." In the case of the last Ming emperor, inappropriate thrift was also a major factor: just when Emperor Chongzhen should have spent every coin in the treasury to shore up his armies fighting the Manchus to the north of the Great Wall and the peasant rebels in the northern provinces, the emperor chose "to practice austerity in food and clothing, and to live like a humble gate keeper." The result was that while "the frontier defense troops had been unpaid for years, and were dressed in rags," the rebels, when they seized Beijing in 1644, "looted huge sums from the palace treasury." Thus instead of boosting the morale of the regular forces, the emperor sent "all the treasure out of the palace to supply the rebels with rations." The policy of Emperor Chongzhen was contradictory: as Zhang put it, "It was totally pointless for the late emperor to daily accumulate wealth, to daily control expenditures, to daily apportion multifarious taxes, and to daily borrow money."

However one chose to assess the abilities of all the previous Ming emperors who had ruled the dynasty in sequence since its founding, the sixteenth and last, Emperor Chongzhen, was doomed for all time to be remembered as the one who presided over the final disintegration. Zhang Dai offered an astute interpretation of Emperor Chongzhen's character, focusing especially on Chongzhen's contrariness in switching advisers constantly, like a "man playing chess." At different times in his seventeen-year reign, wrote Zhang, Chongzhen sought his advisers from a wide span of humanity: the recently promoted bureaucrats, the Confucian Study Academy, "hermits in the mountains and forests," noblemen, palace women and eunuchs, commoners and military men; the result was that as "the choices became chancier, things got worse." Zhang Dai linked these erratic personnel choices to the emperor's overcareful fiscal policy: by constantly crying poor, by raising taxes too high yet spending too little on border defenses and the troops' rations and supplies and by sending eunuchs to gouge out extra revenue, the emperor made everyone believe that he and his policies alike were bankrupt. "It seemed that everyone in the world was in his service; however, at a time of national crisis, no one really shared his worries and offered help. Since ancient times, no other ruler has surpassed our late emperor in losing popular support!" The strange irony was that "Emperor Chongzhen not only died more nobly than the last emperors of the Han, Tang, or Song dynasties," wrote Zhang, but that he had been, in general, "hardworking, frugal and intelligent"; it was the irresponsible people around the ruler who "jointly destroyed their country" and thus managed to transform "a noble ruler who could have restored the dynasty into an incompetent king who lost it."

For that very reason, Zhang concluded, it would not be correct to blame just an individual Chinese rebel like Li Zicheng for the catastrophe. China's crisis was cumulative and the responsibility for catastrophe had to be shared. Blaming Li, wrote Zhang, was like claiming that "one man had felled the Ming tree with his axe, when in fact the tree was riddled with insects from within and bored through by others from without." Nor could one say the Ming fall was "like a deer hunt," as some people had done. It was true in one sense that Li Zicheng had captured the stag, but he only did so because "others were holding it up by the horns, while yet others trapped its legs and made it stumble." Zhang underscored this point with yet another metaphor: wasps and scorpions gave what looked like the final sting, but "the flies and maggots were already writhing in the privies before the bandits got there." That was the true legacy of corruption that Zhang and his fellow survivors had regretfully inherited.

CHAPTER NINE

RECLAIMING THE PAST

Being back at Dragon Mountain and writing in the Happiness Garden did not make Zhang feel closer to his children:

> My eldest son travels the world,
> Barely managing to make a living.
> My second son claims to be studying,
> Yet only desires the pleasures of wine.
> My third son loves to jest and play,
> Taking his friends for his only life.
> My fourth son has great hopes for himself,
> And does not fear to boast.
> My two youngest sons are young, and know only to cry,
> Tugging at my coat for water chestnuts and lotus roots.
> This old man's body is weak,
> And it's hard to know if he will make it to next year.

Once again, Zhang found his voice through Tao Qian, whose celebrated poem on his own five sons' shortcomings was an inescapable part of China's poetic heritage: "Not one of them is fond of brush and paper," Tao had written, regretting their inability to change their ways. Indeed, so profound was their laziness, Tao wrote, sardonically, that he was compelled to drink all the more to make up for his sons' shortcomings.

Yet despite their wandering ways Zhang's two eldest sons were decent scholars and by 1654 were ready to have a try at the provincial examinations in Hangzhou. Zhang had noted that in the former Jiangxi battle zones many scholars and students still refused to take the examinations, considering such a refusal a way to express their hostility to the new Qing regime, but apparently Zhang no longer felt that rejection was significant, and let his sons make their own attempt. They did not pass, but their effort brought their father back to the once-beloved city with its famed West Lake, which he had not seen since 1643, the year before the Ming was overthrown.

The experience was shattering. In his twenties Zhang had written confidently of the fierce joy that pain could bring, cleansing the thoughts like a boil being lanced or a splinter being shifted loose with an awl. Now at fifty-seven he found the experience hard to bear, and in a preface to a book about West Lake that he compiled near the end of his life Zhang recalled the shock and ambiguity of his feelings upon revisiting the scene of his ancient pleasures. "I was born at an unlucky time and have been kept far from West Lake for twenty-eight years. Nevertheless there has not been a day that West Lake has not been a part of my dreams, and the West Lake in my dreams has, in fact, never been gone for a single day. On two occasions, in 1654 and 1657, I went back to West Lake; and all that remained of places like the Shang family's serried halls by the Yongjin Gate, or the more casual dwellings of the Qi Family, or the separate residences of the Qians and Yus, along with my own family's special gardens—of that whole stretch of lakeside villas nothing was left but shards of broken tile. So all those things that were present in my dreams were, in reality, not there beside West Lake at all. As for the view from Broken Bridge, all those delicate willows and tender peach trees of olden days, all those pavilions for singers and dancers, were as if washed away by a vast flood, and not one in a hundred was spared.

"I therefore fled from the place as quickly as I could, saying to myself that it was because of West Lake that I had come there, but now I could see things were in such a state that I should strive to protect the West Lake of my dreams, so that I could keep it entire and unharmed. At that point it occurred to me how different my own dream was from that of Li Bo. When Li Bo dreamed of Tian-mu, he saw her as a goddess or a famous beauty; he dreamed of something he had never seen, and thus his dream was illusion. But when I dream of West Lake, it is like my family garden and my old home; I dream of what was truly there, and thus this dream is genuine.

"I have now been living for twenty-three years in a house rented from someone else, but in my dreams I am still in the place where I used to live. The young servant who looked after me long ago now is white-haired, but in my dreams his hair is still done up in the black tufts of a little boy."

Such dreams were Zhang's enigma: "My old dreams are all I

have to cling to, my stream of scenes and moods from West Lake, all perfectly in order and motionless. When my children ask me about this, I sometimes tell them about it. But that is just giving them dream talk from within my dreams. Either I am caught in a nightmare or I am sleep-talking."

Thus however precise the dream might be, Zhang Dai knew that something was always lost in the telling. He felt like a man from the hills, he wrote (echoing an image he had used when talking about acting), a man who returned to his village after an ocean voyage and tried to share all the wonders he had seen and tasted. As the man talked, "The villagers crowded close around him, and licked his eyes." But the true taste was not to be had like that: "For how could licking the eyes ever satisfy the craving?"

Despite his intense disappointment over his children and what had happened to the pleasure centers of Hangzhou where he had once lived to the full, Zhang was back there again in 1657. This time he had a direct invitation, sent to him by the newly appointed educational commissioner in Hangzhou, Gu Yingtai. Gu had been a successful candidate in the second of the postconquest countrywide examinations in Beijing, and had risen swiftly in the Qing bureaucracy. Arriving in Hangzhou in the summer of 1656, Gu brought with him his own almost completed manuscript entitled *A Comprehensive History of the Ming Dynasty* in eighty chapters arranged by topic. Gu set up a history compilation office on the shore of West Lake to help him complete the project and, knowing of Zhang Dai's expertise on Ming history, invited Zhang to join his editorial staff. Zhang worked with Gu through the year 1657, and the assignment must have brought him much-needed money. Gu was so impressed by Zhang's scholarship that he borrowed scores of segments from the *Stone Casket* history and inserted them at relevant spots in his own *Comprehensive History*.

The historiographical assignment gave Zhang access, as an especial bonus, to Gu's own collection of the *Capital Gazette* for the entire Chongzhen reign from 1628 to 1644 as well as drafts of the state history of the same reign. Zhang saw at once the immense value of this source, which carried weekly information about the government of the realm before the Ming fall. Zhang's own great-uncle, Rufang, had worked in the *Gazette* office for two decades, as Zhang had mentioned in his biography. Well before he had finished the *Stone Casket* history, Zhang used the invaluable *Gazette* source as a means to deepen the detail of the *Stone Casket* and to launch the sequel to his own Ming history, designed to cover the final years from 1628 into the late 1640s. This continuation was well under way and several chapters written when Gu's project was completed and Zhang returned early in 1658, at the age of sixty-one, to the Happiness Garden and his family in Shaoxing. For the next six years he worked steadily on the vast project, and by 1664 could consider the *Stone Casket* completed, while he struggled to finish the sequel.

Since Zhang Dai, by his own testimony, had been writing his Ming history since 1628, when Chongzhen, the man who was to be the last emperor, had just ascended the throne, it is virtually certain that some of Zhang's conclusions about the past had already been reached before the Ming fall—and, having been written during the Ming dynasty itself, showed a mixture of reticence and frankness over what could and could not be discussed. But despite problems caused by such changes in focus, his *Stone Casket* offers an absorbing panorama of the fifteen very different men who ruled China between 1368 and 1627: of their attitudes to power and to usurpation, to border policy and the handling of foreign policy, to astonishing military skill and starkly incompetent strategies, to problems of domestic taxation and military expenditure, to genuine artistic abilities and grandiose programs of palace building.

One can see from some passages how Zhang had to be cautious toward whichever dynasty he was writing under: one clear example was the usurpation of the throne in 1402 by Yongle, uncle to the young ruler who had been made successor to the throne by the founding emperor himself. Zhang's delicate wording shows that the power of reprisal from the state still hung heavily over the historian who made a rash remark. So, as Zhang tactfully phrased it, even if it might be true that the usurper's actions "left something to be desired," yet "how can we judge the wisdom and achievements [of Yongle] through the overcautious mind frame of later generations?" As for the young ruler whose throne was taken from him, Zhang placed him in the context of some earlier figures from Chinese history who had also had the mandate snatched from them, with the comment that "their sacrifices for the country have few comparisons in history; but I can, at most, emit a heart-felt sigh and feel the weight of my brush. No faithful subject is allowed to record their history." Only with his discussions of the running sores that marked the growing incapacity of two of the three emperors who ruled between 1572 and 1627 did Zhang's *Stone Casket* history show clearly how post-1644 knowledge of the Ming collapse affected the way that he phrased the weaknesses (and occasionally the strengths) of those under whose reigns he had lived.

Any kind of history had its problems, Zhang Dai knew: "Political history," he had written, often "suffers from factual errors; whereas family histories are distorted by flattery." The third basic genre of history, what was termed "untamed" or "unofficial history," often consisted of "nothing but fabrications." But what of finding some other organizing principle, something that could place the Zhang family members within the history of the country as a whole, and yet keep their eccentricities and inner natures whole? Zhang saw a way one could avoid the problem of flattery by following Sima Qian's own example of sharp commentary combined with brevity. At the same time, he curbed the sense of passion and excess that had lain at the heart of his series of informal family biographies written in 1651.

As a historian, Zhang had to decide how much space to allocate to members of his own family; some of them were remarkable people, and it is not surprising that in the biographical sections of the *Stone Casket* history certain signs of family and emotional ties appeared. Zhang gave to great-grandfather Wengong, for instance, a prominent place among the classical scholars of the Ming dynasty. In his lengthy biography, Zhang concentrated mainly on Wengong's philosophical interest in the volatile world of late Ming political theory, though not before presenting his great-grandfather as a man of outstanding moral character: "manly and stern" even as a youngster, passionate about moral issues and an early and devoted believer in the intuitionist philosophical theories of the great Ming scholar Wang Yangming. Without going into details in the biography, Zhang merely mentioned that great-grandfather had shown exemplary courage in defending his father during the protracted trial arising from the botched military campaigns in the southwest.

Zhang took the time needed to give his view of his great-grandfather's character: "In the year 1570 he studied in the imperial university, passing the national examinations the next year. Following the final-round interviews, he was declared the highest score of all first-tier examinees and received the position of secretary in the Confucian Study Academy. Thus, he obtained his first taste of royal benevolence. It propelled him to swallow his pride and engage in further studies, hoping to establish a name for himself among scholars and officials." Great-grandfather's method was simple, Zhang continued. "Every day, after finishing his official duties as scribe, he would search in the imperial library for documents on government and law and read them thoroughly. In this way, he organized and refined his literary knowledge. Settling down in a stately residence, Wengong prided himself on his writings. After but a brief time at court, he began to look beyond his official duties for new endeavors, gathering a group of students and lecturing them about the ways of the world. He would remember even those he had barely met and the shoes of his students often blocked his doorway. Occasionally, he would comment on national affairs with his close friends. He did not tolerate extremism, always seeking a balance between strong views."

The portrait, carefully and skillfully built up, left readers with the sense of Wengong as an activist within a great Confucian philosophical tradition, one who valued deeds over words and yet was ultimately destroyed by his own inability to get his father exonerated of all the charges leveled against him by jealous and corrupted officials in the southwest. This failure to reverse injustice ate away at Wengong's self-respect and sense of duty, and eventually killed him. Zhang Dai presented a deathbed scene in which Wengong, attended to the last by his students, suddenly shouted out the words "Your Majesty" several times before murmuring, "And yet this court does not lack for talented men." In a revealing slip—if slip it was—in his final comments Zhang twice referred to the deceased Wengong as "my ancestor," rather than by his name as any writer not connected to the family would have done. As Zhang Dai wrote in his closing lines of the biography, "Whilst Wang Yangming's teachings often lost themselves in Buddhist vagueness, my ancestor managed to maintain a solid moral standard."

Tucked in by Zhang Dai at the beginning of Wengong's biography was great-great-grandfather, and at the end Zhang made room for grandfather Rulin. As a perfect example of the ways that the compiler of the history could tilt the contents at intervals toward his own family, grandfather appeared again, a page or two later, this time at much greater length, in the biography of one of great-grandfather's closest friends and classmates, Deng Yizan. In the protracted anecdote that Zhang Dai included in the *Stone Casket* biography of Deng, grandfather's scholarly commitment and abilities were challenged by Deng during a visit to Shaoxing sometime after great-grandfather's death. The story has Deng bitterly criticizing grandfather for irresponsibly wasting his life, only to have grandfather triumphing in the end and responding to Deng's criticisms by writing a flawless essay on a theme from the Confucian classics, leaving Deng to exclaim that the young man would go far after all and bring further renown to the Zhang family. In a happy ending twist, Zhang Dai wrote that immediately after this test, grandfather took the provincial exams and came out as number six in the whole province. And the following year, grandfather traveled to Beijing and passed the state examinations successfully.

There were other family members and friends elsewhere in the *Stone Casket*. In a short biographical section on "artists of special skill," Zhang Dai included second uncle Zhongshu, praising him for his range and talent as both a collector and a painter. "As a child," wrote Zhang Dai, Zhongshu "understood the principles of painting; since his maternal uncle Zhu Shimen had a great collection of early masters, from dawn to dusk [Zhongshu] could study and compare them, and as a young man was able to visit many other famous collections." Zhang Dai especially praised his uncle's subtlety of brushstroke and the "spirited refinement" of his long landscape scrolls, writing that in this regard Zhongshu excelled even the great landscape masters of the Yuan dynasty. Zhang quoted from the most famous of the late Ming artists, Dong Qichang, who had written approvingly that Zhongshu had "the wisdom and experience gained from reading thousands of books and traveling thousands of miles, yet had kept his emotional responses spacious and spontaneous." In a concluding sentence, Zhang added the personal detail that Chen Hongshou was his uncle Zhongshu's son-in-law, which was why Chen had learned so much from Zhongshu in terms of style and technique.

It was natural, perhaps, for Zhang Dai to add Chen Hongshou to the *Stone Casket* in the same fine arts category of biographies. Chen had died in 1652, after his brief service to the prince of Lu, a short period as a shaven-headed monk and a final wild burst of energy as a painter, during which he had created an astonishing outpouring of forty-two paintings in eleven days, one of them devoted entirely to Tao Qian's poem on the endless and compelling quest for wine. Though short, this biography too must have shown readers that Zhang Dai knew Chen well as a person. After mentioning Chen's service with the prince of Lu in Shaoxing (though not his drunken vomiting) and his particular skills in landscape and flower paintings, as well as in renderings of spirits and immortals, Zhang proceeded to a frank summary of his friend's artistic career: "Though Chen's contemporaries paid handsome prices for his paintings, he himself was extravagant and reckless, never managed to get a proper financial base, and when he died did not even have a grave site ready. As [Chen] wrote on one of his self-portraits, 'Without thinking about it I achieved an empty fame and have ended up a poverty-stricken ghost. Failing to die as the dynasty fell, I was neither loyal nor filial.' " It was a curious way to say farewell to an old friend: the reason may well be that in 1650 Chen had finally abandoned any pretense of being a Ming loyalist on the run, and had made his peace with powerful collaborators whose patronage he now accepted.

Other—sometimes less obvious—linkages to Zhang's own past or his prior interests also slipped into the massive book. Thus in the monographic section on astronomy, Zhang showed the ongoing interest in Matteo Ricci, which his grandfather had first encouraged, by noting that Ricci had worked closely with several Ming astronomers, but that the Western man's influence on the Chinese sciences had been minimal, due to the fact that "the imperial appointees to the bureau of astronomy considered [Ricci] to be a foreign barbarian and thus regarded him slightingly, so that after Ricci had died, his skills and the practical importance of this Western learning were all erased."

When Zhang at last completed it in 1664, the *Stone Casket* history was almost two and a half million characters in length, and covered in detail all the years from the rise of the Ming founding emperor in the 1360s down to Emperor Tianqi's death in 1627. The *Sequel* was naturally shorter, since it dispensed altogether with the topical essays on virtually every aspect of governance from cosmology to economics, which were thoroughly covered in the *Stone Casket* history, so it only had to span some twenty years of chronological outlines in the "annals" of the rulers and the later princely contenders. But because of the complexity and intense detail of Zhang's fifty-six biographical chapters, the *Sequel*'s final draft still contained around five hundred thousand characters, making a total of over three million words for the work as a unified whole.

In a letter about history writing that he sent to a close friend in 1669 (or perhaps a little later), Zhang claimed that he had at last achieved a kind of calmness about the past, that he was able to detach himself from events and view them with tranquility. "I have been trying to keep my heart like reflections in still water or a Qin bronze mirror, rather than to render my own independent judgments. Therefore, when I put brush to paper and portray things, the beauty and the ugliness just present themselves. I dare not say I am describing [the past] with chiseled vividness; I am only trying to catch the likeness of things as they are, without distortion." In reality, Zhang as historian was a passionate witness to the past that had ended up almost destroying him. And especially in the overtly personal comments that he made at the end of each section of the *Sequel* (and sometimes in an introductory reflection that acted as the opening for a given theme) he tried to catch some of the pithiness, brevity and moral sharpness that he believed were a signature of Sima Qian.

Zhang spent much of the *Sequel* assigning blame for the Ming fall and charting how different people reacted to the crisis as it was coming upon them. The last of the Ming emperors, Chongzhen, as Zhang explained, had been a decent person whose rule failed helplessly because of his predecessor's incompetence and Chongzhen's own inability to use creatively the resources that he did have. He was a man to be pitied as much as blamed. However, for the prince of Fu, who briefly held court in Nanjing during late 1644 and early 1645, Zhang Dai felt only a deep contempt, which he reinforced by a historiographical judgment, refusing to acknowledge him with inclusion in the annals of the dynasty: "I could have attached the prince of Fu to the annals [placed just after Emperor Chongzhen]," wrote Zhang in his commentary, "but decided not to, based on the fact that the prince of Fu was not only stupid but also recklessly promiscuous," and employed the worst possible men as ministers in his brief reign. The prince was "like a person intending to poison a tiger taking the arsenic himself: he is only concerned with killing the tiger, yet has forgotten that he himself has taken arsenic and will collapse first!"

And what could one say of the prince of Lu, briefly protector of the realm in Shaoxing and later for many years a fugitive, except that as a musician he showed a "certain facility with the *qin*"? The prince of Lu had no other obvious strong points, unless one counted his initial ability to please. As Zhang put it, presumably reflecting on his own brief experience in the prince's entourage, the prince of Lu would trust you one minute and abandon you as "worthless" or "intolerable" as soon as somebody new came along. "Finally the prince had many advisors yet could not benefit from one advisor; he heard many kinds of advice yet could not benefit from one piece of advice. His court was crowded with retainers, but the prince was unaided. The advisors left him in disappointment, and scattered like duckweed. A rudderless boat will float with the wind and never reach any destination. The prince of Lu's wisdom was even inferior to that of a boatman. How could one plan matters concerning national fate together with him?"

In such an atmosphere of graft, greed and incompetence, "generals" like Fang Guo'an rapidly emerged to power. Despite the disasters that Fang personally had brought on him and his family, Zhang's biographical entry on General Fang was surprisingly fair, even though it started with some harsh words: "Fang Guo'an was a native of Zhuji, Zhejiang. When he was young, he was a rascal indulging himself in gambling, wine, and fighting with people, and was detested by his community. When he secretly took his clansman's farming ox to sell and was discovered by its owner, his clansmen unanimously decided to banish him and forbade him to enter the ancestors' shrine. So Guo'an went away and joined the army under Zuo Liangyu, Marquis of Ningnan. . . . Guo'an was short and stout, and always marched at the head of his troops. From being a soldier of the lowest rank, he ascended to be the commander of a whole army."

After a summary of Fang's many campaigns during the upheavals of the 1640s, Zhang offered his own evaluation of the man: "Guo'an was illiterate. When he received official documents, he had people read them aloud to him, so that when he dictated revisions, they were usually clear and properly written. In face of the gravest danger, he had no fear, but chatted and laughed at ease instead. He was strict about rewards and punishments. He often set up big prizes of cash, and did not grudge wine at the celebrations of birthdays. With transgressors, he showed no leniency to those below the rank of deputy commander. He attacked with extraordinary strategies beyond the comprehension of most people. His soldiers were good at one-to-one combat and various tactics of risky movements and deception. When not engaged in work, they were given to petulant behavior. Consequently, his troops were imperious, yielding to no one."

As he had in the *Stone Casket* history, so in the *Sequel* Zhang had to decide how much to insert his friends' and family's stories. He did not push this in any forceful way, but in the section in the *Sequel* on "outstanding artists" he repeated the short biographies of second uncle Zhongshu and Chen Hongshou that appeared in the *Stone Casket* history. (Indeed it is quite possible that he wrote these two biographies initially for the *Sequel* and decided only later to insert them into the *Stone Casket* history as well.) And Zhang did, in the biography of the treacherous official Ma Shiying, insert a copy of the whole letter that he had written as a "cotton-robed commoner" to the prince of Lu. Furthermore, in the section on martyrs from Jiangxi province, Zhang pointed out in his concluding commentary that he had visited the war-torn

areas of Jiangxi in person and had talked to the rebellious survivors there.

Zhang's comments in the *Sequel* constantly shine through
with emotions that link to his own experience—not just in the
extensive chapters on the suicides and resisters across the years of
fighting in the 1640s and 1650s, but even in sections such as that
on "the world of letters." There Zhang echoed some of his
thoughts from *The Night Ferry* and pointed out that many of the
most published writers of the day were mere "repositories of
knowledge" who "lacked spontaneity and originality" and might
just as well have been "walking bookshelves" rather than authors, since "they all read without digesting, and their writings
had nothing striking in them." Zhang mocked the claim that the
outstanding writers of the Ming dynasty had all been holders of
the highest examination degrees; as a counterweight, he wrote,
he preferred to devote at least half his space to "underprivileged
scholars" to show for all time that "literary excellence cannot be
judged by social status or success in the civil examinations."

In the midst of developing his panorama of combat and dynastic fall, in which Zhang sought to give coverage to those from
all walks of life—the rebels as well as the defenders of the realm,
the martyrs and the brave as well as the traitors, women as well
as men, low born and high, artists and eunuchs—the idea of the
meaning and significance of loyalty was always a dominant
theme. In his preamble to the section on "heroic deaths during
the upheaval year of 1644," Zhang tried to think through the
ramifications of loyalty and sacrifice, themes he had first explored in his author's preface to the *Profiles of Righteous and Hon-*

orable People through the Ages, written during the 1620s. As he now rephrased it: "We often comment that this person died a glorious death, or that person died a shameful death. To draw a comparison, it is like a chaste woman who follows her husband in death, saying 'I give my life,' whereas a wanton woman dies of sexual abandon, also saying 'I give my life.' Death itself comes to both alike, but the causes of death vary." Shifting to a different metaphor, Zhang noted, "Fire fighters die of fire, and people taking advantage of a conflagration to loot also die of fire. Although both die of fire, we cannot say the two situations make no difference." Most officials in China during the bleak years, Zhang felt, were like the looters in that second category: "Despite outbreaks of war all over the country, the officials thought that it was none of their business, until the fire scorched their houses, jade and stone burned together, moths beating at the lamp and swallows living in the main hall both became ashes. How could those ministers who followed Emperor Chongzhen in death during 1644 excuse their former dereliction of duty by merely giving their trivial lives?"

And what was one to make of those who gave their lives as martyrs to the incompetent and lecherous prince of Fu or the hapless prince of Lu? Were their deaths a meaningful response to the needs of their dynasty and their personal definitions of loyalty and duty? Or, to the contrary, were such people just like women "married to an alcoholic and violent husband. The husband beats his wife and concubine because of his alcoholism, but his wife and concubine do not hate him for the abuse. On the day when the husband perishes, the wife and concubine are still willing to follow him in death to maintain their reputation for chastity. Isn't their case much more difficult than that of a married couple who are deeply in love, so the wife is willing to die with the husband to eternalize their relationship?"

It is hard to believe that as he wrote those passages Zhang Dai was not thinking of his friend Qi Biaojia. For though the biography of Qi that he wrote and inserted in the *Sequel* was long and laudatory, Zhang's final comment was in its way unsparing. Many years before, on the night he drowned himself, Qi Biaojia had written a poem and left it for his family. Qi had written that the collapse of the Ming dynasty left him only two clear choices for action: One was to build and lead a strong resistance, so as to reclaim the soil of China for the Chinese people. The other was to commit suicide to show his loyalty to the old order and to avoid bringing shame either to his ancestors or to his descendants. Regaining China from its conquerors would perhaps take generations and an intuitive sense of when to act. Qi wrote:

> To die as a martyr, that is something easier,
> And so it is I choose the easier way.
> What I most desire is to keep myself unsullied,
> And leave the more difficult path to the worthies of a later
>   time.

The exact timing of his death was unimportant, Qi had written. No matter whether he had served the Ming fifteen years earlier or later, the basic point would have been the same. Therefore the decision seemed to Qi clear enough:

So with a smile I go down to the Yellow Springs,
But my life-energy will remain with the earth and sky.

Sometime during his own years of flight, Zhang Dai wrote a
matching poem in response to his dead friend, a poem that was
designed to be a rebuttal to Qi's logic concerning the two choices
he had faced:

It is true the chaste woman and the loyal official
Give service to one, but never to two.
Yet hiding away as a recluse is only a temporary gesture,
And in the circumstances could be the most timely strategy.
Over the past years I have thought this over carefully;
And to die is truly something that is not easy! . . .

Qi had claimed that dying fifteen years earlier or later made
little difference in the long run of moral action. But, said Zhang,
the exact moment of death mattered profoundly, if only because
delaying one's death gave one more time to wonder what was the
best course of action.

Now in the *Stone Casket*'s *Sequel* Zhang felt the need to make
a definitive judgment; though it was hard to say so, he felt that
Qi had made a mistake in giving his own life, especially for
someone as worthless as the prince of Fu or the later pretenders.
And yet the mistake itself had been courageous, even exemplary:
"Alas! As to Qi Biaojia's death, it is appropriate to call him loyal,
but not appropriate to call him really shrewd. Nobody in the position he was in would have any real reason to die. However, the

current situation was getting worse to such an extent that he felt there was absolutely no way out. As a sharp-sighted person he decided that death was the only choice! [Qi] Biaojia gave his life when he felt it was the right time. He made up his mind promptly and went ahead without fear. He was able to practice moral conduct, because his intelligence was stimulated by crisis events." It was because of his clarity of judgment and decisiveness that Qi was to be admired and included in the pantheon of the truly virtuous.

Interest in the Ming as history was spreading, now that any realistic hopes for the Ming loyalist cause had vanished except in the hearts of a few tenacious believers. In 1659 a concerted attack by Ming sympathizers on the Nanjing region failed, though many local people—from the gentry to the farmers—showed their support for the insurgents. The last active Ming pretender to an imperial title—even if of his own making—was cornered and killed in 1662 by pro-Manchu troops on the borders of Burma. That same year the prince of Lu, who had drunk so copiously at Zhang's home back in 1645 and had been drifting around coastal China in search of a resting place ever since his flight from Shaoxing, died on the island of Quemoy. A year later, in 1663, cousin Pei, blind doctor and imaginative military planner, son of sixth uncle, ten years younger that Zhang Dai, died after a short illness, at the age of fifty-six. According to Zhang, Pei's death came swiftly and unexpectedly: "He took to his bed and was unable to rise from it again." Zhang presided at the funeral services and offered eulogies as befitted Pei's eldest living relative. He also contrasted Pei with another blind scholar— brilliant but bitter and reclusive—whom Zhang had known well. It was Pei's wonderful agility and freshness that Zhang Dai remembered best.

Despite the newfound public recognition of his historical skill by Gu and other scholars, it was in 1663 and 1664 while finishing the *Stone Casket* that Zhang Dai wrote his bleakest poems about the struggles that he still faced to keep himself and his family fed. Though he presumably had received some kind of stipend for his contributions to Gu Yingtai's history, there is no sign that his family in Shaoxing was living any better as the years drifted by. In several poems written around the time of Pei's death, Zhang wryly featured his own ineptitude—slopping night soil out of the bucket as he tried to restore the wilting eggplants and pumpkins, or envying his neighbors who fed silkworms from their leafy mulberry trees. "Of what use now," he asked as he helplessly circled his courtyard viewing his almost barren trees, "are all my scholarship and knowledge of economics?"

Some of Zhang's poems lay within the conventional realms of bucolic verse and echoed the themes of loss and retribution that appeared so often in his writings. But sometimes he broke through the genre into a franker world: in one such poem he gave his exact age as sixty-seven, which enables us to place the writing of the poem to the year 1664. Invoking Liang Hong, as Zhang did in line three, gave the poem a special edge of melancholy; Liang Hong, a famous poet who lived a century before Tao Qian, had initially been poor and forced to husk rice for a living. He was helped in this task by his wife, who, though she herself was from a wealthy family, worked at his side and served Liang loyally during the hardship years. Zhang called his poem "Pounding Rice":

Working with mortar and pestle,
I have to rest twice in just a hundred strokes.
Chanting verse on the talents of Liang Hong,
I attempt to muster what feeble strength I have.
I was born to a wealthy family, surrounded by ritual
    objects,
Never learning agricultural skills.
Rice was plentiful in the granaries,
A hundred people worked for my meals.
Several dozen servants
Attended my needs with the utmost care.
When my meals were served to me on a platter,
The cooks looked on anxiously for my reaction.
If I was pleased, all would be pleased,
If I was angry, all would fear.
Now, they have left me,
Not one out of a hundred remains.
My sons are scattered in all directions,
Their own children wailing at their knees.
I buy several bushels of rice from the market,
Finding my remaining sons to be restlessly hungry.
The old man then carries out the mortar,
How dare he delay in pounding the rice for a minute?
After a few dozen strokes,
His breath becomes ragged.
I now regret that, when I was young,
I never learned to use the mortar and pestle.
Counting up my years,
I am sixty-seven now,

A useless man.
Pounding rice was never my responsibility.
Yet how can my arms be strengthened?
Only by pounding rice in the village.
I look back at my young sons,
Who are toiling painfully away at their studies.

As Zhang had written in another poem a few years before, his surviving concubines were far from showing the grace and courtesy of Liang Hong's wife:

My two concubines are old, withered like monkeys,
And can barely draw water from the well.
They clamor for both wheat and firewood,
Filling the day with their angry roaring.
Each day at dawn, I rise to no breakfast,
Forced to run about for food before the sun has risen.
I have lived in this fashion for eleven years,
And feel ashamed to even speak of it.

Perhaps it was cousin Pei's sudden death that gave Zhang the idea of writing what he called his "Self-written Obituary," completed in 1665. Such "obituaries" were a venerable genre, as Zhang Dai knew, and had been practiced not only by his greatly admired Tao Qian, but also by great-grandfather's close friend Xu Wei. Zhang Dai gave a hint of the context of his decision within the obituary itself: "After the events of 1644 I was in a complete daze: I could neither find a noble death, nor work out how to live. With my white hairs wildly fluttering I inhabited a space on the edges of the human world, fearing that some dawn I would die in the morning dew, rotting away like the grass and the twigs. It occurred to me that some men of an earlier time, such as Wang Ji, Tao Qian, and Xu Wei, had written their own tomb inscriptions. Why should I not try to do the same thing? So I jotted down some preliminary thoughts, but soon realized that neither my own character nor my literary skills were of the right order of excellence. So I laid down my writing brush. But at once I picked it up again, for it occurred to me that there might be some point in passing on to others an ordered list of my obsessions and my faults."

Zhang's concept of how to present his shortcomings was lyrical and imaginative, though initially given a touch of restraint by his use of the third-person mode to describe himself, just as he had done in many of his other most personal writings. He began his obituary in these words: "Zhang Dai, a man whose family hailed from the realm of Shu, had the courtesy name Taoan. As a youth he was a real dandy, in love with the idea of excess: he loved exquisite shelter; he loved pretty maidservants; he loved handsome serving boys; he loved bright-colored clothes; he loved perfect food; he loved handsome horses; he loved colorful lanterns; he loved fireworks; he loved the theatre; he loved the trumpets' blare; he loved antiques; he loved paintings of flowers and birds. Besides which, seduced by tea and ravished by oranges, poisoned by stories and bewitched by poems, he drained to the lees the first half of his life, which has now become just dreams and illusions." Still writing in the third person, Zhang proceeded to contrast this early manhood with the years that followed: "When he turned fifty, his country was obliterated, his

family erased. He hid his traces by dwelling in the mountains. . . .
He wore cotton clothes, ate coarse vegetables, and often could
not even keep his stove alight. Casting his mind back to a time
twenty years before, it all seemed as if the world had been cut
adrift."

If occasionally he chanced to scrutinize himself, Zhang continued, it seemed that he had lived with seven paradoxes:

> The first was that in the past, even when wearing
> simple clothes, he compared himself to lofty dukes
> and earls; but in the present time, though coming
> from a distinguished family, he classed himself with
> lowly beggars. Thus were the wealthy and debased
> confounded.
>
> The second was that with property that was not
> even of the middling range, he felt himself able to
> compete with the richest man who ever lived; in a
> world with many routes to riches, he kept solitary
> watch by the stump [as a simple-minded peasant
> awaits a rabbit for his supper]. Thus the ideas of poor
> and the rich grew contradictory.
>
> The third was that, though raised among books, he
> went stomping off with the cavalry on the battlefield;
> aspiring to be a general, all he knew was being in an
> office pushing papers. How could he thus muddle up
> civilian life with the martial calling?
>
> The fourth was that though feeling himself a fit
> companion for the Jade Emperor above, without any
> need for flattery, on earth he consorted with beggar

children from the orphanage without being arrogant. Thus were the lines between honor and contempt kept blurred.

The fifth was that when he was weak, and people spat in his face, he left the spittle to dry by itself; when feeling strong, he whipped up his steed himself and advanced against the foe. Thus did flexibility and firmness stand opposed.

The sixth was that when competing for profit or fame, he was quite content to bring up the rear. But if it was in recreation, or in play, he let no one but himself be in the van. Thus did lightness and seriousness absurdly mingle.

The seventh was that when betting on a game of chess, or gambling with the dice, he never knew the difference between winning and losing; but when choosing the water for infusing his tea, he would carefully distinguish between adjacent streams. Thus, in him, did smartness and stupidity run together.

Exactly how one should disentangle these paradoxes, Zhang wrote, he would leave to others. For himself, he was content to let all the inconsistencies stay in place, especially since he had failed at almost everything he attempted, from scholarship to swordsmanship, from the norms of good conduct to the magical arts, from writing to horticulture.

A certain innate pride, however, led Zhang Dai to list all the books he had worked on to date: heading the list was the *Stone Casket* history and the biographies of Zhang family members.

Listed, too, were his other collections of biographies of worthies of the past as well as several studies of canonical texts from the Chinese scholarly traditions, such as the Four Books and *The Book of Changes*. Zhang included *The Dream Recollections of Taoan*, which he had completed in 1646, and *Tracing West Lake in a Dream*, which he was still working on. There were fifteen titles in all, though most were still in draft, and only the early volume of *Profiles* had been published for general distribution.

In a concluding section of his obituary, Zhang abruptly switched to the first person. After presenting some asides on his childhood health problems and his youthful precocity with words and wordplays, Zhang set the scene for his own impending departure: "I have prepared my tomb on Cock's Head Mountain in King Xiang Village, and my friend Li Yanzhai has written an inscription for it, containing these words: 'Alas! Here is the tomb of the Ming dynasty writer and scholar Zhang Changgong, who goes by the name Taoan.' A lonely orphan can become a lofty scholar, the tomb mound is ready for the steadfast loyalist; thus I am prepared for my journey to [King] Xiang Village. Next year will be my seventieth one, but since I do not yet know the exact day and month of my death and burial they are not given here."

Death did not come so promptly, for Zhang lacked his father's predictive powers. Instead, he continued writing and exploring the ways of controlling the past. The *Stone Casket*'s *Sequel* grew longer and longer as new material became available, though now he had to watch for Qing dynasty censors rather than Ming ones. The perfidy of late Ming officials and the clumsiness or stupidity of their rulers had become open terrain for the historian, but there was still the need for great caution as he dealt with those who had led the Qing armies to victory or laid waste the countryside. Though he listed them in his table of contents, some of the more controversial figures never did get into his history. It was just too dangerous. Zhang loved to tinker and to polish, and he continued to modify manuscripts like his *Tracing West Lake in a Dream*, his notes on the Four Books, and *The Night Ferry*; he updated his *Historical Gaps* to include Ming material and added new *Ming Profiles* to his earlier collection of the same name.

Zhang was also thinking back to the first collection he compiled as the Ming fell, and in 1674, at seventy-seven, he composed a new preface for those *Dream Recollections of Taoan*. It began with a disclaimer: "Of all my various work," he wrote, "I take the most pride in the *Stone Casket* history. [By contrast] *The Dream Recollections* was full of colloquial diction and folk chanting, of humorous stories and trivial details. And to those I added certain colorful strokes, to get the version of the essays we have here. Reading it, one feels one has penetrated mountains and rivers, that one has seen the customs of the places, and glimpsed the 'beauty of the palaces and ancestral temples.' But is not the spirit of the book closer to the recluses of past times, or those who mourned the wild grasses growing, even if it seems to be told in a jocular or lighthearted way? I was writing a series of set pieces, and had no intention of gaining fame from them. From south of the Yangzi I gathered everyone into my nest, the Taoists and the swordsmen, the ritual experts, the performers and the artisans.

"As it happened those days were a time of peace and the whole world seemed at ease. I made my home in Dragon Neighborhood, amid the loveliest gardens, pavilions and ponds, the finest orchards and rice fields. My annual income was in the thousands. As time went by I sank into a dissolute life in every way possible: there were cockfights and hunting with falcons, gambling and kickball, the music of the *qin* and all sorts of other performing arts—there was nothing I did not try. From now back to those times is thirty years; I have kept my house gates closed and said 'no' to visitors, and the visitors have gradually distanced themselves from me. Now if I lean on my stick and go into town, there are many who do not know my family of origin. This secretly delights me. I have even taken a couple of new names, 'The butterfly dreamer,' and 'Old man stone.'

"As to that book I wrote, *The Stone Casket* history, I have buried it inside my Langhuan Mountain; and this little volume of *Dream Recollections*, which you see before you and for which I have written this preface, that too I shall store away."

Over the space of many years, Zhang had been assembling his occasional writings into a collection he called his *Langhuan Wenji* (Collected writings from the land of Langhuan). Langhuan, he told us in a short essay, was a "paradise-place" first visited by a scholar in the Jin dynasty, centuries before. Such visions of the accidental discovery of a previously secret and hidden world, Zhang knew full well, had lain at the very center of Chinese sensibility ever since in the fifth century Tao Qian wrote his celebrated tale "The Peach Blossom Spring." In that story, Tao told of a fisherman who, traveling along a winding stream, found himself in a forest of blossoming peach trees, whose petals covered the water. As the stream narrowed, he came across a fissure in the rocky walls around him and, squeezing through, he found himself in a tranquil and perfect land of prosperous farms and contented families. The people living there welcomed him and told him that long ago they had escaped the fighting and the terror that accompanied the Qin dynasty's unification of the Chinese empire by coming to this spot, and here they had lived in peace for many centuries, oblivious to the rise and fall of dynasties that had been going on in the world outside. They entertained the fisherman well and listened with amazement to his stories. But when he finally departed, none of them chose to accompany him; their only request was that he not tell anyone that they were there. Disregarding their pleas, the fisherman marked the entrance through the rock with care and hurried to tell the local governor what he had seen. At once a search party was sent out, but though they found the markings of the route, none of them could find the way back into the valley.

Zhang Dai wrote an essay on Tao's vision of the Peach Blossom Spring in which he discussed the rarity of finding such a description of a space that was beyond all types of formalized time. In a world that elsewhere was dominated by calendars, cyclical dates, dynastic labels, seasonal solstices and festivals, the people of Peach Blossom Spring "knew heat and cold but not summer or winter, knew germination and harvest but not spring and autumn. Without rulers or officials, they were spared the anguish of taxes and examinations." Instead of trying to force the calendar of the outer world on the people of Peach Blossom Spring, wrote Zhang, how much better would it be if the outer world accepted the forgotten valley's dateless calendar, which proceeded according to the natural rhythms of life and death.

Despite this praise for the open and unstructured world of the Peach Blossom Spring, Zhang Dai took a rather different stance in his own rendering of the Paradise of Langhuan. True, in Zhang's telling there was still a traveler who lost his way, but this one was a scholar, not a fisherman. And the scholar found, not a stream covered with blossoms and a village full of happy and carefree farmers, but a sardonic sage dozing on a rock. After greeting the sage courteously enough, Zhang Dai's scholar became boastful, telling the sage that—apart from the books written in the past twenty years or so—he had read all the books of earlier times. Smiling quietly, the sage opened a door concealed in the rocks and ushered the scholar into a series of secret chambers. There, that scholar found, lay all the written knowledge of the world, from every country and every time. In one of these rooms were stored all the Chinese books yet known, in another, all the history and geographies both of China and of all the foreign lands. They came to one more heavy door, this one bearing the sign PARADISE OF LANGHUAN. Two great dogs guarded the site, and inside the scholar found "all the histories of ancient generations prior to the Qin and Han, and unheard-of countries far across the seas." After the sage had offered him wine and fruit "of a heavenly freshness," the scholar who had visited the book-filled paradise stepped out of the rock enclosure, saying that he wished "to find lodgings for the night but would return another day to read all these books." The sage just smiled, and once the scholar was outside, the rock gates slammed shut behind him. Searching for the entrance with care, the scholar could find no trace of it: "All he could see was a boulder covered with moss, with wild grasses, and with ivy."

Zhang Dai's grandfather had known an earlier version of this story and used the term *Paradise of Langhuan* to describe the

Happiness Garden when he first took Zhang there as a little child. Zhang Dai later used a more personal version of the same name for a place he built in his mind, as he lay in hiding in the hills, and began to gather his swirls of memory into some kind of order for his *Dream Recollections of Taoan*. "*The Dream Recollections*," he wrote, "must have a relation to the karma. Often in my dreams I come to a hermitage of rock, close to a mountain with deep grottos, before which flows a fierce stream whose waters tumble like snow. Among the strangely shaped and ancient pines and rocks, all kinds of famous flowers bloom. In my dream I sit in their midst. A servant boy brings me choice tea and fruits. Shelves full of books are all around me. Opening the different volumes I take a look, and find the pages covered with writings in unknown scripts—tadpole traces, bird feet markings, twisted branches. And in my dream I am able to read them all, to make sense of everything despite its difficulty. Peacefully beyond care, I dream this dream each night, and think about it when I wake."

This, said Zhang, was the retreat that he would build one day. The spaces would be clean and precisely aligned, the trees growing thickly all about. There would be water and hills and flowers, with paths that led down to the river. There would be pavilions with views of the mountains. There would be a stele with the inscription PARADISE OF LANGHUAN. There would be a shrine with a memorial inscription marking it as the site of Zhang's own grave, and monks from the monastery nearby would gather there and burn incense in his name. There would be study halls, with a view over a lake shrouded by willows, where he could read in peace. A small, sinuous stream would give access to his boat in case he wished to travel on the lake. A larger river would take him to the north.

But before he embarked on that great journey, he would come to a bridge that spanned the river. It was an old bridge built of stone and shaded by trees and shrubs. If he chose to, he could pause there on the bridge and under the trees. He could sit there and listen to the wind. And, under the trees and touched by the wind, he would rest from the cares of the world and "be at one with the moon."

Of Zhang's very last years we get only some fleeting glimpses. He was eighty-one when he lovingly recalled, in poetry and prose, the sound of his mother's voice as she recited the sutra of the white-robed Guanyin at the time of his birth. The following year he wrote a brief poem entitled simply "New Year's Day, 1679." At this time civil war against the Qing regime was being waged in the south by former collaborators, and the poem seems to suggest a quickening of his blood at the thought of the re-newed conflict, interspersed with the ambiguous invocations of those twin Chinese symbols of longevity, the pine trees and the crane:

> Old men are always worrying about something,
> As one gets thinner one can't even fill one's clothes.
> Halberds are raised, the words grow more incisive;
> Muscles dissected, we see their intricate connections.
> The pine is gnarled, it need not wait for age;
> The crane is gaunt—is that because of hunger?
> Here am I in the land of plenty:
> But still I need victory in battle to make me fat.

The last writing of any kind that we have from Zhang's own hand is dated from the eighth lunar month of 1680, just around the time of his eighty-third birthday. It is in the form of a preface to a not yet completed book entitled *Portraits with Commentary of the Imperishable Worthies of the Shaoxing Region in the Ming* and shows how, even during these late years of his life, Zhang was still busy with his plans to organize the past. In the preface, he discusses how he had been busy for some years making a collection of the portraits of these worthy figures. In particular, he had been accumulating images and writing comments on those who had "three imperishable attributes—namely their integrity, their accomplishments, and their words." With Xu Wei's grandson for a literary collaborator and companion, wrote Zhang, he had been going from door to door among the Shaoxing residents, seeking those who had pictorial records from the past to share with him.

As word of his quest spread, wrote Zhang, people responded accordingly, "some sending family images of famous figures from many hundreds of miles away," though it had also to be said that with other families, "One might wait for years and years, but never receive a single one."

As the collection began to grow, Zhang continued, the power of these dead exemplars soon entered his being and affected him profoundly: "In the presence of the masters of moral teaching, I trembled as one does in bed at night; in the presence of the loyal and the filial, I felt ashamed that I lacked those same virtues; facing those who were pure and principled, I blamed myself for worrying about fame and profit; in the presence of the great scholars of classical studies, I regretted the shallowness of my own readings in the canonical poems and the histories; facing those who had dedicated themselves to public service, I regretted how I had let the locusts make clean pickings of the fertile crops; and before the geniuses in literature and painting, I realized that I myself lacked even the smallest skill." So strong was the power of their example that "I felt a deep sense of shame, so that my spirit shattered out of fear, my very features were totally transformed, and no matter whether sleeping or awake I felt their force. Yet this ability to arouse and inspire me took me to the point where, without my even knowing it, my hands and feet began to dance."

Zhang and Xu collected a total of 108 portraits. Many, of course, were strangers whom Zhang had never known in person. Others, like his great-great-grandfather Tianfu and great-grandfather Wengong, had died before his birth, but their resonances had colored much of his upbringing. Yet others had, with their presence, shaped his very life and consciousness. Grandfather was there, along with Granny Zhu's father and second uncle Zhongshu. General Zhu, the skilled administrator and reckless eater, at whose funeral Zhang Dai had seen the tidal bore, was there. So were Zhang's two close companions from that fabled moment, Chen Hongshou and Qi Biaojia, who kept him company at the seawall as the water crashed around them. Both were smiling slightly, Qi in his embroidered robe of office and Chen dressed as a simple commoner. "I placed these images on the altar in my family school room," wrote Zhang in 1680, "[and] made offerings of jujubes and pears before them; morning and evening I paid them my respects. Whenever I opened a book to read, I would be sitting face-to-face with them." It was his hope, wrote Zhang, that these portraits along with his commentary would themselves become "an imperishable record of the past" and that "people of countless future generations will read this volume." He signed his preface with yet another new name he had recently adopted for himself: "Old Man with an Ancient Sword."

Though Zhang Dai had known so many people across the years, though he had so many children, though he had labored so long to catch the lives of others as they glided by, it seems that nobody took the trouble to record the exact time or the circumstances of his final journey. So we are free to remember him at the end, if we wish, as giving birth to his final words like the leper woman giving birth to her baby, calling at once for a light so that he could see if his cherished offspring was free from blemish. Or we can remember him sitting bent over the study table, as so many from his family had sat before, staring fixedly at his final collection of images from the past: an old man who, without his having willed it in any deliberate way, found suddenly that his hands and feet were dancing.

NOTES

PROLOGUE

1   **Ming society:** For basic coverage in English, see *The Cambridge History of China*, vol. 7, pt. 1, and vol. 8, pt. 2 (1988 and 1998); and *The Dictionary of Ming Biography*, 2 vols. (1976). The journal *Ming Studies* (*Mingshi yanjiu*), 1975 to present, has excellent coverage of current research and new publications on the Ming in all fields of scholarship. Three fine and accessible introductions to Ming society are Timothy Brook, *The Confusions of Pleasure*; Ray Huang, *1587, A Year of No Significance*; and Craig Clunas, *Superfluous Things*.

1   **Zhang Dai's life:** The first biographical study in English was that by Fang Chao-ying, "Chang Tai" [Zhang Dai], in Arthur Hummel, ed., *Eminent Chinese of the Ch'ing Period* (1943), a fine example of Dr. Fang's scholarship. The first extensive Western-language study of Zhang's famous *Taoan Mengyi* was Philip Kafalas's "Nostalgia and the Reading of the Late Ming Essay: Zhang Dai's Tao'an Mengyi." (1995). I have benefited greatly from Hu Yimin's two studies of Zhang Dai published in 2002 and She Deyu's 2004 study of Zhang's family. For the life and writings of a near contemporary of Zhang Dai, Li Yu (1610–80), who, like Zhang, was a scholar, sensualist, professional writer and director of acting troupes, see the absorbing study

by Patrick Hanan, *The Invention of Li Yu*. For a valuable annotated French translation of *Taoan Mengyi*, see Brigitte Teboul-Wang.

4   **Ming population:** Figures drawn from *The Cambridge History of China*, vol. 8, pt. 2, p. 438.

5   **Ming landholding:** A recent analysis with extensive backup sources is in Xue Yong's "Agarian Urbanization," Yale University, History PhD, 2006.

7   **Ming politics:** For a recent study of the Ming founder, see Sarah Schneewind, ed., "The Image of the First Ming Emperor." On eunuchs and scholars, see John Dardess, *Blood and History*; on morality and governance, see Charles Hucker, *Censorial System*, Cynthia Brokaw, *Ledgers of Merit and Demerit*, and Joanna Handlin, *Action in Late Ming Thought*. The Buddhist revival at the time is analyzed in Yü Chün-fang, *Renewal of Buddhism*.

8   **The Ming wall:** Two comprehensive studies are Arthur Waldron, *The Great Wall of China*, and Julia Lovell, *The Great Wall*. For the failed Ming campaigns against the Mongols, see *Cambridge History of China*, vol. 7, pt. 1, pp. 416–21.

9   **Manchu conquest:** Two major surveys are Frederic Wakeman, *The Great Enterprise*, and Lynn Struve, *The Southern Ming*.

12   **Zhang Dai's *Dream Recollections*:** The most comprehensive study is Philip Kafalas, *In Limpid Dream: Nostalgia and Zhang Dai's Reminiscences of the Ming*, EastBridge, 2007. I have also benefited greatly from the translation of the whole *Taoan Mengyi* into French by Brigitte Teboul-Wang (Paris, 1995). A fine analysis of the short vignette or essay form favored by Zhang Dai, with extensive translations, is given by Ye Yang, *Vignettes from the Late Ming: A Hsiao-p'in Anthology*.

CHAPTER ONE: CIRCLES OF PLEASURE

13   **Nanjing pleasures:** Zhang Dai, *Taoan Mengyi* [Dream recollections of Taoan] (hereafter cited as *TM*), section 4, number 2 (4/2). French translation of *TM* by Brigitte Teboul-Wang (hereafter cited as *T-W*), #48, p. 72. Zhang is describing the festival of the fifth day of the fifth lunar month, in Nanjing, on the Qinhuai River.

14   **First lanterns:** *TM* 4/10, "Shimei tang deng"; *T-W* #56, pp. 81–82 and notes; Xia ed. *TM*, p. 59, n. 3.

14   **Cheap lanterns:** *TM* 6/4; *T-W* #81, pp. 112–13.

15 **Shaoxing streets:** *TM* 6/4, "Shaoxing dengjing"; *T-W* #81, pp. 112–13. Kafalas (2007), pp. 86–87, has a full translation.

15 **Temple lanterns:** *TM* 6/4; *T-W* #81, pp. 112–13.

16 **Giant fish:** *TM* 6/15; *T-W* #92, pp. 123–24. On the donor, Tao Yunjia, see *TM,* ed. Xia, p. 108, nn. 5–7 and pp. 63–64, n. 1. Also in Kafalas (1995), pp. 86–87, and (2007), p. 37.

16 **The tidal bore:** *TM* 3/5, "Baiyang chao." For two fine prior translations of this celebrated passage, to both of which I am much indebted, see Kafalas (2007), p. 104, and *T-W* #35, pp. 58–59. Haining was across Hangzhou bay, west of the city. For the Kan and Zhe outcrops against which Zhang notes the wave also struck, see *Shaoxing fuzhi*, pp. 108–9. For the end of the tidal impact area, see ibid., p. 165, "chaozhi." (Special thanks to Shiyee Liu.) The funeral was for the deceased Minister Zhu Xieyuan; see *Mingshi*, pp. 2825–28, for his career and extraordinary girth. See also Qi Biaojia, *Qi Zhongmin Gong riji* (1992 ed., p. 1129), under Chongzhen 11th year, 8/4, for Qi's parallel diary entry. This source shows 1638 was the correct year; some variants of *TM* have 1640. See also *Qi Zhongmin Gong riji* (1937), *ce* 5, pt.1, pp. 23b–24.

17 **Shrine spring:** *TM* 3/3 and *T-W* #33, pp. 56–57.

18 **Snow Orchid tea:** *TM* 3/4 "lanxue cha" and *T-W* #34, pp. 57–58. Recipes: *TM* 4/8; see especially *T-W* #54, p. 79, for an elegant translation. Kafalas (2007), p. 47, discusses milk products.

19 **Polluted spring:** *TM* 3/6; *T-W* #36, pp. 59–60. Zhang and his friends played their own guessing games with water sources—see *TM* 3/7 "Min Laozi cha"; *T-W* #37, pp. 61–62; Ye, *Vignettes*, pp. 88–90, Kafalas (2007), pp. 82–83.

20 **Water circulated:** *TM* 7/13 "Yugong"; *T-W* #106, pp. 137–38, Kafalas (2007), pp. 93–94.

21 **Lantern craftsmen:** *TM* 4/10; *T-W* #56, pp. 81–82.

21 **Young conservator:** *TM* 4/10; *T-W* #56, pp. 81–82.

21 ***Qin* club:** *TM* 3/1; *T-W* #31, pp. 53–54, translates the manifesto. For the date of the club's founding, see *TM* 2/6. (*T-W* #21, p. 43, has the correct date of 1616 [not 1676 as in Xia edition *TM*, p. 27 n. 1].) The *qin* Zhang Dai is describing was somewhat longer and more resonant than the models in Europe at that same time.

22 **Fan's playing:** *TM* 2/6; *T-W* #21, p. 43.

22 **Quartet:** *TM* 2/6; *T-W* #21, p. 44.

23   **Cockfights:** *TM* 3/13; *T-W* #43, p. 67; Zhang's essay is translated in
      Robert Joe Cutter, *The Brush and the Spur*, p. 128. On cock training,
      see Cutter, pp. 16, 99; on key characteristics, ibid., p. 118; metal spurs
      and mustard, p. 119; betting on fights for gold, p. 118; three rounds
      and fight to the death, p. 119; Wang Bo's manifesto, pp. 58 and 174,
      n. 3; the Tang emperor's loss, p. 99. Also Kafalas (2007), p. 48.

24   **Football:** *TM* 4/7; *T-W* #53, p. 78; *TM* 5/12 describes lute players,
      cockfights and ball playing all at one festival site; for similar con-
      junctions, see Cutter, *The Brush and the Spur*, pp. 17, 20, 99, 113.

24   **Poetry circle:** Many examples are in *TM* passim. For a 1637 example,
      see *TM* 1/12; *T-W* #12, pp. 31–32.

25   **Cards and Yanke:** *TM* 8/11; *T-W* #121, p. 154.

25   **Other clubs:** See grandfather's and father's biographies in *Zhang Dai
      shiwenji* (cited hereafter as *ZDSWJ*), pp. 253–56. The Humor Club is
      in *TM* 6/11; *T-W* #88, p. 120.

25   **Crab-eating Club:** *TM* 8/8; *T-W* #118, p. 151, has an exquisite trans-
      lation. Also translated in Ye, *Vignettes*, pp. 96–97, and Kafalas (2007),
      p. 31.

26   **Snow in 1627:** *TM* 7/8, "Longshan xue," and Xia ed. *TM,* p. 116, n.
      3; *T-W* #101, pp. 133–34. Translated in Kafalas (1995), pp. 145–46,
      and (2007), pp. 102–3.

27   **Snow on West Lake:** Owen, *Anthology*, has a fine translation on p. 818,
      as do Kafalas (1995), p. 143; Campbell (1998), pp. 36–37; and Ye, *Vi-
      gnettes*, p. 90. See also *TM* 3/15, "Huxinting kan xue"; *T-W* #45, pp.
      68–69; Kafalas (2007), p. 100.

28   **Boat song:** *TM* 7/9; *T-W* #102, p. 134; Xia ed. *TM*, p. 117, n. 1.

29   **The moon watchers:** *TM* 7/3, "Xihu qiyue ban"; *T-W* #96, pp. 128–
      29. This is one of Zhang Dai's most famous passages. See the full
      translations in Strassberg, *Inscribed Landscapes*, pp. 342–45; Ye, *Vi-
      gnettes*, pp. 93–95; Owen, *Anthology*, pp. 816–17; Pollard, *Chinese Es-
      say*, pp. 86–88; Kafalas (1995), pp. 133–34, and (2007), pp. 88–90.

30   **Old Bao:** *TM* 3/12; *T-W* #42, pp. 65–66. Bao was a close friend of
      Zhang Dai's grandfather—see Xia ed. *TM*, p. 53, n. 1.

30   **Hunting:** *TM* 4/4; *T-W* #50, pp. 74–75.

32   **Yangzhou brothels:** *TM* 4/9; *T-W* #55, pp. 79–80; Xia ed. *TM*, p. 67,
      nn. 1–8. A full translation is in Strassberg, *Landscapes*, pp. 347–48.
      On Yangzhou city during this period, see Finnane, *Speaking of*

Yangzhou, and on the city's postconquest recovery, see Meyer-Fong, *Building Culture*.

32 **"Lean Nags":** *TM* 5/16; *T-W* #77, pp. 105–7. This piece is also one of Zhang Dai's most celebrated. See translations in Pollard, *Chinese Essay*, pp. 90–92; Mair, *Anthology*, pp. 597–98; Kafalas (1995), pp. 137–38 and (2007), p. 95.

33 **The wedding:** *TM* 5/16, following Pollard translation in *Chinese Essay*, pp. 91–92.

34 **Dangling shoes:** *TM* 8/1; *T-W* #111, p. 144. The passage is discussed in Brook, *Confusions*, p. 236.

34 **Women and wine:** *TM* 8/1; *T-W* #111, p. 144. The same section describes a woman dressed as a man disporting herself in a male brothel.

35 **Woman on the lake:** *TM* 3/16; *T-W* #46, p. 69. Also in Kafalas (1995), pp. 125–26, and (2007), pp. 75–76.

35 **Scholarly courtesans:** See Chang, *The Late Ming Poet*, passim; Brook, *Confusions*, pp. 229–33.

36 **Wang Yuesheng:** See *TM* 2/3; *T-W* #18, p. 40, for an excursion with Wang Yuesheng to Swallow Rock.

36 **Wang Yuesheng's career:** *TM* 8/2; *T-W* #112, pp. 145–46. Translated in Pollard, *Chinese Essay*, pp. 88–89, and Ye, *Vignettes*, pp. 95–96.

36 **Wang's silence:** *TM* 8/2; *T-W* #112, p. 146; Pollard, *Chinese Essay*, p. 89. In the Chinese text her two words were *chu jia* ("I am leaving for home").

37 **Poem for Wang:** *ZDSWJ*, pp. 45–46, "Quzhong ji Wang Yuesheng" [For the singer prostitute Wang Yuesheng]. The date is not given, but the next poem in the collection, written for his friend Qi Biaojia, is dated 1636 (*bingzi* year). For an English translation of Zhang's rather boastful account in *TM* 3/7 of his own friendship with the tea connoisseur Min, see Ye, *Vignettes*, pp. 88–90 and Kafalas (2007), pp. 82–83.

39 **Kunqu opera:** For a good introduction, see Nienhauser, *The Indiana Companion to Traditional Chinese Literature*, pp. 514–16, under *K'un-ch'u*; and ibid., pp. 13–30, "Drama" by Stephen West.

39 **Pock-marked Liu:** *TM* 5/7; *T-W* #68, pp. 95–96. Translated in Ye, *Vignettes*, pp. 92–93, and Pollard, *Chinese Essay*, pp. 89–90.

40 **Early troupes:** *TM* 4/12; *T-W* #58, pp. 83–84; Kafalas (2007), p. 50.

40 **Female troupes:** Compare *TM* 4/12 with the names listed in *TM* 7/8 on the outing in the snow.

41 **Zhang on actors:** *TM* 4/12; *T-W* #58, pp. 83–84. For another use by Zhang of the same seafarer's image, see Owen, *Anthology*, p. 820, on West Lake. On mutual fame, *TM*, 7/16; *T-W* #109, p. 141.

41 **Teacher Zhu:** *TM* 2/5; *T-W* #20, pp. 42–43.

42 **Zhu's excesses:** *TM* 2/5; *T-W* #20, pp. 42–43.

42 **Gateway of swords:** *TM* 7/16; *T-W* #109, p. 141.

42 **Floating stages:** *TM* 8/4; *T-W* #114, p. 147.

43 **Young actresses:** *TM* 7/12; *T-W* #105, pp. 136–37. For their full names and Pingzi's troupe, see *TM* 4/12.

43 **Actress Liu Huiji:** *TM* 5/14; *T-W* #75, pp. 103–4.

44 **Teacher Peng:** *TM* 6/1; *T-W* #78, pp. 109–10. Peng's native place, Xia ed. *TM*, p. 93, n. 1. Translated in Owen, *Anthology*, pp. 818–19.

44 **Peng's performances:** *TM* 6/1; *T-W* #75, p. 109. Translated in Owen, *Anthology*, pp. 818–19.

44 **Actress Zhu:** *TM* 5/15; *T-W* #76, pp. 104–5; Xia ed. *TM*, p. 91.

45 **Zhu's sadness:** *TM* 5/15; *T-W* #76, p. 105.

46 **Gold Mountain:** *TM* 1/6; *T-W* #6, p. 26. Translated in Ye, *Vignettes*, pp. 87–88, Owen, *Anthology*, pp. 815–16, Kafalas (1995), pp. 153–54, and Kafalas (2007), p. 110. The passage is discussed by Timothy Brook, *Praying for Power*, pp. 37–38.

CHAPTER TWO: CHARTING THE WAY

47 **Examination system:** The most comprehensive guide to the system and its details is Benjamin Elman's *A Cultural History of Civil Examinations in Late Imperial China*. Shaoxing prefecture's incredible success record is discussed by James Cole, *Shaohsing*. On the problems of cheating and memorizing packaged essays at this time, see Chow Kai-wing, "Writing for Success," especially pp. 126–27.

48 **Tianfu's ambitions:** Tianfu's exams: *ZDSWJ*, p. 244; *Dictionary of Ming Biography* (hereafter cited as *DMB*), pp. 110–11 under Chang Yuan-pien; and *Shaoxing fuzhi*, 48/52, reprint p. 137.

49 **Tianfu's grading:** The episode is in Zhang Dai's biography of Tianfu, *ZDSWJ*, p. 244. The examiner was Xu Wenzhen from Huating (Songjiang). Tianfu's elder brother, who received the *juren* degree in 1516, according to the *Shaoxing fuzhi* (32/37), continued to study with Tianfu in the Tianyi Temple.

49   **Tianfu's study:** *TM* 1/7; *T-W* #7, pp. 26–27. For its location, see Xia ed. *TM*, p. 13, nn. 1–2. Discussed in Kafalas (2007), pp. 62–63.

50   **Ai and exams:** Zhang's essay on the exams, quoting Ai Nanying, is in Zhang's *Shigui shu* (hereafter cited as *SGS*), *juan* 17, pp. 1–6b (Shanghai reprint, vol. 318, pp. 419–22). The essay is also summarized in Chow Kai-wing, *Publishing, Culture, and Power*, pp. 94-95, and in Kafalas (2007), p. 128. Ai's biography is in *Mingshi*, *juan* 288 (reprint pp. 32–41). For display boards, see Ai in *SGS*, *juan* 27, p. 3b (Shanghai reprint p. 420).

51   **Eight-legged system:** Zhang in *SGS*, *juan* 27, pp. 1b–2 (Shanghai reprint pp. 419–20). Ai's judgment: *SGS*, *juan* 27, p. 6b (Shanghai reprint p. 422).

51   **Wengong's health:** *Mingshi*, p. 3191 (*juan* 283), joint biography of Deng Yizan and Zhang Yuanbian (Wengong).

52   **White-haired candidate:** (*Zhuang yuan*), *ZDSWJ*, pp. 248–49. For a synopsis of the Xu Wei (Hsu Wei) story and the Yunnan campaign, see *DMB* biographies of Hsu and Chang Yuan-pien (Wengong).

52   **Wengong's model:** *ZDSWJ*, pp. 250–51. Wengong's slowness: *ZDSWJ*, p. 247. Wengong's friends: His main study friends were Zhu Geng and Luo Wanhua. Their *jinshi* degrees with dates and *zhuang yuan* status are given in *Shaoxing fuzhi*, pp. 728–29 (30/46b–47).

53   **Grandfather's studying:** *ZDSWJ*, pp. 251–55. He must have been born in 1556 or 1557; he took his *juren* degree in 1594 and his *jinshi* in 1595. For Xu Wei (Hsu Wei) (1521–93), see *DMB*, pp. 609–12 (Xu was in prison for murder from 1566 to 1573). Xu's nature: *DMB*, p. 611.

54   **Grandfather's eyes:** *ZDSWJ*, p. 252.

54   **Grandfather's provincial exam:** *ZDSWJ*, p. 252. For aspects of the evaluation system that more or less fit Zhang Dai's version, see Etienne Zi, *Pratique*, pp. 107, 130, 142–43, 152, 159. Grandfather was placed sixth, which was considered an honorary spot. See Zi, op cit., p. 153. (Thanks to Taisu Zhang.) For the system in general, see Elman, *Examinations*.

56   **Grandfather's dismissal:** His erratic exam choices are explored in *ZDSWJ*, p. 253.

57   **Father's exams and eyes:** *ZDSWJ*, p. 255.

57   **Seventh uncle:** *ZDSWJ*, p. 265.

58   **Tenth uncle's rage:** *ZDSWJ*, p. 273. Ibid., p. 272, states that Lady

Chen was mother of both of them. *Shaoxing fuzhi*, reprint 732 (31/53b) confirms 1628 as the date of ninth uncle's *jinshi* degree.

58 **Tenth uncle's special exam:** *ZDSWJ*, pp. 274–75, "Guizhou Section." For Zhang Dai's feeling that tenth uncle echoed the would-be assassin, Jing Ke, see *ZDSWJ*, p. 276.

59 **Eyeglass costs:** The price of four to five taels was the norm between 1570 and 1640. See Chow Kai-wing, *Publishing, Culture, and Power*, p. 262, appendix 4.

59 **Pei's eyes:** Pei's alternate name was "Boning"; see *ZDSWJ*, p. 280. Apparently Pei grew worse after his grandfather Zhiting took the boy with him in 1612 on a posting to Xiuning. But the gazetteer of that region, the *Xiuning xianzhi* (1693), gives no indication that the region was especially famous for its sugared or other sweet products.

59 **Pei's memory and medicine:** *ZDSWJ*, p. 280. Zhu Xi's work is the *gangmu*. The nine schools were as classified by Liu Xin and the "hundred names" were the *baijia*. See also the brief biography in *Shaoxing fuzhi*, 70/23a (reprint p. 692), and also, for the eleven-year age gap, Zhang Dai's obituary of Pei in *ZDSWJ*, p. 359.

62 **Grandfather and the Happiness Garden:** "Kuaiyuan Ji" in *ZDSWJ*, pp. 181–82. (Special thanks to Xin Dong.)

62 **Zhang's pavilion:** *TM* 7/6; *T-W* #99, p. 132. Zhang Dai says he was "six *sui*," which would be five years old by Western reckoning.

65 **Pavilion's demolition:** *TM* 7/6; *T-W* #99, p. 132.

65 **Visit to Huang:** *TM* 1/11; *T-W* #11, pp. 30–31.

66 **Huang's life:** The complex intersections of grandfather's and Huang's careers are clearly shown in *ZDSWJ*, pp. 252–53. For Huang Ruheng's various names, see Xia ed. *TM*, p. 16, nn. 2–3; *T-W*, p. 165, nn. 54–57; and *DMB* 79. Zhang's 1626 return visit is in *TM* 1/11; *T-W* #11, p. 31.

67 **Zhang given books:** *TM* 2/15; *T-W* #30, pp. 51–52; Kafalas (1995), p. 103, and (2007), pp. 59–60.

68 **Zhang and commentaries:** The key source is Zhang Dai's preface to his *Sishu yu*, also reprinted in *ZDSWJ*, pp. 107–8. The translations here are drawn mainly from Duncan Campbell, "The Body of the Way," pp. 38–39.

69 **Zhang's depression:** Qi Biaojia diary (and 1992 reprint) for 1635, 10/28 and 11/1. For Zhang's other childhood illnesses, see *ZDSWJ*, p. 296.

69 **Zhang's exam hopes:** Preface to *Sishu yu*, translated in Campbell, "The Body of the Way," p. 39.

70 **Rusen the drinker:** "Zhang the Beard" (1565?–1632). See *ZDSWJ*, pp. 270–72.

71 **Grandfather's essay:** Incorporated in the biography, *ZDSWJ*, pp. 270–72. I have changed the alternate name Zhongzhi to "Rusen" for consistency.

73 **Zhang Dai on liquor:** See *TM* 8/3; *T-W* #113, pp. 146–47. Also Kafalas (2007), p. 30. Zhang was obviously not totally averse to drink himself, despite his remarks to the contrary. In a conclusion, he mentioned similarities between Rusen's drinking and the mood of Qu Yuan's celebrated poem "Lisao."

73 **Library dispersal:** *TM* 2/15; *T-W* #30, pp. 51–52.

74 **Grandfather's Rhyme Mountain:** *TM* 6/5 (*yunshan*); *T-W* #82, pp. 113–14. Kafalas (2007), pp. 31–32, has a full translation.

76 **Hiding the manuscript:** *TM* 6/5; *T-W* #82, p. 114, and nn. 122, 391; Xia ed. *TM*, p. 98, n. 9, places the mountain nine *li* due south of Shaoxing and gives its variant names.

CHAPTER THREE: ON HOME GROUND

77 **Father's elixir:** *TM* 3/10; *T-W* #40, p. 64. Also translated in Kafalas (1995), pp. 84–85, and (2007), pp. 42–43.

78 **Mother's prayers:** Zhang gives these details in the preface and poem "In Praise of the White-robed Guanyin" (*Baiyi Guanyin zan*), *ZDSWJ*, p. 328. For representations of white-robed Guanyin, see Yü Chün-fang, *Kuan-yin*, pp. 126–30.

79 **Sutra wheel:** Zhang Dai, *Xihu mengxun*, ed. Xia, p. 255 ("*Gaoli si*"). The episode is discussed in Timothy Brook, *Praying for Power*, p. 43, as part of his analysis of Zhang Dai and Buddhism.

80 **Shaoxing community:** See the family biographies in *ZDSWJ* and the *Shaoxing fuzhi*. On Shaoxing exam successes, see James Cole, *Shaohsing*. On the Tao family itself, see *Shaoxing fuzhi*, 34/37b (reprint p. 813), and Xia ed., *TM*, p. 63, n. 1.

80 **Lady Liu:** *ZDSWJ*, pp. 245–46. Her son Zhang Yuanbian has a biography in *DMB*, pp. 110–11.

81 **Lady Wang and husband:** *ZDSWJ*, p. 250. She was from the Liuhu region.

83 **Illicit execution:** For the killing of Yang Jisheng by order of Yan Song, see *DMB*, p. 110; *ZDSWJ*, p. 247; *SGS, juan* 201, p. 42b.

84 **Uplifting poems:** See great-grandfather's biography in *Mingshi*, p. 3191, joint biography with Deng Yizan. These poems form the famous "Zhounan" and "Shaonan" sections of the poetry classic. See Legge, *She king*, prefaces, pp. 36–41. Wengong's death: *Mingshi*, joint biography, p. 3191. Zhang Dai records a similar and more elaborate account in *SGS* (vol. 320, p. 82), *juan* 201, p. 43b.

85 **The pledge:** *ZDSWJ*, p. 254. Zhu Geng's biography is in *Mingshi*, p. 2538. The Chinese date for the pledge was Jiajing 35, seventh month, seventh day.

85 **Zhang and Zhu:** The dates they each obtained their provincial degrees can be seen in *Shaoxing fuzhi*, 32/47b and 32/48 (reprint pp. 763–64).

85 **Zhu Geng:** *TM* 3/10; *T-W* #40, pp. 63–64; On Zhang Jiucheng, see Xia ed. *TM*, p. 52, n. 3.

86 **Zhongshu's head:** Described in Zhang Dai's biography of his uncle, *ZDSWJ*, p. 259.

87 **Sanshu's shards:** *ZDSWJ*, p. 262.

87 **Zhongshu's tears:** For timing of great-grandfather's trip and the children's separation and response, see *ZDSWJ*, pp. 249, 259, 262.

88 **Zhang supervision:** *ZDSWJ*, pp. 254–55.

88 **Zhu family influence:** *ZDSWJ*, p. 255.

89 **Zhongshu's collection:** *TM* 6/10 ("Zhongsju gudong"); *T-W* #87, p. 119.

90 **Second uncle:** *ZDSWJ*, p. 260.

90 **Ironwood table:** *ZDSWJ*, p. 260; *TM* 6/10; *T-W* #87, p. 119.

90 **Art collection:** *TM* 6/9; *T-W* #86, p. 118. On the art scene in the late Ming, see especially Craig Clunas, *Superfluous Things*, which also has several references to Zhang Dai; James Cahill, *The Painter's Practice*; and Hongnam Kim, *Life of a Patron*.

90 **Uncle's villa:** *ZDSWJ*, p. 260. The other four collectors named by Zhang Dai were Wang Shouren, Zhongshu's maternal uncle Zhu Shimen, Xiang Yuanbian, and Zhou Mingzhong.

91 **Houseboat:** *TM* 5/1; *T-W* #62, p. 90.

91 **Best art:** *TM* 6/3; *T-W* #80, p. 111 and p. 179, nn. 379–83; Xia ed. *TM*, p. 95, nn. 1–3, for Zhang Dai's general discussion of porcelain. Three treasures: *TM* 6/10; *T-W* #87, p. 119, on Zhongshu's acquisitions.

92 **Bronzes:** *TM* 6/10; *T-W* #87, p. 119.

92   **Huge profits:** *TM* 6/10; *T-W* #87, p. 119.

92   **Stolen objects:** *TM* 6/16; *T-W* #93, p. 124. The objects had been stolen from the tomb of Prince Jing of Qi.

93   **Mother's thrift:** See father's biography in *ZDSWJ*, p. 296.

94   **Family lantern display:** *TM* 8/1 "Longshan fangdeng"; *T-W* #111, pp. 143–44. A full translation is in Kafalas (1995), pp. 151–52; and further analysis in Kafalas (1998), pp. 71–74, and (2007), pp. 112–13.

96   **Zhang's baby brother:** See Zhang Dai's obituary for Shanmin in *ZDSWJ*, p. 292. For Zhang Dai's younger brothers born to Lady Tao, see Hu Yimin, *Zhang Dai yanjiu*, p. 170; and She Deyu, *Zhang Dai jiashi*, pp. 68–75.

97   **Shanmin's skills:** *ZDSWJ*, pp. 292–94. Among his younger brother's patrons, Zhang Dai lists Jiang Yuegang (the senior libationer of the National Academy) and Zhao Weihuan (*DMB*, ref. 774). The poets in his brother's circle included Zeng Hongjiang, Zhao Wofa, and Lu Ruzi.

98   **Shanmin's art collection:** *ZDSWJ*, pp. 293–94.

99   **Mother's ingenuity:** *ZDSWJ*, p. 258. For the lesser-known Min Ziqian, see Confucius, *Analects*, book 11, ch. 2 and 4. Zengzi was one of the best-known disciples.

99   **Spirit of dreams:** *TM* 3/2; *T-W* #32, pp. 54–55, 170–71, nn. 167–79, on Zhang's many allusions. Zhang dates his petition to 1612.

100   **Feng Tang parallel:** Sima Qian, tr. Watson, *Records of the Grand Historian, Han Dynasty*, vol. 1, pp. 472–75.

101   **Father indulged:** *ZDSWJ*, pp. 255–56. For father's intestinal illness, see *ZDSWJ*, pp. 112–14. The cyclical date given there (*gengchen* or 1580) is apparently a misprint for *gengxu* (1610).

101   **Mother's credit:** *ZDSWJ*, pp. 258–59.

102   **Father's gluttony:** *ZDSWJ*, p. 258.

102   **Father's illness:** *ZDSWJ*, pp. 112–14.

103   **Father's plight:** *ZDSWJ*, p. 258.

103   **Grandfather's concubines:** *ZDSWJ*, p. 253.

104   **Zhu's wife:** *TM* 3/10; *T-W* #40, pp. 64–65.

104   **Zhongshu's concubine:** *ZDSWJ*, p. 261.

105   **Father's concubine:** *ZDSWJ*, p. 257. For the story of Bo Pi, see Nienhauser, *Grand Scribe's Records*, vol. 7, pp. 55–59.

106   **Zhang's mother-in-law:** Zhang Dai's powerful eulogy is preserved in *ZDSWJ*, pp. 348–51. Zhang Dai wrote that there were "nineteen

years" between their deaths. In Western reckoning, that is equivalent to eighteen years of the solar calendar.

108 **Dr. Lu:** Zhang Dai's eulogy to Dr. Lu Yungu is in *ZDSWJ*, pp. 285–86. Zhang's poem of thanks is in *ZDSWJ*, p. 34. (Especial thanks to Zhang Taisu.)

109 **Closing eulogy:** *ZDSWJ*, p. 350.

CHAPTER FOUR: THE WORLD BEYOND

112 **Father in Lu:** *ZDSWJ*, pp. 256–58. For the post and its responsibilities, see *Yanzhou fuzhi* (1596), *juan* 10, p. 8b, "Changshi si." Prince's pine branch, *TM* 6/12; *T-W* #89, p. 121.

112 **Glories of Lu:** "Lu fan yanhuo," *TM* 2/4; *T-W* #19, pp. 41–42. Translated and beautifully analyzed in Kafalas (1995), pp. 155–56, as a moment that "shares with memory the ambiguousness of artifice" (ibid., p. 156). I have slightly modified his translation following Teboul-Wang. See also Kafalas (2007), pp. 115–16.

114 **Mount Tai:** Zhang Dai's own account is included in *ZDSWJ*, pp. 150–59, "Daizhi" section. A fine analysis of the trip and several lengthy sections of translation are given in Wu Pei-yi, "Ambivalent Pilgrim," pp. 72–85; for his dating of Zhang's trip, see ibid., p. 73. The term *ya-jia* seems more equivalent to a manager than to a guide.

114 **Taxes:** A second account by Zhang Dai is in *TM* 4/15; *T-W* #61, pp. 87–88. Also translated in Wu Pei-yi, "Ambivalent Pilgrim," p. 75, and by Strassberg, *Inscribed Landscapes*, pp. 339–41.

115 **Lodging and catering:** *TM* 4/15; *ZDSWJ*, pp. 151–52. Translations also in Wu Pei-yi, "Ambivalent Pilgrim," pp. 74–75, and Strassberg, *Inscribed Landscapes*, p. 341.

115 **Entertainments and extras:** *ZDSWJ*, pp. 151–52; Wu Pei-yi, "Ambivalent Pilgrim," p. 77. On Zhang, see also Dott, *Identity*, pp. 96–99.

116 **Beggar's coins:** *ZDSWJ*, p. 152; Wu Pei-yi, "Ambivalent Pilgrim," p. 77.

116 **Weather patterns:** *ZDSWJ*, p. 150.

117 **Bixia Palace:** *ZDSWJ*, p. 155; and brief history in Wu Pei-yi, "Ambivalent Pilgrim," pp. 79–80, Dott, *Identity*, pp. 265–67.

117 **Offerings and guards:** *ZDSWJ*, pp. 155–56; Wu Pei-yi, "Ambivalent Pilgrim," pp. 78–79.

117   **The descent:** *ZDSWJ*, p. 156. (Especial thanks to Zhang Taisu.)

118   **The return:** *ZDSWJ*, pp. 156–57; Wu Pei-yi, "Ambivalent Pilgrim,"
       pp. 81–82.

118   **Final evaluation:** *ZDSWJ*, p. 153; Wu Pei-yi, "Ambivalent Pilgrim,"
       pp. 77–78.

119   **Confucius's home:** *TM* 2/1; *T-W* #16, pp. 37–38. Translated in
       Strassberg, *Inscribed Landscapes*, pp. 338–39; Kafalas (2007), p.29.

120   **The mad monk:** *TM* 3/14; *T-W* #44, pp. 67–68.

121   **Pilgrimage to Putuo:** *ZDSWJ*, pp. 159–72, "Haizhi" section. Zhang
       Dai's trip is discussed in Timothy Brook, *Praying for Power*, pp.
       46–49, and in Wu Pei-yi, "Ambivalent Pilgrim," p. 83. The pilgrim-
       age area is described in detail by Yü Chün-fang in her essay "P'u-t'o
       Shan: Pilgrimage and the Creation of the Chinese Potalaka."
       (Zhang Dai's own Putuo pilgrimage is in Yü, pp. 227–29.) Zhang
       Dai's surviving revision, dated 1658, does not include the preface by
       Xiao. See also Yü, pp. 202–3, for economic background and a de-
       tailed map of Putuo.

122   **Hangzhou hubbub:** *TM* 7/1; *T-W* #94, pp. 125–27. Commentary in
       Wu Pei-yi, "Ambivalent Pilgrim," pp. 83–84.

122   **Putuo as destination:** *ZDSWJ*, pp. 159–60. Ibid., p. 170, on Qin
       Yisheng. Numbers of shrines and temples, ibid., p. 169. Maternal
       grandfather Tao Lanfeng, see *ZDSWJ*, p. 163.

122   **Pilgrim boats:** *ZDSWJ*, p. 169. Also discussed in Wu Pei-yi, "Am-
       bivalent Pilgrim," p. 83, and Yü, "P'u-t'o Shan," p. 241, n. 25. For
       "tiger boats," see *ZDSWJ*, pp. 169–70. Sailors' superstitions are in
       ZDSWJ, p. 161.

123   **Zhang on deck:** *ZDSWJ*, p. 161.

123   **Nightlong vigil:** *ZDSWJ*, p. 164, and Yü, "P'u-t'o Shan,"
       pp. 227-28.

124   **The beach:** *ZDSWJ*, p. 165. The distant islands are in *ZDSWJ*,
       p. 166.

125   **Dinghai meal:** *ZDSWJ*, p. 168. Also, Yü, "P'u-t'o Shan," p. 241, n. 25.

125   **Tai and Putuo:** *ZDSWJ*, p. 272. (Thanks to Zhang Taisu.)

126   **The night ferry:** See Zhang Dai, *Yehang chuan*, p. 1 (preface) and p.
       334 on foreign countries. (The Shaoxing Library also has a fully an-
       notated earlier edition, Liu Yaolin ed., Hangzhou, 1987.) On the
       role of the night ferries in the Yangzi delta rural economy, see Xue
       Yong, "Agrarian Urbanization," especially pp. 356, 360–62.

127 **Ferry categories:** See full contents table of *Yehang chuan*, and Zhang's preface, undated. Partly translated in Xue Yong, "Agrarian Urbanization," p. 360. Also Kafalas (2007), pp. 190–91.

128 **Foreign lands listed:** *Yehang chuan*, section 15, 2004 ed., pp. 331–37.

128 **Grandfather on Ricci:** Zhang Rulin, "Xishi chaoyan xiaoyin" (page number illegible), in Yang Tingyun, *Juejiao tongwen ji* (1615). The comment is on Ricci's *Qiren shipian* of 1608. See also *DMB*, p. 1141; D'Elia, *Fonti Ricciane*, vol. 2, pp. 301–6; and Spence, *Memory Palace*. On the editor Yang Tingyun, see *Eminent Chinese of the Ch'ing Period (1644–1912)* (hereafter cited as *ECCP*), p. 894.

128 **Grandfather on the text:** Zhang Rulin, Xishi chaoyan xiaoyin (no page numbers), first page, lines 5–7.

129 **Ricci's legacy:** Zhang Dai, *GS* reprint, vol. 320, pp. 205–7; original pagination, *juan* 204, "Fangshu liezhuan" (practitioners of unusual arts), pp. 45b–49. Alien peoples or tribes are called *Lu*. For a deeply erudite and comprehensive analysis of the Jesuit Chinese sources in this period, see the work of Hui-hung Chen, "Encounters in Peoples, Religions, and Sciences: Jesuit Visual Culture in Seventeenth Century China," Brown University, PhD thesis, 2003.

133 **Zhang on Ricci:** *GS*, vol. 320, p. 207 (*juan* 204, p. 49). For a variant sketch of Ricci's life by Zhang's contemporary and fellow *Xiaopin* writer Yuan Zhongdao, see Ye, *Vignettes*, p. 60.

134 **Asoka temple:** "A-yu wang si sheli," *TM* 7/15; *T-W* #108, pp. 139–40. Also anthologized in Victor Mair, *Columbia Anthology*, pp. 594–95 (from the translation in Strassberg, *Inscribed Landscapes*, pp. 350–51), and discussed in Timothy Brook, *Praying for Power*, p. 43. Asoka ruled from 268 to 232 BC. For Zhang's friendship with Qin Yisheng, see also *TM* 1/13, *T-W* #13, p. 33.

134 **The vision:** *TM* 7/15, following the translation in Strassberg, *Inscribed Landscapes*, p. 351.

135 **Zhang's concision:** See Qi Biaojia's comment in his preface to Zhang's first piece of history writing, discussed in Hu Yimin, *Zhang Dai pingzhuan*, pp. 85–87; Qi Biaojia's own comments are cited in Hu Yimin, *Zhang Dai yanjiu*, pp. 102–3.

135 **Qin's fate:** This final comment is mine, not Qi Biaojia's.

CHAPTER FIVE: LEVELS OF SERVICE

137 **Emperor Tianqi and Wei:** *Cambridge History of China*, vol. 7, pt. 1. *The Ming Dynasty*, Chapter 10; John Dardess, *Blood and History in China*, gives a detailed analysis of late Ming court politics.

139 **Book of *Profiles*:** Zhang Dai's *Gujin yilie zhuan*, preface, is cited fully in Hu Yimin, *Zhang Dai pingzhuan,* pp. 85–87, which discusses the two extant editions: one from 1628, one slightly later. Both have prefaces by Qi Biaojia.

140 **Excitement of history:** From preface by Zhang, cited in Hu Yimin, *Zhang Dai pingzhuan*, p. 86.

142 **History and spontaneity:** Zhang's methodology (*fanli*), cited in Hu Yimin, *Zhang Dai yanjiu*, p. 62.

142 **Horses and dogs:** Zhang's *fanli*, as summarized in Hu Yimin, *Zhang Dai yanjiu,* p. 63. Unfortunately these pages are so badly damaged as to be mostly illegible in the Library of Congress edition.

143 *Ice Mountain (Bingshan):* For basic biography of Wei Zhongxian, see *ECCP*, pp. 846–47. For the opera performance, see *TM* 7/17; *T-W* #110, p. 142.

143 **Yang Lian:** Dardess, *Blood and History*, ch. 3, "Political Murders." For basic biography, see *ECCP*, pp. 892–93. See other references in *DMB*, pp. 237, 707, 1569.

144 **Town laborer Yan:** *TM* 7/17; *T-W* #110, p. 142. On the urban riots, see Spence and Wills, *From Ming to Ch'ing*, pp. 293–95, 316.

144 **Shandong performance:** *TM* 7/17; *T-W* #110, p. 142. The play transcript has not yet been found; Qi Biaojia lists it in his survey of late Ming drama, but not with Zhang as author. See Qi's *Ming qupin jupin*, p. 87.

144 **Mu and Yunnan:** *ZDSWJ*, p. 245; *Mingshi, juan* 283, p. 3194. For great-grandfather's white hair, see *ZDSWJ*, p. 248; *SGS, juan* 201, pp. 41b–45, reprint pp. 81–83.

145 **On Luo:** The *zhuang yuan* of 1568, see *DMB*, p. 739, and *ZDSWJ*, p. 248. On Zhang Zhuzheng's relations with Wengong, see *ZDSWJ*, p. 249; this passage is almost exactly echoed in the *SGS, juan* 201, p. 44, reprint p. 82. For Zhang Dai glosses on Wengong, see *SGS, juan* 201, pp. 44b–45a, reprint pp. 82–83.

146 **Grandfather's impracticality:** *ZDSWJ*, p. 251. For Mao Shounan's appointment as magistrate from 1587 to 1592, see *Shaoxing fuzhi*,

27/28b, and his biography in ibid., 43/17. (Thanks to Huang Hongyu.)

146 **Rulin as magistrate:** *Qingjiang xianzhi* (1870 ed.), *juan* 5, p. 49b, reprint p. 668. Grandfather served there from 1598 to 1604. For Mao's policies, see *Shaoxing fuzhi*, 43/17.

147 **Father's campaign:** *ZDSWJ*, p. 256. For disruptions in this region at this time, see Wakeman, *Great Enterprise*, pp. 429–31.

147 **Father in Lu:** *ZDSWJ*, p. 257, for father in Jiaxing jail, and ibid., pp. 256–57, on Zhao Eryi and family deficits.

148 **Great-uncle Rufang:** *ZDSWJ*, p. 268, using his given name Rufang throughout, in place of Ruiyang or his other alternate names.

150 **Rufang's boat journey:** See *ZDSWJ*, p. 268.

150 *Capital Gazette:* The journal clearly circulated as widely in the late Ming as it did in early Qing—Zhang Dai read it regularly, too. See also Spence, *Treason by the Book*, passim, for the *Gazette* in the early eighteenth century. Barbara Mittler, *A Newspaper for China*, pp. 173–207, gives a helpful history of the *Gazette*.

151 **Ming contracts:** See *Tian Collection, Contracts* (3 vols., Beijing 2001), especially vol. 3, items 587–809 (covering the years 1585–1681), with summaries and facsimiles.

151 **Chu politics:** See *DMB*, pp. 768–70 (under Kuo Cheng-yu); *Mingshi*, *juan* 116, reprint p. 1499; Rufang in Beijing: *ZDSWJ*, p. 269.

152 **Chu case:** For the main story on Hua Kui, see *Mingshi*, *juan* 116, reprint, pp. 1498–99, and *Ming shilu* (Wanli reign), *juan* 383, 385, 387. The key ministers involved were Guo Zhengyu and Shen Yiguan—see their biographies in *DMB*, pp. 768–70, 1179–82.

153 **Rufang's scheme:** His biography containing the details is in *ZDSWJ*, pp. 268–70.

154 **Rufang's return:** *ZDSWJ*, p. 270.

155 **Untitled nobility:** Sima Qian, tr. Watson, *Shiji*, Han vol. 2, p. 437; *ZDSWJ*, p. 270, for Zhang Dai's comment.

156 **Rufang's success:** *ZDSWJ*, p. 270. See Sima Qian, tr. Watson, *Shiji*, Han vol. 2, p. 433. Taogong is Fan Li's alternate name. Zhang Dai also cites other figures famous for poverty or self-destructive integrity.

156 **Tao Qian's ballad:** Poem translated in Hightower, *T'ao Ch'ien*, pp. 268–69; original in *Tao Yuanming ji*, Taipei, 2002, pp. 328–37.

157   **Tao's ballad:** Following Hightower, translation p. 269, with minor changes.

158   **Third uncle:** *ZDSWJ*, p. 262, which also has references to He Shiyi and Xu Fanggu, who had been prefect of Shaoxing in 1626–27.

159   **Third uncle's character:** *ZDSWJ*, p. 264.

160   **The Xu case:** *ZDSWJ*, p. 263.

162   **Sanshu's fall:** Fuller details are in *ZDSWJ*, pp. 263–64, and in the *Mingshi*, *juan* 253, reprint p. 2869, biography of Xue Guoguan, discussing Shi Fan's fate (Zhang is miswritten "Liu" in one passage). Ninth uncle has a brief biography in *Mingshi*, *juan* 291, reprint p. 3272, and in *Shaoxing fuzhi* 31/53, reprint p. 732.

163   **Third uncle as Cai Ze:** *ZDSWJ*, p. 264. For Cai Ze, see Sima Qian, tr. Watson, *Shiji*, *juan* 79, in the Qin volume, p. 157, end of the joint biography of Fan Ju and Cai Ze.

164   *The Outlaws of the Marsh*: See Zhang's poems in *ZDSWJ*, pp. 333–45 (Wu Song on p. 333); and Zhang's praise of Chen Hongshou in *TM* 6/7; *T-W* #84, pp. 116–17. For Chen's series of forty illustrations, see Weng Wan-go, *Chen Hongshou*, vol. 3, pp. 62–71. For a translation of the entire novel, see Shi Nai'an, tr. Sidney Shapiro, *Outlaws of the Marsh*. Discussed in Kafalas (2007), pp. 66–68, 207–12.

165   **Wu Daozi images:** *TM* 6/7; *T-W* #84, pp. 116–17.

165   **1632 drought:** *TM* 7/4; *T-W* #97, pp. 130–31. On tides and sea, *Shaoxing fuzhi*, 80/27b, reprint p. 964. On 1598–99 drought and famine, see *Shaoxing fuzhi*, 80/26, reprint p. 963.

166   **Lookalikes:** *TM* 7/4; *T-W* #97, pp. 130–31; Xia ed. *TM*, p. 113. Also translated in Kafalas (1995), pp. 121–22.

166   **Mottoes:** *TM* 7/4; *T-W* #97, p. 131.

167   **Zhang's analysis:** *TM* 7/4; explanatory note in Xia ed. *TM*, p. 113, nn. 11–12. More droughts (in 1625), floods (in 1629 and 1630) and quakes (in 1635 and 1636) are given in *Shaoxing fuzhi*, reprint pp. 963–65.

CHAPTER SIX: OVER THE EDGE

169   **Zhang on his failures:** From his own self-written "obituary." *ZDSWJ*, pp. 295–96; also translated in Kafalas, "Weighty Matters," p. 65.

169   Paradoxes: *ZDSWJ*, p. 295; Kafalas, "Weighty Matters," p. 64.

170   *Historical Gaps*: Zhang Dai's preface to his *Shique*, also printed in
       ZDSWJ, pp. 103–4. Zhang returns to the moon-in-eclipse metaphor
       in his *ZDSWJ* family biographies.

171   The Xuanwu Gate: Zhang, *Shique*, preface, in *ZDSWJ*, p. 103. A
       concise introduction to this famous Tang case is in Hansen, *Open
       Empire*, pp. 196–97.

173   Four simple words: Zhang Dai, *Shique*, pp. 88–89.

173   Passions and flaws: *TM* 4/14; *T-W* #60, p. 86. I translate *pi* as "crav-
       ings" or "obsessions," and *ci* as "flaws." For Zhang's study of Confu-
       cius's *Analects*, see his *Sishu yu* [The four books, transforming
       encounters].

174   Blemishes: *ZDSWJ*, p. 259, introduction to supplementary biogra-
       phies. On Xie Jin, see *DMB*, pp. 554–58, under Hsieh Chin.

174   Passions: Introduction to section of five biographies, *ZDSWJ*, p. 268.

174   Suitability: *ZDSWJ*, p. 259.

174   Seventh uncle Jishu: (Born 1585?, died 1615.) All data here from
       Zhang Dai's *ZDSWJ*, pp. 264–67.

178   Seventh uncle's scrolls: *TM* 6/2; *T-W* #79, pp. 110–11. (With special
       thanks to Shiyee Liu.)

179   Yanke's biography: *ZDSWJ*, pp. 277–80. Yanke died in 1646. Other
       accounts are in *ZDSWJ*, p. 261, and a recapitulation of the garden
       story in *TM* 8/12 and *T-W* #122, pp. 155–57. For Yanke and card
       games, see *TM* 8/11. I standardize his name as "Yanke" throughout.
       There are many further references to Yanke in Zhang's *Kuaiyuan
       daogu*.

181   Lady Shang: The original text has "Lady Wang" as Yanke's wife.
       This is probably a slip for "Lady Shang" since Shang Dengxian was
       Yanke's father-in-law.

182   Gardener Jin: On Jin and the insect and flower names, see *TM* 1/4;
       T-W #4, pp. 23–24. Kafalas (2007), pp. 76–77. Gives a translation of
       the passage, slightly modified here.

183   Crazed landscaping: See the biography in *ZDSWJ*, pp. 277–80, and
       the variant in *TM* 8/12 and *T-W* #122, p. 156.

183   Yanke's trees: Quote is from *TM* 8/12; *T-W* #122, p. 156.

185   Gold fish: This and the following examples are from *ZDSWJ*,
       pp. 277–80.

186   **Yanke's self-naming:** See *TM* 8/12; *T-W* #122, p. 157, and notes in Xia ed. *TM* 8/12.

186   **Yanke's loss:** For Yuhong, see *ZDSWJ*, p. 279; *TM* 8/12; *T-W* #122, p. 157; Xia ed. *TM*, p. 138, n. 9. "The emperor who lost it all" is literally "a ruined Qin Shihuang" in the original, in reference to the founding emperor of the Qin dynasty.

187   **Poem for Qi:** *ZDSWJ*, pp. 46–47, refering to Qi's generosity in 1636 as being "last year."

188   **Famine victims:** Seen by Zhang in Hangzhou, *TM* 7/1; *T-W* #94, p. 126. Kafalas (2007), p. 55.

189   **Tombs violated:** *TM* 1/1; *T-W* #1, pp. 19–21. See careful annotations in Xia ed. *TM*, p. 6. Also translated in Kafalas (1995), pp. 96–97, and (2007), pp. 23–26.

CHAPTER SEVEN: COURT ON THE RUN

191   **Pirates and fishermen:** *ZDSWJ*, pp. 167–68. Zhang Dai was at Fanshan and noted the strangeness of the experience.

192   **Opera *Mulian*:** *TM* 6/2; *T-W* #79, pp. 110–11. Internal evidence suggests the date was either 1613 or 1614.

192   **Seventh uncle and prefect:** The prefect was Xiong Mingqi, who served from 1613 to 1622. See Xia ed. *TM*, p. 95, n. 4, and *Shaoxing fuzhi*, reprint p. 596 (*juan* 26, p. 22). Seventh uncle died in 1615.

192   **Dragon boats:** *TM* 5/13; *T-W* #74, pp. 102–3.

193   **Dinghai maneuvers:** *TM* 7/14; *T-W* #107, p. 139; Xia ed. *TM*, p. 121, n. 1. Translation in Kafalas (1995), p. 149, and (2007), pp. 107–8.

193   **Divers and lanterns:** *TM* 7/14; *T-W* #107, p. 139.

194   **Prince of Lu's display:** *TM* 4/3; *T-W* #49, p. 73.

194   **The acrobats:** *TM* 4/3; *T-W* #49, pp. 73–74; Kafalas (2007), pp. 108–9.

195   **Roving bandits:** See Des Forges, *Cultural Centrality*, pp. 182–84.

195   **Government failures:** Listed in Zhang Dai, *Shigui shu houji* (hereafter cited as *SGSHJ*), p. 493.

197   **Second uncle's skills:** *ZDSWJ*, p. 261. For corroborating local sources, see *Mengjin xianzhi*, reprint pp. 183, 291–93 (*juan* 5, p. 32); *juan* 11, pp. 12b–15, for Wang Duo's account. See also *DMB*, pp. 1432–34. For the Henan region at this time, see the admirable analysis by Roger Des Forges, in *Cultural Centrality*, pp. 182–85.

197   **The Lu fief:** Tables on the incumbents of the Lu fief and their
       deaths by suicide or in war are in *Qingshi*, p. 1133, and commentary
       (under the year 1639) in ibid., p. 1500. In *ZDSWJ*, p. 256, Zhang uses
       an alternate character for the "Xian" of the prince's name. On the
       prince and the pines, see *TM* 6/12; *T-W* #89, p. 121.

198   **Second uncle's death:** *ZDSWJ*, p. 261. "Roving bandits" are *liuzei*.
       On Shi Kefa (Shi Daolin), see *ECCP*, pp. 651–52. On the details of
       the Henan campaigns, see Des Forges, *Cultural Centrality*, Chapter
       5. I use *military coordinator* for *Ssu-ma*. For other options, see
       Hucker, *Dictionary*, #5713.

198   **Sanshu's rage:** *ZDSWJ*, p. 264.

199   **Sanshu's ghost:** *ZDSWJ*, p. 264. In the original, "ninth month" is
       miswritten as "eighth."

199   **Seventh and second uncles:** *ZDSWJ*, p. 266.

200   **Tenth uncle Shishu:** Biography in *ZDSWJ*, pp. 272–76.

201   **Tenth uncle's death:** *ZDSWJ*, pp. 275–76.

203   **Ming fall:** For the main narrative of the fall, see especially Frederic
       Wakeman, *The Great Enterprise*; Roger Des Forges, *Cultural Cen-
       trality and Political Change*; *Cambridge History of China*, vol. 7, *The
       Ming Dynasty*; Lynn Struve, *The Southern Ming*.

204   **Shanmin withdraws:** *ZDSWJ*, p. 293, in Zhang Dai's obituary.
       Zhang uses "Shi Daolin" to designate Shi Kefa.

204   **Qi Biaojia:** *ECCP*, p. 126, under Ch'i Shih-p'ei; Wakeman, *Great
       Enterprise*, p. 320, n. 4; Struve, *Southern Ming*, p. 208, n. 71; Smith,
       "Gardens," passim; and Qi Biaojia "Yuezhong yuanting ji."

205   **Shave foreheads:** Struve in *Cambridge History of China*, vol. 7, pt. 1,
       p. 662.

205   **Zhang on Qi's death:** *SGSHJ*, pp. 307–11, quotation ibid., pp. 310–
       11. In his diary, Qi kept track of his feelings almost until the day he
       died. For the full version of the will and poems, see also Qi's own
       Collected Writings, pp. 221–22, and *ZDSWJ*, p. 392.

207   **On Ma Shiying:** Zha Jizuo, *Lu Chunqiu*, p. 14 (seventh month of
       1645); *SGSHJ*, pp. 389–91; *Mingshi, juan* 308, *liezhuan, juan* 196. A
       biography of Ma is in Qian Haiyue, *Nanming shi*, pp. 5388–94.

208   **Letter to prince of Lu:** Full text in *SGSHJ*, pp. 391–94. According to
       Mencius, Shun in fact exiled three men and executed one. Qian
       Haiyue, *Nanming shi*, p. 288, gives a brief reference to Zhang's letter.

210   **Zhang foiled:** See *SGSHJ*, pp. 398–400, biography of Fang Guo'an.

210   **Prince to Shaoxing:** Zha, *Lu Chunqiu*, p. 15, is clear that this was in the eighth lunar month (i.e., after September 20, 1645).

211   **Prince of Lu's visit:** *TM*, Supplement #1, "Lu Wang." There are four supplements found in the 1775 edition of *TM*, of which this is the first. Teboul-Wang does not include the supplements in her translation, though they are included in most recent Chinese editions of *TM*.

212   *The Oil Seller:* A widely known tale in the late Ming. See Lévy, *Inventaire,* pp. 580–86. A translation of one version of the narrative (*The Oil Vendor*) is in Geremie Barmé, ed., *Lazy Dragon: Chinese Stories from the Ming Dynasty*, pp. 69–116. (This does not include the Prince Kang episode.) A detailed and evocative account of Prince Kang's survival of the Jin invasion and his subsequent rule over the Southern Song is in F. W. Mote, *Imperial China*, pp. 289–99.

213   **Prince's drinking:** *TM*, Supplement #1. The Prince's attendants are the *Shutang guan*. On the "one-of-a-kind studio," see *Qi Biaojia ji, juan* 8, p. 189, and Smith, "Gardens," p. 68.

214   **Zhang's post:** Hu Yimin, *Zhang Dai pingzhuan*, p. 357. The exact title was *Fangbu Zhushi*. See also Hucker, *Dictionary*, #1420. On the initial enthusiasm in Shaoxing, see Struve in *Cambridge History of China*, vol. 7, pt. 1, p. 666. Chen Hongshou's position was *Hanlin taichao*, Hucker, *Dictionary*, #2150. Hu Yimin, ibid., p. 357.

214   **Yanke's service:** *ZDSWJ*, p. 279. Yanke took on the role of *Zongrong*. Hucker, *Dictionary*, #7107, suggests this is an "unofficial reference to a regional commander."

215   **Pei and Yanke:** *ZDSWJ*, pp. 281–82. "Eyes . . . made useless": Zhang Dai literally wrote "had his eyes gouged out" in a specific reference to Sima Qian's account of Jing Ke and the minstrel.

216   **Zhang withdraws:** *TM*, Supplement #4. This was in the ninth lunar month—which in 1645 spanned October 19 to November 17. Chen Hongshou and cousin Zhang Youyu are in Hu Yimin, *Zhang Dai pingzhuan*, p. 357. Details on Chen's Buddhist decision are in Liu Shi-yee, "An Actor," pp. 22–27.

217   **General Fang:** *SGSHJ*, pp. 398–400; *TM* 1/10; *T-W* #10, pp. 29–30; *ECCP*, p. 181; Qian Haiyue, *Nanming shi*, pp. 5510–15, gives a biography of Fang.

218   **Zhang dreams of Qi:** *TM*, Supplement #4. (The passage is not included in Teboul-Wang.) February 26 was the eleventh day of the

first lunar month of 1646. For simplicity, I render "Qi Shipei" as "Qi Biaojia" throughout.

219 **Loss of library:** *TM* 2/15; *T-W* #30, pp. 51–52. On the lootings, kidnappings for ransom and random killing in northeast Zhejiang at this time, see Liu Shi-yee, "An Actor," pp. 193–99.

219 **Death of Yanke:** *ZDSWJ*, p. 279. Zhang Dai's description of Yanke's death is a complex set of analogies and wordplays from the *Shiji* of Sima Qian, *juan* 129 (vol. 10, p. 3257), concerning Fan Li, Wu Zixu and the war between the states of Wu and Yue. After the war, Fan Li took the name "Old Wine Skin." For English translations, see Nienhauser, *Grand Scribe*, vol. 7, pp. 58–60, on Wu Zixu, citing *Shiji*, *juan* 66; and Sima Qian, tr. Watson, *Records of the Grand Historian*, Han Dynasty, vol. 2, pp. 437–38. On wrapping valorous deceased fighters in horsehide, see *SGSHJ*, p. 438.

CHAPTER EIGHT: LIVING THE FALL

221 **Temple hideouts:** Hu Yimin, *Zhang Dai pingzhuan*, pp. 357–58. The poems cited as evidence by Hu can be found in *ZDSWJ*, pp. 36, 357, 393. For an analysis of many other Ming fugitives to the countryside, see Wang Fansen, *Wanming qingchu*, pp. 217–30 and 243–47.

221 **Hunger:** From the preface to *TM*, *ZDSWJ*, p. 110. Zhang admits he did not even know how to prepare persimmons for eating: *TM* 7/2; *T-W* #95, p. 127.

222 **Wild appearance:** See translation in Owen, *Remembrances*, p. 134.

223 **The *Dream Recollections*:** This celebrated preface by Zhang to his *Taoan Mengyi (TM)* was published separately from the book itself and is in *ZDSWJ*, pp. 110–11. For full translations, see Owen, *Remembrances*, pp. 134–35, and Owen's accompanying essay; and Kafalas (1995), pp. 71–72, and (2007) pp. 10–14, 46, an almost complete translation, with commentary. (There are slight variants in different Chinese versions.) Also see Martin Huang, *Literati*, pp. 106–7 and 157, n. 17. Teboul-Wang in her introduction (*T-W*, p. 10) presents the different hypothesis that this work did not appear until after 1657 and was drawn from Zhang's own extensive notebooks. Zhang's own words seem to suggest both the earlier date and the informal composition. Kafalas's 1995 and 2007 studies give the most detailed and insightful analysis that I have seen of the *Recollections*.

223 **Retribution:** I am drawing here on two prior translations: Owen's *Remembrances*, p. 134, and Kafalas (2007), 11 (though I have tried to reconcile the two somewhat differing versions).

224 **Jewel of life:** See Owen's translation, *Remembrances*, p. 135. Owen defines *śarî* as "the jewel . . . found in the ashes of Buddha."

224 **Tao Qian:** The analysis and translation of Tao Qian (Tao Yuanming) cited here is from James Hightower, *The Poetry of T'ao Ch'ien*. For his translation of "Inspired by Events," see his poem 46, pp. 165–66. Zhang Dai's matching poem is in *ZDSWJ*, pp. 24–25. For "In Praise of Impoverished Gentlemen," see Hightower, poem 50, pp. 203–15. Zhang Dai's seven matching poems are in *ZDSWJ*, pp. 21–23. For Chen Hongshou's painting sequences on Tao Qian, see Liu Shi-yee, "An Actor," passim, especially ch. 3. Also Weng Wan-go, *Chen Hongshou*, vol. 2, pp. 222–30.

226 **Commentators on Tao:** Hightower, *T'ao Ch'ien*, p. 204, comments on poem 50:1. *ZDSWJ*, p. 21, colophon, gives the Zhang family locations. In the third line of his poem Zhang refers punningly to the "destruction" of the Ming and in the ninth line to the "whirlwind force" of the Qing.

226 **Tao's full poem:** Translation in Hightower, *T'ao Ch'ien*, pp. 203–4.

227 **Zhang's matching poem:** *ZDSWJ*, p. 21. (Thanks to Zhang Taisu.)

227 **Broken possessions:** *ZDSWJ*, pp. 294–95.

228 **Happiness Garden:** On moving back to the Kuaiyuan garden, see *ZDSWJ*, p. 1, colophon dated ninth lunar month of 1649. In that year the ninth lunar month was equivalent to October. Hu Yimin, *Zhang Dai pingzhuan*, p. 359, notes that in poem #8, the reference to "the heart's history" (*xinshi*) is to the *Stone Casket* history. On the profits that could be made from such grand gardens, see Craig Clunas, *Fruitful Sites*. For other details and Zhang's earlier visits with grandfather, see *ZDSWJ*, pp. 181–83. His joke on the miserable people in Happiness Garden is told to a Mr. Lu, *ZDSWJ*, pp. 182–83.

229 **Family composition:** *ZDSWJ*, pp. 31–32, dated to 1654.

230 **Family shipwreck:** *ZDSWJ*, p. 33, poem for his second son. For other family details, see She Deyu, *Zhang Dai jiashi*; ibid., pp. 76–77, underscores how little we know of Zhang Dai's own children.

230 **Lady Chen:** Zhang's greetings for her fiftieth birthday, with colophon, are in *ZDSWJ*, p. 52.

230 **Qi Zhixiang:** Zhang's eightieth birthday poem for this elder brother

of Qi Biaojia is in *ZDSWJ*, p. 59. For his identity, see Xia ed. *TM*,
p. 73, nn. 1–2. For Zhang's depiction of him as a spirited man of passion, see *TM* 4/14; *T-W* #60, p. 86.

231 **The conversations:** Zhang Dai, *Kuaiyuan daogu* (Shaoxing ms, second preface). A rather different version of the preface is given in She
Deyu, *Zhang Dai jiashi*, p. 125.

232 **Six Satisfactions:** Zhang Dai, *Kuaiyuan daogu*, *juan* 13, p. 39. (My
thanks to Dong Xin.)

232 **Family biographies:** Collected in *ZDSWJ*, pp. 243–82.

233 **Biographies organized:** *ZDSWJ*, p. 259, explaining his "add on" to
the paternal line. On Xie Jin, scholarly editor of the *Yongle dadian*,
see *DMB*, pp. 554–57, "Hsieh Chin." See also Kafalas (2007), p. 52.

233 **On obsessions:** *ZDSWJ*, p. 267. Zhang had used the same sentence
before, in his reminiscences of Qi Zhixiang. See *TM* 4/14; *T-W* #60,
p. 86.

234 **Paternal line:** *ZDSWJ*, p. 243. See Nienhauser, *Companion*, pp. 543–
45, and *DMB*, pp. 841–45, on Li Meng-yang (d. 1529); and Nienhauser, ibid., pp. 369–70, and *DMB*, pp. 408–9, under Chung Hsing
(d. 1624). Neither source mentions the two works highlighted by
Zhang Dai.

234 **Biographical procedures:** *ZDSWJ*, p. 244. In some cases, of course, so
tightly entwined in time were the two projects of *Stone Casket* history and the family biographies that Zhang Dai could slide material
across from one to the other, leaving readers unsure which was being the supplement to the other.

236 **Zhang and the leper woman:** *ZDSWJ*, pp. 243–44. The passage originally came from the works of Zhuangzi. See *Chuang-tzu, Complete
Works*, ch. 12, trans. Burton Watson, p. 140.

236 **Tao Qian and the leper woman:** Hightower, *T'ao Ch'ien*, p. 35, poem
9, "On naming my son." Unlike Watson, Hightower talks of the
child's father's being the leper. Wen Honglong in his *Tao Yuanming
ji*, pp. 33, 37–38, gives an ungendered paraphrase.

237 **Message to his children:** *ZDSWJ*, p. 267. I use "fundamental nature"
for the Chinese phrase *hunpo* or "uncarved block." Zhang used the
designation "Hanyang" to refer to Zhang Tianqu.

238 **Dirge:** Tao Qian's three "coffin-pullers dirge" poems can be found
in Hightower, pp. 248-54 (under the title "Bearers' Songs").

239   *Stone Casket* history: ZDSWJ, pp. 99–100. Like the preface to the
       Dream Recollections, this preface was also published separately.
       (Thanks to Zhang Taisu.)

238   **Stone caskets:** The term is analyzed in Brook, *Praying for Power*,
       p. 41.

240   **History writers:** From Zhang's preface to the *Shigui shu*, ZDSWJ, p. 99.
       The passage is translated in Kafalas, "Weighty Matters," pp. 59–60,
       and Kafalas (2007), p. 187. For an analysis of Wang Shizhen
       (1526–90), see Hammond, "Chalice." Among those who sought to
       pressure Su, according to Zhang, were Ouyang Xiu and Wang An-
       shi.

241   **Sima Qian:** A fine introduction to Sima's work is provided by Bur-
       ton Watson in *Ssu-ma Ch'ien: Grand Historian of China*.

242   **Jiangxi battlefields:** Included by Zhang Dai as his "commentary" on
       the Jiangxi martyrs in SGSHJ, p. 379 (*juan* 46). In 1653 the eighth
       lunar month spanned September 22–October 20. For the identifica-
       tion of his cousin Dengzi, see Hu Yimin, *Zhang Dai pingzhuan*, p.
       360. On the Jiangxi visit, see also Brook, *Praying for Power*, p. 50.

243   **On Wanli:** SGS, vol. 318, p. 192. An evocative picture of Wanli's
       character and lethargy is given by Ray Huang in *1587, A Year of No
       Significance*, ch. 1.

244   **Ming lesions:** Zhang Dai, SGS (reprint vol. 318), p. 208, commentary
       on reign of Xizong (Tianqi emperor, r. 1621–27). This passage also
       makes references to the Zhengtong (1438–65) and Zhengde
       (1506–22) reigns. "Cancerous lesion" is *yong*. "Kidneys" are *ming-
       men*. (Especial thanks to Huang Hongyu.) The greatest doctors:
       Zhang Dai, SGS (reprint vol. 318), p. 208. Zhang Dai's phrase is
       "even had Liezong (i.e., Chongzhen) been Bian Que" in reference to
       the great physician of the past.

245   **Losing the country:** SGSHJ, p. 58.

246   **Pointless policy:** SGSHJ, p. 58.

246   **Chongzhen's problems:** Zhang's lengthy analysis is in SGSHJ, p. 59.
       Supplemented by ibid., p. 71, judgment included in the chronicle of
       the prince of Fu. (Thanks to Huang Hongyu.)

247   **Legacy of corruption:** See Zhang's introduction to "biographies of
       the bandits," SGSHJ, p. 493.

310 NOTES

CHAPTER NINE: RECLAIMING THE PAST

249 **Zhang's sons:** *ZDSWJ*, p. 32, referring to the "Jiawu" year of 1654. This passage is extracted from a longer poem. (Thanks to Zhang Taisu.)

250 **Tao's sons:** Hightower, *T'ao Ch'ien*, pp. 163–64, poem 45, "Finding Fault with My Sons."

251 **Ravaged West Lake:** Preface to Zhang's *Xihu Mengxun* in *ZDSWJ*, pp. 144–45. Translated in full in Owen, *Anthology*, pp. 819–20, and in Ye, *Vignettes*, pp. 102–3. This is another of Zhang Dai's most celebrated passages. (Different Chinese texts contain slightly different times and dates.)

252 **The ocean voyager:** Owen, *Anthology*, p. 820; *ZDSWJ*, p. 145. Zhang used the same metaphor, with a different twist, as a way of defining the subtleties of Chinese opera troupes. See *TM* 4/12; *T-W* #58, p. 84.

252 **Gu's history office:** Hu Yimin, *Zhang Dai pingzhuan*, pp. 361–62; *ECCP*, p. 426, under "Ku Ying-t'ai"; Gu's book was the *Mingshi jishi benmo*. Qing *jinshi* tables show Gu received his degree in Shunzhi fourth year (1647), ranked fiftieth in class two. On Rufang (Ruiyang) and the *Gazette*, see *ZDSWJ*, pp. 268–70. For Zhang's discussion of the *Gazette* as a source, see *SGSHJ*, p. 121, biography of Mao Wenlong. Shi-yee Liu (2003), pp. 220–21, discusses Chen Hongshou's reading of the *Gazette*. The extensive borrowings by Gu from Zhang Dai's work are discussed in Hu Yimin, *Zhang Dai pingzhuan*, p. 91. For an immensely detailed analysis comparing passages of Zhang's *Shigui shu* with other Ming histories, see Ming, "A Study of Zhang Dai's *Shigui shu*," vol. 2.

254 **Yongle usurpation:** *SGS*, vol. 318, p. 53. Zhang wrote a "comment" after each emperor's annals. For Jianwen, who lost his throne, see ibid., p. 30.

255 **Three types of history:** Preface to *SGS* in *ZDSWJ*, pp. 99–100. I translate *Guoshi* as "political history"; "family history" is *jiashi*; "untamed" is *yeshi*. See also Kafalas (2007), p. 187.

255 **Wengong's biography:** *SGS*, vol. 320, pp. 81–83 (original *juan* 201, pp. 41b–45).

257 **Grandfather and Deng Yizan:** *SGS*, vol. 320, pp. 84–85 (original *juan* 201, pp. 46b–49b). Much of this material was also in the *ZDSWJ* biography of grandfather.

258   **Second uncle and Chen Hongshou:** *SGS*, vol. 318, p. 725. (The original *juan* has been amended and is possibly 56, pp. 1–2.) This small supplement, with only five painters, is separate from the main entry on painters, which comes in *SGS*, vol. 320, pp. 175–83. It is clearly an afterthought, and may have been transferred wholesale to *SGS* from *SGSHJ*, where the same five sketches appear on pp. 485–86.

259   **Chen's biography:** *SGS*, vol. 318, p. 725. On Chen's wild burst of energy expressed in painting for Zhou Lianggong, see the vivid description by Liu Shi-yee, "An Actor," pp. 188–90. Also discussed in Kim, *Life of a Patron*, pp. 75–79.

260   **On Ricci and science:** *SGS*, vol. 318, p. 589.

260   **Lengths of volumes:** Based on my count of the numbers of characters per page multiplied by the number of pages. Hu Yimin calculates the length of *Shigui shu* as three million characters, presumably including the *Sequel* in that total. See his *Zhang Dai pingzhuan*, p. 62.

260   **Zhang's detachment:** Zhang's letter to Li Yanweng, *ZDSWJ*, pp. 232–34 (at p. 232). (Especial thanks to Huang Hongyu.) Zhang told Li he had been "writing *Shigui shu* . . . for over forty years," presumably including the *Sequel* in that figure.

261   **Prince of Fu:** *SGSHJ*, pp. 67–68. (Among the ministers, Zhang emphasized Ruan Dacheng and Ma Shiying.) The poison tigers metaphor is in the preamble to the "Yiyou" martyrs, ibid., p. 263.

262   **Prince of Lu:** *SGSHJ*, p. 85, on "the hereditary household of the prince of Lu." The *Qin* comment is in ibid., p. 67, preamble on the five hereditary princes.

262   **General Fang Guo'an:** *SGSHJ*, pp. 398, 400, biography of Fang Guo'an. (Thanks to Liu Shi-yee.)

263   **Artists' biographies:** *SGSHJ*, *juan* 60, pp. 485–86, for Zhang Ribao (i.e., Zhongshu) and Chen Hongshou. Apart from one accidentally dropped character, these are word-for-word copies of the two biographies in *SGS*, vol. 318, p. 725. This *miaoyi* section is discussed in Liu Shi-yee (2003), pp. 68–69.

264   **Zhang's own history:** Letter to prince of Lu, *SGSHJ*, *juan* 48, pp. 391–94. War-torn Jiangxi, ibid., *juan* 46, p. 379, second comment. Biography of Qi Biaojia, ibid., *juan* 36, pp. 307-11, with Zhang's extensive comments on p. 11. The "world of letters," ibid., *juan* 58, pp. 473–74. Zhang pointed out that neither Li Bo nor Du Fu had the

highest degree, and that of course Tang literature would not be Tang literature without them!

264 **Meaning of death:** *SGSHJ*, *juan* 20, p. 183, opening remarks.

265 **Alcoholic husband:** *SGSHJ*, *juan* 32, p. 264, last lines of preamble.

266 **Qi chooses suicide:** *Qi Biaojia ji*, pp. 221–22.

267 **Zhang's rebuttal:** *ZDSWJ*, p. 392.

268 **Qi's decision:** *SGSHJ*, *juan* 36, p. 311, biographies of "yiyou mar-tyrs." I translate *min* as "shrewd." (Thanks to Zhang Taisu and Huang Hongyu.)

268 **Pei's death:** *ZDSWJ*, p. 282, gives the date of death but not the cause. Pei was born in 1607. The date of 1663 is much later than any other event in the biographies of "Five Obsessive Men" and this item may have been added later. Other mourning poems for Pei are in ibid., pp. 356–57.

269 **Historians seek Zhang:** Among those historians were Zha Jizuo (d. 1676), Tan Qian and Mao Qiling. (See *ECCP* for Zha and Mao.) For sources on this period, see Hu Yimin, *Zhang Dai pingzhuan*, p. 368; and ibid., pp. 72, 89–90, on Xu Wei's grandson Xu Qin.

269 **Farm poems:** *ZDSWJ*, p. 36 on manure, p. 30 on silk worm raising, including the phrase on economics.

269 **"Pounding Rice":** *ZDSWJ*, p. 35. Liang Hong and his wife Meng Guang are celebrated in the *Hou Han shu*, "Yimin liezhuan" section. (Especial thanks to Zhang Taisu.)

271 **Old concubines:** *ZDSWJ*, p. 31. On p. 32, in another poem, Zhang calls the two women "old concubines [*laoqie*] hunched and short." He does not mention having any younger companions.

271 **"Self-written Obituary":** Printed in *ZDSWJ*, pp. 294–96, and the most celebrated of Zhang's shorter writings. There is a full transla-tion in Ye, *Vignettes*, pp. 98–101, and an almost complete translation in Kafalas (1995), pp. 21–23. Kafalas (1998), pp. 61–68, has a detailed analysis and lengthy translations. On such "obituaries" as a Chinese genre, see Wu Pei-yi, *Confucian's Progress*, pp. 24–32, "self-written necrologies." A partial translation is also in Brook, *Praying for Power*, pp. 40, 43, and in Martin Huang, *Literati*, pp. 4–5. Though indebted to all these versions, I have tried to combine them with my own renderings.

272 **Zhang's passions:** *ZDSWJ*, p. 295; Kafalas (1995), p. 21; Kafalas (1998), p. 63; Kafalas (2007), p. 53; Brook, *Praying for Power*, p. 40.

273   **Seven paradoxes:** *ZDSWJ*, p. 295. There are fine translations of the entire passage in Martin Huang, *Literati*, p. 4; Campbell, "The Body of the Way" pp. 45–46; Ye, *Vignettes*, p. 99; and Kafalas (1998), p. 64. Kafalas ibid., p. 80, n. 29, discusses some of the ways his version differs from Huang's. I have attempted my own composite rendering here.

275   **Tomb inscription:** *ZDSWJ*, p. 297; Kafalas (1995), p. 23. "Lofty scholar" and "steadfast loyalist" are literally "Bolan" (i.e., Liang Hong) of the later Han, and Yaoli of the late Chunqiu period. The inscription ends with a densely allusive series of three character references to Zhang's foibles, translated in Ye, *Vignettes*, p. 101.

276   **Missing biographies:** Among those biographies marked in Zhang's *SGSHJ* contents as "missing" (*que*) are those of Wu Sangui, Qian Qianyi, Hong Chengchou and Zheng Zhilong.

277   **New preface for *Dream Recollections*:** As printed in p. 5, *Taoan Mengyi*, ed. Chen Wanyi, from a copy in the Yueyatang congshu. The "beauty of the palaces" reference is from *Analects*, 19:23.

277   **"The Peach Blossom Spring":** For translation and discussion, see Hightower, *T'ao Ch'ien*, pp. 254–58; Owen, *Anthology*, pp. 309–10 (Tao's prose passage only).

278   **The natural calendar:** Zhang Dai's essay "Taoyuan li xu" is in *ZDSWJ*, p. 115.

279   **Langhuan story:** Zhang Dai's first telling of this story, in *ZDSWJ*, pp. 148–49 ("Langhuan fudi ji"), is taken almost verbatim from the Yuan version of Yi Shizhen's preface to his collection "Langhuan ji." Discussed and part translated in Kafalas (1995), pp. 77–79. There is also a useful paraphrase of the Yuan version in *T-W*, pp. 183–84, n. 490.

279   **Grandfather's garden:** *ZDSWJ*, p. 182.

280   **Zhang's own Langhuan:** *TM* 8/13, fully translated in *T-W* #123, pp. 157–59, and in Ye, *Vignettes*, pp. 97–98. "Be at one with the moon" is my attempt to catch the meaning of Zhang's concluding phrase *"Keyue."* Also translated in Kafalas (2007), pp. 18–19.

281   **New Year's poem, 1679:** *ZDSWJ*, p. 96. There were originally three poems, but two are lost.

282   **Zhang's last book:** The preface is in Hu Yimin, *Zhang Dai pingzhuan*, pp. 89–90, and in a rather broken up form in the 1973 Taiwan reprint ed., vol. 77, pp. 3–4. The eighth lunar month in 1680

was equivalent to late August and early September in the Western calendar. In his self-written obituary Zhang wrote that he was born on the twenty-fifth day of the eighth month of 1597. See *ZDSWJ*, p. 296.

282   **Completing the quest:** The original is in Hu Yimin, *Zhang Dai pingzhuan*, p. 90.

283   **The portraits:** Zhang Dai and Xu Qin, *Youming Yüyue sanbuxiu tuzan* [1918], reprinted Taipei 1973. For those mentioned here, see 1973 reprint, pp. 41, 67, 213, 219, 223, 237, 259, 261. Though Zhang Dai collected the images, many of the blocks were not carved until 1689 or later. See Hu Yimin, p. 89, and reprint vol. 77, pp. 5–6.

284   **Dates of death:** Over the centuries, estimates for Zhang's age when he died have ranged from sixty-nine to ninety-two. (See Hu Yimin, *Zhang Dai pingzhuan*, p. 370, n. 2.) Hu's own estimate, which I accept, is the eighth month or later of the year 1680, when Zhang was eighty-three. See Hu, ibid., pp. 71–78, for more discussion.

BIBLIOGRAPHY

Barmé, Geremie, ed. *Lazy Dragon: Chinese Stories from the Ming Dynasty*. Hong Kong: Joint Publishing Co, 1981.

Brokaw, Cynthia J. *The Ledgers of Merit and Demerit: Social Changes and the Moral Order in Late Imperial China*. Princeton, N.J.: Princeton University Press, 1991.

Brook, Timothy. *The Confusions of Pleasure: Commerce and Culture in Ming China*. Berkeley: University of California Press, 1998.

———. *Praying for Power: Buddhism and the Formation of Gentry Society in Late-Ming China*. Cambridge, Mass.: Council on East Asian Studies, Harvard University, 1993.

Cahill, James. *The Painter's Practice: How Artists Lived and Worked in Traditional China*. New York: Columbia University Press, 1994.

The Cambridge History of China, *The Ming Dynasty, 1368–1644*, vol. 7, pt. 1, and vol. 8, pt. 2, eds. Denis Twitchett and Frederick W. Mote. Cambridge: Cambridge University Press, 1988–98.

Campbell, Duncan. "The Body of the Way Is without Edges: Zhang Dai (1597?–1684) and His Four Book Epiphanies." *New Zealand Journal of East Asian Studies*, 6:1 (June 1998), pp. 36–54.

Chang, Kang-I Sun. *The Late Ming Poet Ch'en Tzu-lung: Crises of Love and Loyalism*. New Haven: Yale University Press, 1991.

Chen Hui-hung. "Encounters in Peoples, Religions, and Sciences: Jesuit

Visual Culture in Seventeenth Century China." PhD thesis, Brown University, Dept. of History of Art and Architecture, Sept. 2003.

Chow Kai-wing. *Publishing, Culture, and Power in Early Modern China*. Stanford, Calif.: Stanford University Press, 2004.

———. "Writing for Success: Printing, Examinations and Intellectual Change in Late Ming China." *Late Imperial China*, 17:1 (June 1996), pp. 120–57.

Chuang-tzu [Zhuangzi]. tr. Burton Watson. *The Complete Works of Chuang-tzu*. New York: Columbia University Press, 1968.

Clunas, Craig. *Fruitful Sites: Garden Culture in Ming Dynasty China*. London: Reaktion Books, 1996.

———. *Superfluous Things: Material Culture and Social Status in Early Modern China*. Urbana and Chicago: University of Illinois Press, 1991.

Cole, James H. *Shaohsing: Competition and Cooperation in Nineteenth-Century China*. Monograph no. 44. Tucson, Ariz.: Association for Asian Studies, 1986.

Confucius. *The Analects (Lun yü)*, tr. D. C. Lau. New York: Penguin Books, 1979.

Cutter, Robert Joe. *The Brush and the Spur: Chinese Culture and the Cockfight*. Hong Kong: Chinese University Press, 1989.

DMB. See *Dictionary of Ming Biography*.

Dardess, John W. *Blood and History in China: The Donglin Faction and Its Repression, 1620–1627*. Honolulu, Hawaii: University of Hawaii Press, 2002.

D'Elia, Pasquale. *Fonti Ricciane* [Sources on Matteo Ricci], 3 vols. Rome: Libreria dello Stato, 1942–49.

Des Forges, Roger V. *Cultural Centrality and Political Change in Chinese History: Northeast Henan in the Fall of the Ming*. Stanford, Calif.: Stanford University Press, 2003.

Dictionary of Ming Biography, 1368–1644, eds. L. Carrington Goodrich and Chaoying Fang, 2 vols. New York: Columbia University Press, 1976.

Dott, Brian R. *Identity Reflections: Pilgrimages to Mount Tai in Late Imperial China*. Cambridge, Mass.: Harvard University Asia Center, 2004.

ECCP. See *Eminent Chinese of the Ch'ing Period*.

Elman, Benjamin A. *A Cultural History of Civil Examinations in Late Imperial China*. Berkeley: University of California Press, 2000.

Eminent Chinese of the Ch'ing Period (1644–1912), ed. Arthur W. Hummel, 2 vols. Washington, D.C.: The Library of Congress, 1943.

Fang Chao-ying. "Chang Tai" [Zhang Dai]. Biographical essay in *Eminent Chinese of the Ch'ing Period*, ed. Arthur Hummel, vol. 1, Washington, D.C.: The Library of Congress, 1943, pp. 53–54.

Finnane, Antonia. *Speaking of Yangzhou: A Chinese City, 1550–1850*. Cambridge, Mass.: Harvard University Asia Center, 2004.

Hammond, Kenneth J. "The Decadent Chalice: A Critique of Late Ming Political Culture." *Ming Studies*, 39 (Spring 1998), pp. 32–49.

Hanan, Patrick. *The Invention of Li Yu*. Cambridge, Mass.: Harvard University Press, 1988.

Handlin, Joanna F. *Action in Late Ming Thought: The Reorientation of Lü K'un and Other Scholar-Officials*. Berkeley: University of California Press, 1983.

Hansen, Valerie. *The Open Empire: A History of China to 1600*. New York: W. W. Norton, 2000.

Hightower, James R. *The Poetry of T'ao Ch'ien*. Oxford: Clarendon Press, 1970.

Hu Yimin. *Zhang Dai pingzhuan* [A critical biography of Zhang Dai]. Nanjing: Nanjing University Publishers, 2002.

———. *Zhang Dai yanjiu* [A study of Zhang Dai]. Hefei, Anhui: Haitang Wencong, 2002.

Huang Guilan. *Zhang Dai shengping ji qi wenxue* [Zhang Dai's life and literature]. Taipei: Wenshizhe chubanshe, 1977.

Huang, Martin W. *Literati and Self-Re/Presentation: Autobiographical Sensibility in the Eighteenth Century Chinese Novel*. Stanford, Calif.: Stanford University Press, 1995.

Huang, Ray. *1587, A Year of No Significance: The Ming Dynasty in Decline*. New Haven: Yale University Press, 1981.

Hucker, Charles O. *The Censorial System of Ming China*. Stanford, Calif.: Stanford University Press, 1966.

———. *A Dictionary of Official Titles in Imperial China*. Stanford, Calif.: Stanford University Press, 1985.

Kafalas, Philip A. *In Limpid Dream: Nostalgia and Zhang Dai's Reminiscences of the Ming*. Norwalk, Conn.: East Bridge, 2007.

———. "Nostalgia and the Reading of the Late Ming Essay: Zhang Dai's Tao'an Mengyi." PhD thesis, Stanford University, Dept. of Asian Languages, 1995.

———. "Weighty Matters, Weightless Form: Politics and the Late Ming Xiaopin Writer." *Ming Studies*, 39 (Spring 1998), pp. 50–85.

Kim, Hongnam. *The Life of a Patron: Zhou Lianggong (1612–1672) and the Painters of Seventeenth-Century China*. New York: China Institute, 1996.

Legge, James, tr. *The She king*, or *The Book of Poetry*, in his *The Chinese Classics*, vol. 4, Preface. Hong Kong, 1871.

Lévy, André. *Inventaire analytique et critique du conte chinois en langue vulgaire* [Analytical and critical inventory of vernacular Chinese tales]. *Mémoires*, vol. 8-2. Paris: College de France, Institut des hautes études chinoises, 1979.

Liu Shi-yee. "An Actor in Real Life: Chen Hongshou's Scenes from the Life of Tao Yuanming." PhD dissertation, Yale University, Dept. of the History of Art, 2003.

Lovell, Julia. *The Great Wall: China against the World, 1000 BC–AD 2000*. London: Atlantic Books, 2006.

Mair, Victor, ed. *The Columbia Anthology of Traditional Chinese Literature*. New York: Columbia University Press, 1994.

Mengjin xianzhi [The Gazetteer of Mengjin County, Henan], ed. Xu Yuancan, 1709. Taiwan: Cheng-wen chubanshe reprint, 1976.

Meyer-Fong, Tobie. *Building Culture in Early Qing Yangzhou*. Stanford, Calif.: Stanford University Press, 2003.

Mingshi [History of the Ming], ed. Zhang Tingyu, 1739, 336 *juan*. Taipei: Guofang yanjiuyuan reprint, 6 vols., 1963.

Ming Shilu (Shenzong) [Veritable records of the Wanli reign], ed. Yao Guangxiao et al., in 3375 *juan*. Nanjing, 1940.

Ming Yau Yau. "A Study of Zhang Dai's *Shigui shu*," 2 vols. MPhil thesis, University of Hong Kong, December 2005.

Mittler, Barbara. *A Newspaper for China? Power, Identity, and Change in Shanghai's News Media, 1872–1912*. Cambridge, Mass.: Harvard University Asia Center, 2004.

Mote, F. W. *Imperial China, 900–1800*. Cambridge, Mass.: Harvard University Press, 1999.

Nienhauser, William H., Jr., ed. *The Grand Scribe's Records*, vol. 7, "The Memoirs of Pre-Han China by Ssu-ma Ch'ien." Bloomington: Indiana University Press, 1994.

———. *The Indiana Companion to Traditional Chinese Literature*. Bloomington: Indiana University Press, 1986.

Owen, Stephen. *An Anthology of Chinese Literature: Beginnings to 1911*. New York: W. W. Norton, 1996.

————. *Remembrances: The Experience of the Past in Classical Chinese Literature*. Cambridge, Mass.: Harvard University Press, 1986.

Pollard, David. *The Chinese Essay*. London: Hurst, 2000.

Qi Biaojia. *Ming qupin jupin* [Ming dramas and plays], ed. Zhu Shangwen. Tainan: Yen wen, 1960.

————. *Qi Biaojia ji* [Collected writings of Qi Biaojia]. Shanghai: Guohua shuju, 1960.

————. *Qi Zhongmin Gong riji* [The diary of Qi Biaojia], 10 vols. Shaoxing County Gazetteer Revision Committee, 1937.

————. *Qi Zhongmin Gong riji* [The diary of Qi Biaojia], 15 *juan,* in *Qi Biaojia wengao*, 3 vols., pp. 921–1447. Beijing: Shumu wenxian, 1992.

————. "Yuezhong yuanting ji" [Record of the gardens and pavilions of Shaoxing] in *Qi Biaojia ji* [Collected writings of Qi Biaojia], *juan* 8, pp. 171–219. Shanghai: Zhongua shuju, 1960.

Qian Haiyue. *Nanming shi* [History of the southern Ming], 14 vols. Beijing: Zhonghua Shuju, 2006.

Qingjiang xianzhi [Gazetteer of Qingjiang County], 5 vols., comp. Pan Yi [1870]. Taipei: Chengwen chubanshe reprint, 1975.

Qingshi [History of the Qing dynasty], comp. Guofang yanjiu yuan, 8 vols. Taipei: Lianhe chubanshe, 1961.

Ricci, Matteo. *Qiren shipian* [Ten chapters on the subtle men], in *Tianxue chuhan* [Collected writings on Catholicism], vol. 1, comp. Li Zhizao. Taiwan: Taiwan Students Press reprint, 1965.

Schneewind, Sarah, ed. "The Image of the First Ming Emperor, Zhu Yuanzhang." *Ming Studies*, 50 (Fall 2004), special issue.

SGS. See Zhang Dai, *Shigui shu*.

SGSHJ. See Zhang Dai, *Shigui shu houji*.

Shaoxing fuzhi [Gazetteer of Shaoxing prefecture], revised ed., Gioro Ulana, 1792, 80 *juan;* Shanghai shudian reprint, in 2 vols., 1993.

She Deyu. *Zhang Dai jiashi* [The family history of Zhang Dai]. Beijing: Beijing chubanshe, 2004.

Shi Nai'an and Luo Guanzhong. *Shuihu zhuan* [Outlaws of the marsh], tr. Sidney Shapiro, 2 vols. Beijing Foreign Languages Press and Indiana University Press, 1981.

Sima Qian, *Shiji*, tr. Burton Watson. *Records of the Grand Historian: Qin Dynasty* and *Han Dynasty*. New York: Columbia University Press, (1961) 1993.

Smith, Joanna F. Handlin. "Gardens in Ch'i Piao-chia's Social World:

Wealth and Values in Late Ming Kiangnan." *Journal of Asian Studies*, 51:1 (Feb. 1992), pp. 55–81. (See also under Handlin, Joanna.)

Spence, Jonathan. "Cliffhanger Days: A Chinese Family in the Seventeenth Century." *American Historical Review*, 110:1 (Feb. 2005, pp. 1–10).

———. *The Memory Palace of Matteo Ricci*. New York: Viking, 1986.

———. *Treason by the Book*. New York: Viking, 2001.

Spence, Jonathan, and John E. Wills, Jr., eds. *From Ming to Ch'ing: Conquest, Region and Continuity in Seventeenth-Century China*. New Haven: Yale University Press, 1979.

Strassberg, Richard. *Inscribed Landscapes: Travel Writing from Imperial China*. Berkeley: University of California Press, 1994.

Struve, Lynn A. *The Ming–Qing Conflict, 1619–1683: A Historiography and Source Guide*. Ann Arbor, Mich.: Association for Asian Studies, 1998.

———. *The Southern Ming, 1644–1662*. New Haven: Yale University Press, 1984.

Tao Yuanming (Tao Qian). *Tao Yuanming ji* [Collected works of Tao Qian], ed. Wen Honglong. Taipei: Sanmin shuju, 2002.

Teboul-Wang, Brigitte. See Zhang Dai, *Taoan mengyi*.

Tian Collection, Contracts. See *Tiancang qiyue wenshu cuibian* [Traditional Chinese contracts and related documents from the Tian collection (1408–1969)], ed. Tian Tao, Hugh T. Scogin, Jr., and Zheng Qin, 3 vols. Beijing: Zhonghua Shuju, 2001.

TM. See Zhang Dai, *Taoan mengyi*.

T-W. See under Zhang Dai (tr. Brigitte Teboul-Wang), *Taoan mengyi*.

Wakeman, Frederic, Jr. *The Great Enterprise: The Manchu Reconstruction of Imperial Order in Seventeenth-Century China*, 2 vols. Berkeley: University of California Press, 1985.

Waldron, Arthur. *The Great Wall of China: From History to Myth*. Cambridge: Cambridge University Press, 1992.

Wang Fan-sen. *Wanming qingchu sixiang* [Thought in the late Ming and early Qing]. Shanghai: Fudan University Press, 2004.

Watson, Burton. *Ssu-ma Ch'ien: Grand Historian of China*. New York: Columbia University Press, 1958.

Weng Wan-go. *Chen Hongshou: His Life and Art*, 3 vols. Shanghai: People's Fine Arts Publishing House, n.d.

Wu Pei-yi. "An Ambivalent Pilgrim to T'ai shan in the Seventeenth Century," in *Pilgrims and Sacred Sites in China*, eds. Susan Naquin and Chün-fang Yü, pp. 65–88. Berkeley: University of California Press, 1992.

————. *The Confucian's Progress: Autobiographical Writings in Traditional China*. Princeton, N.J.: Princeton University Press, 1990.

Xia ed. *TM*. See Zhang Dai, *Taoan mengyi,* ed. Xia Xianchun.

Xia Xianchun. *Mingmo qicai—Zhang Dai lun* [Talents of the late Ming—The case of Zhang Dai]. Shanghai: Shehui Kexue yuan, 1989.

Xiuning xianzhi [Gazetteer of Xiuning County Anhui], 8 *juan* [1693], ed. Liao Tenggui, 3 vols. Taipei: Chengwen chubanshe reprint, 1970.

Xue Yong. "Agrarian Urbanization: Social and Economic Changes in Jiangnan from the Eighth to the Nineteenth Century." PhD thesis, Yale University, Dept. of History, 2006.

Yang Tingyun. *Juejiao tongwen ji* [Collected essays and translation on Western writings and Christianity], preface dated 1615, 2 *juan*.

Yanzhou fuzhi [Gazetteer of Yanzhou prefecture], comp. Yu Shenxing [1596], 6 vols. Tsinan, 1985.

Ye Yang, tr. and ed. *Vignettes from the Late Ming: A Hsiao-p'in Anthology*. Seattle: University of Washington Press, 1999.

Yi Shizhen. *Langhuan ji* [Records from Langhuan], Yuan dynasty, Baibu congshu jicheng ed., n.d., pp. 1, 2. Taiwan, 1967.

Yü Chün-fang. *Kuan-yin: The Chinese Transformation of Avalokiteśvara*. New York: Columbia University Press, 2001.

————. "P'u-t'o Shan: Pilgrimage and the Creation of the Chinese Potalaka," in *Pilgrims and Sacred Sites in China*, eds. Susan Naquin and Chün-fang Yü, pp. 190–245. Berkeley: University of Calilfornia Press, 1992.

————. *The Renewal of Buddhism in China: Chu-hung and the Late Ming Synthesis*. New York: Columbia University Press, 1981.

ZDSWJ. See Zhang Dai, *Zhang Dai shiwenji*.

Zha Jizuo [Cha Chi-tso]. *Lu Chunqiu* [Chronicle of the Lu regime], Wen xian congkan, vol. 118. Taipei, 1961.

Zhang Dai. *Gujin yilie zhuan* [Profiles of righteous and honorable people through the ages]. Zhejiang?: 1628. (Preserved in the Library of Congress.)

————. *Kuaiyuan daogu* [Times past in the Happiness Garden], vol. 1, *juan* 1–5, and vol. 2, *juan* 12–15. Preface, signed by Zhang Dai at Dragon Mountain, 1655. (Ms in Shaoxing Municipal Library.)

————. *Kuaiyuan daogu* [Times past in the Happiness Garden], dated 1655, transcribed by Gao Xuean and She Deyu. Hangzhou, Zhejiang: Zhejiang guji chubanshe, 1986.

————. *Langhuan Wenji* [Collected writings from the land of Langhuan]. Shangai: Zhongguo wenxue, 1935 (reprint of 1877 edition).

————. *Mingji shique* [Ming supplement to the *Shique*], n.d. Taipei: Xuesheng shuju, 1969.

————. [*SGS*], *Shigui shu* [Book of the stone casket]. Combined mss. from Nanjing and Shanghai Libraries, 208 *juan,* in *Xuxiu siku quanshu* [Continuation of the Four Treasuries], vols. 318–320. Shanghai: Shanghai guji chubanshe, ?1995.

————. [*SGSHJ*] *Shigui shu houji* [The sequel to the book of the stone casket], 63 *juan.* Taipei: Zhonghua shuju, 1970.

————. *Shique* [Historical gaps], n.d., 14 *juan,* (1824). Reissued Taipei: Huashi chubanshe, 1977.

————. *Sishu yu* [The four books, transforming encounters]. Hangzhou, Zhejiang: Zhejiang guji chubanshe, 1985.

————. [*TM*], *Taoan mengyi* [The dream recollections of Taoan], ed. Chen Wanyi. Taipei: Jinfeng chubanshe, n.d.

————. *Taoan mengyi* [The dream recollections of Taoan], ed. Xia Xianchun. Shanghai: Shanghai guji chubanshe, 2001.

————. [*T-W*], *Taoan mengyi: souvenirs rêvés de Tao'an* [Taoan's dream recollections], tr. Brigitte Teboul-Wang. Paris: Gallimard, 1995.

————. *Xihu Mengxun* [Tracing West Lake in a dream], ed. Xia Xianchun. Shanghai: Shanghai guji chubanshe, 2001.

————. *Yehang chuan* [The night ferry], ed. Tang Chao. Chengdu: Sichuan wenyi chubanshe, 1998, rev. ed. 2004.

————. [*ZDSWJ*], *Zhang Dai shiwenji* [The collected poetry and short prose of Zhang Dai], ed. Xia Xianchun. Shanghai: Guji chubanshe, 1991.

Zhang Dai and Xu Qin. *Youming yüyue sanbuxiu tuzan* [Portraits with commentary of the imperishable worthies of the Shaoxing region in the Ming], 1918 ed. with preface by Cai Yuanpei, reprinted in the *Mingqing shiliao huibian*, series 8, vol. 77, pp. 1–272, Taipei: Wenhai chubanshe, n.d. (1973?); boxed ed. in four vols., Shaoxing Library. Beijing: Chinese Archive Publishers, 2005.

Zhang Rulin. "Xishi chaoyan xiaoyin" [A short introduction to the Western scholar's moral teachings], included in Yang Tingyun, ed., *Juejiao tongwenji* [1615].

Zi, Etienne. *Pratique des examens littéraires en Chine* [The Chinese system of civil examinations]. Shanghai, *Variétés Sinologiques,* no. 5, 1894.

INDEX

Li Mengyang, 234, 235

Li Yanzhai, 275

Li Zicheng, 196, 202, 247

Liang dynasty, 186

Liang Hong, 269, 271

Liaodong, 187, 188

Linqing, 198, 199

Liu (father-in-law), 92, 107, 108

Liu family, 80

Liu, Financial Commissioner, 147

Liu Huiji, 43

Liu Jiezhu, 43

Liu, Lady (great-great-grandmother), 80–81, 87, 110, 154

Liu, Lady (wife), 102, 103, 108, 139

Liu, Pock-marked, 39–40

Liu, Widow (mother-in-law), 106–8, 109–10

Lord Pang's Lake, 27–28

Lu Baoshan, 89

Lu, fiefdom of, Yanzhou, 112–14, 147, 152, 194, 203

Lu, prince of (Xian, under whom Zhang Dai's father served), 112, 164, 207

Lu, prince of (nephew of Xian; older brother of Zhu Yihai), 197, 207

Lu, prince of (Zhu Yihai; "protector of the realm"), 197, 203, 205, 207–11, 213–14, 215, 216, 217, 218, 219, 220, 221, 228, 230, 239, 258–59, 261–62, 263, 265, 268

Lu Yungu, 108

Luo Wanhua, 145

Ma Shiying, 205, 207–8, 209–10, 217, 220, 263

Ma Xiaoqing, 26

Manchus, 9, 10, 11, 12, 138, 187, 195, 197, 199, 205, 209, 210, 212, 214, 220, 245; hairstyle, 205, 216, 222, 243; Ming loyalist resistance to, 203, 204–7. See also Qing dynasty

marriage, 1, 84, 131–32

maternal grandfather. See Tao Lanfeng

medical treatments, 4, 60–61, 78, 102, 108–9, 140, 177, 187, 188, 201–2

Meng Guang (wife of Liang Hong), 269, 271

Mengjin region, Henan province, 92, 197

military spectacles, 192–95

Min, Master, 36, 37

Min Ziqian, 99

Ming dynasty, 1, 3, 4, 6–8, 25, 188–89, 212, 253, 264, 268; decay, 138, 243–45; fall (1644), 1, 9, 10, 12, 245–47, 261. See also Zhang Dai, writings: Book of the Stone Casket (history of the Ming dynasty)

Ming loyalists, resistance to Manchus, 203, 204, 205, 207, 243, 268

Ming princely families, 111, 114, 151–53. See also Fu, prince of; Lu, prince of

Mongols, 7, 8, 138, 139

moon viewing, 28–30

mother-in-law. See Liu, Widow

Mount Putuo, shrine on, 121

Mount Tai, 107, 114–19, 125, 135

Mozi, 132

Mu (Yunnan strongman), 144–45

Mulian (opera), 192

music, 21–22, 41

Nanjing, 7, 13, 21, 27, 35, 36, 37, 39, 66, 120, 129, 162; as resistance capital, 203, 205, 207, 208, 209, 239, 261, 268; surrender to Manchus (1645), 205, 217; tomb of Ming founder, 189

Nanzhen, 99–100

national exams, 48, 52, 54, 58, 69, 81, 252, 258. See also jinshi degree

naval spectacle, 193–94

Ni Zan, 91

Ningbo, 121, 122; Asoka temple,
133–34
ninth uncle. *See* Zhang Jiushan
Northern Song dynasty, 212

obituaries, self-written, 271–75
obsessions, 183, 186, 233
officeholding, restrictions on, 79
Oil Seller, The (drama), 212–13
omens, 2, 189. *See also* divination;
dreams
operatic drama, 39, 40, 42, 44, 143–44,
192, 212–13
Outlaws of the Marsh, The (novel),
164–67

Pan Xiaofei, 26
Pantoja, Diego de, 129
passion, 38, 173–74
peasant rebels, 202, 245, 246
Peng Tianxi, 43–44, 45
pilgrim boats, 122–23
poetry circle, 24
prostitutes, 31–32
provincial exams, 48, 50–51, 54, 56, 250
pulse theory, 60–61
Putuo Island, 121–24, 133, 191

qi (vital energy), 201
Qi Biaojia (Qi Shipei), 69, 129, 135, 179,
182, 187, 188, 204–5, 230, 231, 283;
suicide, 205–6, 231, 266–68; in
Zhang Dai's dream, 218–19, 220,
239–40
Qi family, 204, 251
Qi Lisun, 206
Qi Zhixiang, 230–31
Qian family, 251
Qiantang River, 63, 150, 210, 215, 217,
220
qin (zither), 21–22, 130, 133
Qin dynasty, 278

Qin Yisheng, 122, 133, 134, 135
qing (passion), 38
Qing dynasty, 9, 203, 228, 250, 252,
275–76, 281. *See also* Manchus
Qingjiangpu, 198, 200, 201
Qufu, Shandong province, 119

Red Market, Nanjing, 36
religion, 2, 3, 131, 132–33, 134
Ricci, Matteo, 128, 129–33, 259–60
Ruan Dacheng, 203, 204–5
Ruan Ji, 71

scholars, 47–48, 51, 56, 74–76, 126–27,
132; courtesans, 35–36; resistance to
Qing, 243, 250. *See also* examination
system
second uncle. *See* Zhang Zhongshu
seventh uncle. *See* Zhang Jishu
Shandong province, 114, 119–20, 147,
195
Shang Dengxian, 182
Shang family, 251
Shang, Lady (wife of cousin Zhang
Yanke), 181
Shanghai, 5, 150
Shanyin, Shaoxing, 79, 80
Shao Zhengmao, 208
Shaoxing, 5, 6, 9, 19, 25–26, 35, 63, 76,
79, 80, 97, 146, 156, 212, 213;
drought, 164–66; lantern arts, 14–15,
20, 21, 94–96, 112; Lord Pang's Lake,
27–28; performing arts, 21, 39, 45,
143, 192; portraits of worthy
residents, 282–84; as a resistance
center, 203, 205, 207, 210, 214, 217,
239, 261; Sanshu's career, 158–59,
160; scholars, 48, 56, 80, 127, 187. *See
also* Dragon Mountain
Shen Zhou, 89
Shi Fan, 162
Shi Kefa, 197, 203–4, 216–17

Mao Zedong

From humble origins, Mao Zedong rose to absolute power, unifying with an iron fist a vast country torn apart by years of weak leadership, colonialism, and war. This sharply drawn account brings to life this modern-day emperor and the tumultuous era he shaped. *ISBN 978-0-14-303772-9*

Treason by the Book

In this thrilling story of a conspiracy against China's Qing dynasty, Spence has created a vivid portrait of the rich culture surrounding one of the most dramatic periods in Chinese history. *ISBN 978-0-14-200041-0*

The Memory Palace of Matteo Ricci

In 1577, the Jesuit Priest Matteo Ricci set out from Italy to bring Christian faith and Western thought to Ming dynasty China. Spence's compelling narrative captures the complex emotional and religious drama of Ricci's extraordinary life.

ISBN 978-0-14-008098-8

The Gate of Heavenly Peace
The Chinese and Their Revolution

In this masterful, highly original approach to modern Chinese history, Jonathan Spence shows us the Chinese revolution through the eyes of the artists, writers, and thinkers who shaped and were shaped by the turbulent events of this century.

ISBN 978-0-14-006279-3

To Change China
Western Advisers in China

"To change China" was the goal of foreign missionaries, doctors, teachers, and revolutionaries for more than three hundred years. But the Chinese clung steadfastly to their religious and cultural traditions. As a new era of relations between China and the United States begins, this book will serve as a cautionary history for businessmen, diplomats, students, or any other foreigners who believe that they can transform this enigmatic country.

ISBN 978-0-14-005528-3

The Death of Woman Wang

Life in provincial China in the seventeenth century emerges here as an endless cycle of floods, plagues, crop failures, banditry, and heavy taxation. Against this turbulent background a tenacious tax collector, an irascible farmer, and an unhappy wife act out a poignant drama at whose climax the wife, having run away from her husband, returns to him, only to die at his hands. Magnificently evoking the China of long ago, *The Death of Woman Wang* also deepens our understanding of the China we know today. *ISBN 978-0-14-005121-6*